# Fashion in American Life

Also published by Bloomsbury

*Fashion and Everyday Life: London and New York*, Hazel Clark (authored with Cheryl Buckley)
*Fashion Curating: Critical Practice in the Museum and Beyond*, Hazel Clark (co-editor with Annamari Vänska)
*Fashion Before Plus-Size: Bodies, Bias, and the Birth of an Industry*, Lauren Downing Peters

# Fashion in American Life

Edited by
Hazel Clark and
Lauren Downing Peters

BLOOMSBURY VISUAL ARTS
LONDON • NEW YORK • OXFORD • NEW DELHI • SYDNEY

BLOOMSBURY VISUAL ARTS
Bloomsbury Publishing Plc
50 Bedford Square, London, WC1B 3DP, UK
1385 Broadway, New York, NY 10018, USA
29 Earlsfort Terrace, Dublin 2, Ireland

BLOOMSBURY, BLOOMSBURY VISUAL ARTS and the Diana logo are trademarks of
Bloomsbury Publishing Plc

First published in Great Britain 2024

Selection, editorial matter, Introductions © Hazel Clark and Lauren Downing Peters, 2024
Individual chapters © their Authors, 2024

Hazel Clark and Lauren Downing Peters have asserted their right under the Copyright,
Designs and Patents Act, 1988, to be identified as Editors of this work.

For legal purposes the Acknowledgements on p. xvi constitute
an extension of this copyright page.

Cover design by Adriana Brioso
Cover image: Noel Woodford GNY Install-4945, Shanzhai Lyric. Incomplete Poem
(2015-ongoing). Image courtesy MoMA PS1. Photo by Noel Woodford.

All rights reserved. No part of this publication may be reproduced or transmitted
in any form or by any means, electronic or mechanical, including photocopying,
recording, or any information storage or retrieval system, without prior
permission in writing from the publishers.

Bloomsbury Publishing Plc does not have any control over, or responsibility for, any
third-party websites referred to or in this book. All internet addresses given in this
book were correct at the time of going to press. The author and publisher regret
any inconvenience caused if addresses have changed or sites have ceased to
exist, but can accept no responsibility for any such changes.

A catalogue record for this book is available from the British Library.

A catalog record for this book is available from the Library of Congress.

ISBN:  HB:     978-1-3503-3193-8
       PB:     978-1-3503-3192-1
       ePDF:   978-1-3503-3194-5
       eBook:  978-1-3503-3195-2

Typeset by RefineCatch Limited, Bungay, Suffolk
Printed and bound in India

To find out more about our authors and books visit www.bloomsbury.com
and sign up for our newsletters.

# Contents

| | |
|---|---|
| List of Illustrations | vii |
| List of Contributors | x |
| Acknowledgments | xvi |

Introduction: Fashion in American Life     1
*Hazel Clark and Lauren Downing Peters*

Section One: Refashioning the Everyday     13
*Hazel Clark and Lauren Downing Peters*

1  Sovereignty Every Day: Mobilizing Indigenous Fashion from the Northwest Coast     17
    *Laura J. Allen*

2  Haoles in Hawaiian Shirts     39
    *Andrew Reilly*

3  "Smart Togs for Action": Everyday Clothes for Rural Women in Texas in the 1950s     59
    *Rebecca Jumper Matheson*

4  Examining the Ordinary: Mourning Adornment and Black Death     79
    *Rikki Byrd*

Section Two: Revisiting the Everyday     95
*Hazel Clark and Lauren Downing Peters*

5  *Rags:* The Birth of Personal Style in Print     99
    *Laura McLaws Helms*

6  Playing *Seminole* Indian: The Cultural Appropriation of Seminole Men's Fashion     119
    *Amanda Thompson*

7  Working from the Periphery: The National Association of Fashion and Accessories Designers (NAFAD) and the Promotion of Black Fashion     141
    *Einav Rabinovitch-Fox*

8   Primitivizing Accessories: "Slave Jewelry" and the Construction
    of White Femininity in 1920s America                              159
    *Victoria Rose Pass*

Section Three: Recovering the Everyday                                181
*Hazel Clark and Lauren Downing Peters*

9   Extra-ordinary Americans: Oral History, Workwear, and the US
    Postal Service                                                    185
    *Alison Bazylinski, Lynn Heidelbaugh, and Rachel Lifter*

10  1970s Fashion and Women: Finding the Everyday at the
    Intersection of Image, Archive, and Oral History                  203
    *Alexis Romano*

11  Preserving the Latinx Sartorial Experience Through Digital Archives   227
    *Michelle McVicker*

12  Self-fashioning, Participatory Research, and the "Will to Adorn"  249
    *Diana Baird N'Diaye*

Index                                                                 269

# Illustrations

| | | |
|---|---|---|
| 1.1 | Talaysay Campo modeling Yolonda Skelton's "Raven Transformation" dress. Brooklyn Bridge, Manhattan, May 14, 2022. | 18 |
| 1.2 | Behind the scenes of Figure 1.1, with Yolonda Skelton (left); Patrick Shannon (with camera); and onlookers. | 19 |
| 1.3 | Henry Seaweed and Yolonda Skelton in Skelton's studio. Victoria, BC, September 7, 2019. | 24 |
| 1.4 | Tsimshian robe (AMNH 16/360, left) in the Northwest Coast Hall, American Museum of Natural History, New York, 2022. | 26 |
| 1.5 | Wendy Van Riesen/Dahlia Drive "Big Blouses" commissioned by Chief Marilyn Slett. They are printed with the symbol of the Heiltsuk Nation, a copper. | 30 |
| 1.6 | Chief Marilyn Slett [Ḱáwáziɫ] (center, in red and black button blanket and beige apron) at the opening of the Heiltsuk Nation Big House, Bella Bella, BC, October 2019. | 31 |
| 2.1 | 1930s Hawaiian shirt with images of postcards. | 43 |
| 2.2 | This David Shepard shirt tells a moʻoelo. | 46 |
| 2.3 | Paul wears the "Lahaina Sailor" shirt from Reyn Spooner. | 48 |
| 2.4 | A typical shirt sold at ABC and seen on tourists in Waikiki. | 49 |
| 3.1 | Dana Rusk (later Jumper), about age ten, with her mother, Louise Jenkins Rusk. *c.* 1956. | 62 |
| 3.2 | Everyday rural East Texas fashions, 1958. The Spivey family. | 65 |
| 3.3 | "Interior shot of the Stephen F. Austin State College bookstore when it was located off East College," July 29, 1952. | 66 |
| 3.4 | Frances Maxine (Rose) Leaphart holding daughter Becky, *c.* 1956, Brownwood, Texas. | 67 |
| 3.5 | United States Information Agency, "Manuel Ramirez and members of his family in front of their home in Texas will be relocated as a result of the joint US-Mexico Falcon Dam construction project on the Rio Grande River," *c.* 1951–4. | 69 |
| 4.1 | Kerry James Marshall, *Heirlooms and Accessories* (triptych), 2002. Ink-jet prints on paper in wooden artist's frames with rhinestones, 51 x 46 inches. | 83 |

| | | |
|---|---|---|
| 5.1 | Cover, *Rags*, June 1970. | 100 |
| 5.2 | Mary Peacock and Blair Sabol visit Betsey Johnson at her New York studio for their story on Johnson, which appeared in the first issue of *Rags* in 1970. | 106 |
| 5.3 | "On the street," *Rags*, July 1970. | 109 |
| 5.4 | "Stud & Patch & Paint & Bleach," *Rags*, July 1970. | 111 |
| 5.5 | Cover, *The Very Best of Rags 1970–1971*. | 114 |
| 6.1 | "HOLLYWOOD, FL – MAY 05: Mitchell Cypress and Governor Charlie Crist attend A Celebration of the Seminole Compact at Seminole Hard Rock Hotel on May 5, 2010 in Hollywood, Florida." May 5, 2010. | 119 |
| 6.2 | Charles Bird King, Tuko-See-Mathla. A Seminole chief, from *History of the Indian Tribes of North America*, c. 1843. | 124 |
| 6.3 | Seminole Indians in Florida. c. 1912, colored postcard. | 125 |
| 6.4 | The VFW marching in Seminole Indian dress for Governor's inaugural parade. The Veterans of Foreign Wars, or VFW, was another settler veterans' organization who dressed as Seminoles. 1949. | 127 |
| 6.5 | Patchwork big shirt, early twentieth century. | 128 |
| 6.6 | Patchwork jacket, mid twentieth century. | 131 |
| 7.1 | NAFAD Emblem. | 146 |
| 7.2 | "Cleveland NAFADs to Show Spring, Summer Collection," *Cleveland Call & Post*, March 1, 1958. | 149 |
| 7.3 | Amanda Wicker, Suit Ensemble, c. 1950s. | 152 |
| 7.4 | San Francisco Junior Chapter NAFAD. | 154 |
| 8.1 | Joel Gutman & Co. advertisement for "Slave Jewelry," *The Evening Sun*, Baltimore, March 4, 1926. | 160 |
| 8.2 | At center, "Colleen Moore all bound round with the 'slave bracelets,' dear to the heart of flappers," in *Motion Picture Classic*, January 1925. | 161 |
| 8.3 | Joan Crawford in *Our Dancing Daughters*, 1928. | 162 |
| 8.4 | Cohn & Rosenberger, Inc. Advertisement for "Slave Bracelets," *Women's Wear Daily*, April 1, 1926. | 164 |
| 8.5 | Georges Lepape, Denise Poiret at 'The Thousand and Second Night' party, 1911. Gouache on paper. | 166 |
| 8.6 | Christina Aguilera, featuring Lil' Kim, "Can't Hold Us Down," directed by David LaChappelle. | 173 |
| 9.1 | City letter carrier's uniform manufactured by Maher Brothers of Utica, New York, c. 1900. | 188 |
| 9.2 | Letter carrier in New York City, 2020. | 190 |

| | | |
|---|---|---|
| 9.3 | Ann Salisbury's Post Office Department uniform (left) and her USPS letter carrier's jacket (right). | 192 |
| 10.1 | Andrea at Riding Academy, Rockville Centre, New York, 1972. | 208 |
| 10.2 | Mary Jo in drawing class with her professor, Madame Wibaut, Banff Centre for the Arts, Alberta, Canada, 1978. | 209 |
| 10.3 | Barbara and Kevin Walz, Publicity Poster, Adri for Royal Clothes, *c.* 1971. | 213 |
| 10.4 | Publicity photograph for the Spring 1972 Clothes Circuit collection by Adri. | 214 |
| 10.5 | Joyce surrounded by her grandmother, mother and daughter after Christmas dinner, Baton Rouge, *c.* 1975. | 216 |
| 10.6 | Joyce at work at the copy center, Baton Rouge, 1975. | 217 |
| 10.7 | Andrea at the Law School Prom, St. John's University, New York, 1975. | 220 |
| 11.1 | Mercedes Marina Arambulo, The Bronx, 1980s. | 235 |
| 11.2 | A typical day at the office, *c.* 1991/1992. | 236 |
| 11.3 | Jaime Restrepo, Kristina Lopez's padrino, at the ribbon factory. Long Island City, Queens, late 1980s. | 237 |
| 11.4 | Submitted by @jen.mar10, an ode to her tia. | 238 |
| 11.5 | A little story about my nameplate, submitted by @michelle.korinna. | 240 |
| 12.1 | Rosemarie Reed Miller at the 2013 Smithsonian Folklife Festival. | 250 |
| 12.2 | Rufus Isley outfitting a client at his Mister Mann store in Washington, DC. | 254 |
| 12.3 | Marilyn Davies on the Will to Adorn program runway. | 262 |
| 12.4 | Interns enrolled in the Will to Adorn summer teen program. | 263 |

# Contributors

## Editors

**Hazel Clark**, PhD, FRSA, is Professor of Design Studies and Fashion Studies and currently Director of the MA Fashion Studies program, which she initiated at Parsons School of Design, The New School, New York, USA. She has taught and researched internationally on fashion, culture and everyday life, fashion in the USA and China, fashion curation, and slow approaches to fashion. Her more recent books include the anthology *Fashion Curating: Critical Practice in the Museum and Beyond* (Bloomsbury Academic, 2018) with Annamari Vänska, and *Fashion and Everyday Life: London and New York* (Bloomsbury Academic, 2017), with Cheryl Buckley, which provided a conceptual impetus for *Fashion in American Life*.

**Lauren Downing Peters**, PhD, is Assistant Professor of Fashion Studies and Director of the Fashion Study Collection at Columbia College Chicago, USA. Her research focuses on the history of plus-size fashion, weight bias in the fashion industry, alternative histories of American fashion, and transformed and inclusive fashion pedagogies. Her work has been published in the peer-reviewed journals *Fashion Theory, Design Issues, Critical Studies in Fashion and Beauty, International Journal of Fashion Studies* and the *Journal of Curatorial Studies*, among others. She is the author of *Fashion Before Plus-Size: Bodies, Bias, and the Birth of an Industry* (Bloomsbury Academic, 2023) and the co-curator with Emma McClendon of *(Re)Dressing American Fashion: Wear as Witness* (Bard Graduate Center Gallery, 2025).

## Authors

**Laura J. Allen** is an interdisciplinary scholar and the Curator of Native American Art at the Montclair Art Museum located on Lenape land (New Jersey), USA. Her museum practice focuses on critical and collaborative museology and historical, modern, and contemporary Native art. Her research and publications examine visual and material culture of the Northwest Coast as well as Indigenous and intercultural dress, fashion, and textile history in the Americas. Themes in her writing include Indigenous agency and resurgence; colonialism; materiality and material analysis; and the collection, circulation, and display of cultural objects and designs. Her work has received awards from the Textile Society of America and Bard Graduate Center. Allen earned her MA in Decorative Arts, Design History, and Material Culture from Bard Graduate Center, an AAS in Fashion Design from SUNY Fashion Institute of Technology, and a BS in Biology from Bates College. Integrating these disciplines, her career has spanned the museum, design, and editorial fields and the material and natural world. She has served in the Division of Anthropology and the Exhibition Department of the American Museum of Natural History; consulted for the University of Alaska Museum of the North, Columbia University, and other organizations; and worked for several fashion designers in New York City, where she lives. www.laura-allen.com

**Rikki Byrd** is a writer, educator and curator who works across the academy, arts, and fashion industries. She holds a Bachelor of Journalism from the University of Missouri, a Master of Arts in Fashion Studies from Parsons School of Design and a Master of Arts in Black Studies from Northwestern University, USA, where she is currently pursuing her PhD in Black Studies (2024). She has lectured at the School of the Art Institute of Chicago and Washington University in St. Louis, where she created new courses on fashion and race. Her writing appears across exhibition catalogs, academic journals, and books such as *The Routledge Companion to African American Theatre and Performance, International Journal of Fashion Studies, and the Fashion Studies Journal*, and popular media such as *Hyperallergic, Cultured*, and *Teen Vogue*. She is the co-founder and editor of the Fashion and Race Syllabus and founder of Black Fashion Archive.

**Alison R. Bazylinski** is an assistant curator at the Smithsonian's National Postal Museum, USA She earned her doctorate in American Studies from William & Mary, where her research focused on cultural histories of fabric and clothing in early twentieth century America. She is currently serving as coordinator for an oral history project, "Postal Workwear." Her other specialties include the history of mail-order, commerce and consumption, and postal uniforms.

**Lynn Heidelbaugh** is a curator at the Smithsonian's National Postal Museum, USA, where she specializes in research and acquisitions on the history of postal communications. Heidelbaugh has served as lead curator for exhibitions including *Mail Call: History of U.S. Military Mail* (2011); *Behind the Badge: The U.S. Postal Inspection Service* (2014); *My Fellow Soldiers: Letters from World War I* (2017), for which she received a Smithsonian Secretary's Research Award. She co-edited *Between Home and the Front: Civil War Letters of the Walters Family* (2022) featuring correspondence from the museum's collection. She is a co-creator of the Postal Workwear Oral History Project collaboration.

**Laura McLaws Helms** is a fashion and cultural historian based in New York, USA. She writes for a number of publications and works as an editorial advisor and historian for publishing companies and fashion houses. Laura curated an exhibition, "Thea Porter: 70s Bohemian Chic," at the Fashion and Textile Museum, London (2015), and wrote an accompanying monograph, *Thea Porter: Bohemian Chic*, published by V&A Publications. Ms. Helms worked towards her Ph.D. at the London College of Fashion and holds a Master's Degree in Fashion History, Theory and Museum Practice from the Fashion Institute of Technology.

**Rachel Lifter** is Clinical Assistant Professor and Director of NYU's master's program in Costume Studies. She is author of *Fashioning Indie: Popular Fashion, Music and Gender* (Bloomsbury Visual Arts 2020). Her current projects prioritize oral history within fashion storytelling.

**Rebecca Jumper Matheson** (JD, University of Texas at Austin; MA, Fashion Institute of Technology; PhD, Bard Graduate Center) is a fashion historian. Matheson's research focuses on nineteenth- and twentieth-century American women's dress, using interdisciplinary approaches to discover women's narratives as designers, makers, sellers, and consumers. Her recent projects have dealt with accessories, advertising, teenage fashion, and long-distance train travel. Matheson is the author of two monographs, *The Sunbonnet: An American Icon in Texas* (2009) and *Young Originals: Emily Wilkens and the Teen Sophisticate* (2015). She is an adjunct instructor at the Fashion Institute of Technology in the MA program in Fashion and Textile Studies.

**Michelle McVicker** is the Associate Collections Specialist at the Antonio Ratti Textile Study and Storage Center. She previously worked as the Permanent Collections Associate Registrar at El Museo del Barrio, the Collections and Education Assistant at the Museum at The Fashion Institute of Technology, a Smithsonian Cultural Heritage Fellow at The National Museum of American

History, and a Collections Management Assistant at The Costume Institute. She received her Fashion Studies MA at Parsons School of Design in 2017. Her research interests include how material culture, specifically clothing, embody ever-evolving Latinx representations in the United States.

**Dr. Diana Baird N'Diaye** is an interdisciplinary artist, scholar, writer, and cultural activist whose work interrogates the connections between textiles, personal adornment, history, and identity across global Africa. As Senior Curator and Cultural Heritage Specialist at the Smithsonian Center for Folklife and Cultural Heritage, USA, N'Diaye directs three Smithsonian living cultural heritage Initiatives: The African American Craft Initiative, the Crafts of African Fashion, and the Will to Adorn: African American Style and the Aesthetics of Identity. The latter was the focus for a ten-year participatory research project that resulted in a major ten-day program of the Smithsonian's Folklife Festival, several national events, an exhibition at the Institute for Texan Cultures, online conferences, and publications. The Will to Adorn is the subject of an upcoming book to be published by University of Mississippi Press. Dr. N'Diaye's awards include the Smithsonian Secretary's Research Prize for the 2016 co-authored book, *Curatorial Conversations: Reflections on the Folklife Festival*, the Americo Paredes Prize for folklore work that engages communities. In 2022, N'Diaye was named a Craft Visionary by the American Craft Council.

**Victoria Rose Pass** is Associate Professor at the Maryland Institute College of Art, USA, and a specialist in Visual Culture, particularly in areas of design and fashion. Her essay "Racial Masquerades in the Magazines: Defining White Femininity Between the Wars," was published in the *Journal of Modern Periodical Studies*. Her co-edited the book *Design Beyond the Canon* with Jennifer Kauffman-Buhler and Christopher Wilson was published by Bloomsbury in 2019. She also co-edited the volume, *Women's Magazines in Print and New Media* with Noliwe Rooks and Ayana Weekley, which was published in 2016.

**Einav Rabinovitch-Fox** is a historian of modern American women's and gender who teaches at Case Western Reserve University in Cleveland, USA. Her research examines the connections between fashion, politics, and modernity, particularly the role of visual and material culture in social movements. Her recent book, *Dressed for Freedom: The Fashionable Politics of American Feminism* (2021) explores women's political uses of clothing and appearance to promote feminist agendas during the long twentieth century. Her research has been featured in

*The New York Times*, *Teen Vogue*, and the *Wall Street Journal*, and she has published in academic journals and books including the *Journal of Women's History*, the *International Journal of Fashion Studies, American Journalism: Journal of Media History*, as well as popular media such as *The Washington Post*, *The Conversation*, *Public Seminar*, and *History News Network*.

**Andrew ('Andy') Reilly**, PhD, is a professor in the Fashion Design and Merchandising program at the University of Hawai'i, Mānoa, USA. Dr. Reilly's research areas investigate appearance-related issues surrounding gender and sexuality identity as well as testing and developing new theories of fashion adoption and change. His books include *Handbook of Men's Fashion* (co-edited with Ben Barry and José Blanco F.), *Fashion, Dress, and Post-postmodernism* (co-edited with José Blanco F.), and *Crossing Gender Boundaries: Fashion to Create, Disrupt, and Transcend* (co-edited with Ben Barry). He is past-president of the Textile and Apparel Programs Accrediting Commission, past vice-president for scholarship for the International Textile and Apparel Association, and president-elect for the International Textile and Apparel Association. He is a fellow of the International Textile and Apparel Association.

**Alexis Romano**, PhD, Courtauld Institute of Art, is a writer and educator in the fields of fashion, design history, and visual culture. She teaches at Parsons School of Design, USA, and is US Editor of WeAr Global Magazine. Her work explores women's history and everyday, subjective aspects of dress, with the aim of broadening fashion access and challenging design hierarchies. Her book, *Prêt-à-Porter, Paris and Women: A Cultural Study of French Readymade Fashion, 1945–68*, is published by Bloomsbury (2022). She is also developing a 2023 community-led exhibition for the Newhouse Center for Contemporary Art on local fashion identities. Alexis is a co-founder of the Fashion Research Network and was the 2020–1 Curatorial Fellow at the Costume Institute (Metropolitan Museum of Art). She has contributed to peer-reviewed journals such as *Costume*, *Fashion Theory*, and *Photography and Culture*, catalogues by institutions including the Jewish Museum, Palais Galliera and the V&A, and design publications including *Vestoj*, *Disegno*, and *Address*.

**Amanda Thompson** is a PhD candidate at the Bard Graduate Center whose work considers settler colonialism, gender, and the consumption, management, and appropriation of Native American arts, especially fashion and fiber arts techniques. She has held a Smithsonian American Art Museum Pre-Doctoral

Research Fellowship and the Hagley Museum and Library's H. B. du Pont Dissertation Fellowship in Business, Technology, and Society. Additional research has been funded by the American Philosophical Society, the Bard Graduate Center, and the Decorative Arts Trust. Amanda has over fifteen years' experience managing exhibitions and collections for museums and currently serves on the Board of the Tomaquag Museum, an Indigenous-led institution committed to expanding knowledge of the Native cultures and peoples of Southern New England.

# Acknowledgments

First and foremost, the editors would like to thank our editor, Frances Arnold, for her support, direction, and patience throughout the writing and production of this book. We are also grateful to the anonymous reviewers who believed in the value of this work and who offered valuable guidance as we developed this from a proposal to a book. We would also like to thank MA Fashion Studies student research assistants Katie Ibsen and David Suoth for their assistance in helping to pull the many pieces of final manuscript together, including permissions. It is our contributors, however, to whom we owe the greatest debt of gratitude. Without their wonderful chapters—written and edited during the Covid-19 pandemic—this book would have never come to fruition.

This project began as an academic symposium, which was held at Columbia College Chicago in February 2020. We would like to extend a huge thanks to Columbia for being such a gracious host, as well as to the original lineup of presenters and discussants whose scholarship and contributions helped to lay the foundations for this book. Special thanks to the Columbia student volunteers who helped to produce and run the symposium, and to the Department of Fashion Studies at Columbia College Chicago and the School of Art and Design History (ADHT) and Theory at Parsons School of Design for providing funding for the event. Thanks also to ADHT faculty colleague Mev Luna for suggesting the image, which has been adapted for the cover of the book.

For the editors and authors, having vibrant, full-color images was essential for adequately telling the stories that unfold in the pages that follow. We are therefore grateful for the generous Faculty Development Grant provided by the Office of the Provost at Columbia College Chicago to cover additional production costs, as well as costs associated with indexing and rights and reproduction. Any individual author acknowledgements are included at the end of each chapter; however, the editors would like to extend thanks to all of the archives, galleries, artists, interview subjects, and practitioners who graciously shared imagery.

INTRODUCTION

# Fashion in American Life

Hazel Clark and Lauren Downing Peters

## Fashion

An immediate point of origin of this book was a conference, organized by the editors, and held in Chicago in February 2020. "American Everyday: Resistance, Revolution and Transformation" elicited over forty diverse and fascinating presentations, some of which became chapters for this book. The conference developed our thinking on the role/s of fashion in American life through the lenses of "agency," "identity," and "the everyday," as well as begging many questions, which soon came to be framed by an unexpected turn of events.

Exactly a month after the conference, the United States began to go into lockdown as the potential severity of the Covid-19 global pandemic was recognized, and our everyday lives were put on hold. The pandemic period, during which this volume came into being, enabled us to reflect, in unexpected ways, on the roles of dress, fashion, and self-fashioning in American life. It caused many Americans to re-negotiate their relationships with what they wore on their bodies, highlighting fashion's "multitude of possibilities,"[1] as an active and agential practice. In this volume, authors engage with "fashion," most particularly used as a verb, to refer to the act of fashioning the body, contextualized relative to broader discourses of cultures, periods, and places. Comparatively, "fashion" as a noun, should be understood to signify the contemporary capitalist industry and system of power, originating in Europe, and exported throughout the world by Western imperialism.[2] While this monolithic and market-driven sense of fashion did not disappear during the pandemic period, it encountered challenges as people stayed at home, dressed up less, and bought fewer new clothes. But what was interesting was that self-fashioning did not disappear; in fact, many people attired themselves, often quite creatively, even if just above the waist, as they communicated with one another via computer screens. Fashion did not recede from everyday life; it rather took different forms.

The concept of self-fashioning, introduced by Stephen Greenblatt to demonstrate how selves were formed, or "fashioned" in the Renaissance, in response to powerful social forces, such as the church, state, or family, is valuable to our study.[3] The role of dress and embodiment in human self-fashioning is closely interwoven with culture, society, and time. The period when this book was under construction was unprecedented not only because of the pandemic, but also for the challenges being posed to constructs of American identity and civic life, and as conversations on race and representation came into greater prominence in the public domain.

The Black Lives Matter movement, formed in 2013, highlighted the continuing racial inequality of Black people in America, especially as victims of police brutality. It impacted fashion in a number of ways. The individuals being represented on the covers of fashion magazines, such as *Vogue* and *Vanity Fair*, and those who created the pictures, changed to include Black and Brown bodies, stylists, and image makers. This acknowledgement by the fashion system of the racial and cultural diversity of America, for a moment at least, was striking in its reminder of who had been excluded from the mainstream fashion discourse. However, it was an act that may also be read as the "spectacularization" of the Black body by the media, even in death.[4] An example of this is the depiction of Breonna Taylor, who was fatally shot by police in her home in Louisville, Kentucky, that appeared on the September 2020 cover of *Vanity Fair* from a posthumous painting by Amy Sherald. It is too soon to tell whether such representations mark a significant shift in the fashion media or just a "fashion moment." As this book makes evident, the fashion system (or Fashion, with a capital F) fails to embrace the legitimacy of self-fashioning and its relationship to the formation and expression of identity, and personal agency, which Greenblatt introduced. Commodity driven, mainstream fashion in America has tended, until recently, only to acknowledge (or appropriate) Black and indigenous culture as a source of "inspiration." We might recall how Urban Outfitters was sued by the Navajo Nation for illegally using its name for products bearing offensive interpretations of Navajo motifs in 2016.[5] Or we could reflect on how Hip Hop, a cultural movement that emerged from the grassroots of New York street culture, has come to "influence" fashion at many levels of the market, even as the legacies of its principal arbiters—from Dapper Dan to Carl Jones—have only recently been given due recognition.[6]

Our choices of who and what to include in this book were thus informed by our awareness that the fashion system does not, and never has, represented the range and diversity of people that engage with fashion in America (and elsewhere). Our authors were chosen to present a nuanced set of case studies and approaches that address how people dress and self-fashion day-to-day and in ordinary contexts. In that sense, this anthology begins (but only just) to fill a gap in the conceptualization of and existing literature on "American fashion." But establishing the geographical and cultural parameters of our study, or to put it another way, what and where was America and who was American, was another challenge we faced in framing this collection.

## America

In 1968, the folk-rock duo Simon and Garfunkel released their song "America," inspired by a road trip taken a few years earlier. The refrain focuses on the search of a literal and physical America which seemed to have disappeared, along with the country's ideals. Perhaps the mythic American Dream had already been assuaged, or at least diluted, by the fatigue of the Vietnam War and the impact of the Civil Rights Movement. America was, and remains, a nation predominantly of immigrants. Paradoxically, it is also a nation where Black, indigenous, and people of color (BIPOC) exist as a minority who are struggling for recognition, representation, and appreciation. Thus, the practices of making fashion and self-fashioning to be found across the country are as disparate and diverse as the bodies who wear the clothes, and the cultural practices which have influenced what is worn. This book can only provide a limited window into the range and complexity of fashion, or rather fashions, that are and always have been evident in everyday life in America, present and past, examined from (in our chapters) the 1920s to the present day.

Geographically, the examples included in the book inscribe a trajectory from the noncontiguous state and islands of Hawai'i, through the Pacific Northwest, across into Florida, to the Caribbean, and across the political boundary that separates the United States and Canada. While our authors take examples from within the fifty states, we acknowledge that borders are constructs and who people are, where they originated, and how they choose to fashion themselves is not constrained by national or state boundaries, which can and do shift. Some indigenous people avoid referring to names created by the construction of state and county borders, preferring to use the term "Turtle Island," to refer to the whole continent of North America. Significantly, the chapters make explicit how communities of fashion evolve and function relative to time and place, and how cultural ideas are made manifest in how people dress. Such practices develop and are transmitted within and through human networks, which are themselves subject to change as individuals and groups move and relocate. How people choose to dress is a signifying practice, with deeply symbolic, as well as functional, foundations. The examples mentioned in the chapters do not and cannot provide a comprehensive view of fashion in American life across the twentieth and into the twenty-first century. It was not possible, in one volume, to cover comprehensively the many different culturally, racially, and ethnically determined groups of people who make their lives and identify intersectionally, across the land.

What we are therefore intending to provide is a contribution to fashion studies that revisits and problematizes existing approaches, and which reframes the concepts, practices, and politics of "American fashion." Even a cursory literature review reveals, until recently at least, a predominance of well-trodden accounts of fashion designers and the prevalence of accounts of New York. Much of the fashion we uncover has been under-represented in previous writing or may have been codified as "dress" or "ethnic costume," rather than relative to the broader definitions of fashion, referred to above. That being said, there is much, inevitably, that we were unable to include. We do not reference what has been and is worn and made by the Asian American or Muslim American populations living in the United States, among others. This is an omission, but not an erasure. It is reflective of the fact that uncovering the role of fashion in American life remains a relatively new approach to the scholarship of American fashion and is very much a work in progress. What we present here is content that is current and original in its subject matter and methodologies.

## Everyday life

Our conceptual framework of the everyday builds on the perspectives established by co-editor Hazel Clark and Cheryl Buckley in *Fashion and Everyday Life: London and New York* (2017).[7] This provides us with an overview of concepts such as "the ordinary," "the everyday," and "everyday life" as considered by scholars including Henri Lefebvre, Michel de Certeau, and Ben Highmore.[8] None wrote about fashion or dress, but each offers perspectives which have proved vital to our work. Lefebvre considered the everyday to be a critical arena within capitalist culture; de Certeau highlighted the inventiveness of the everyday; and Highmore continues to recognize the importance of the everyday in his work as a cultural theorist. Their scholarship on the everyday provides us with an opportunity to revisit the narrative(s) of American fashion and to include stories, experiences, and groups that have been forgotten, marginalized, and left out of the fashion canon. Buckley and Clark acknowledge fashion that has gone unrecognized in everyday life, as well as referring to effective tactics of dressing that have usurped the strategic dominance of the fashion system. Sometimes this is realized in a modest way, simply by wearing garments in places or at times other than were originally intended, for example, secondhand clothes. At other times it can be much more intentional, and political, as a form of style activism.[9] Our volume acknowledges the everyday as a critical framework for questioning the very shape and nature of American fashion. Our authors demonstrate how examining fashion in everyday life transcends a sense of the static or the senseless, to reveal the extraordinary possibilities offered and opportunities taken by Americans in their own self-fashioning.

In taking a wider view of "fashion" in two (so called) world "fashion cities,"[10] London and New York, Buckley and Clark look beyond the fashion system to include the everyday choices and experiences of wearers. In her review of their book, Elizabeth Wilson noted that the biggest omission of their book, although one that went beyond its remit, was not to include "different experiences of fashion outside the world metropolis experience."[11] That wider remit is one that has informed this book, while also acknowledging that our coverage in such a short volume can only be partial. Taking a broader geographical and cultural lens on fashion is one that other scholars have also begun to tackle. In their ethnographic investigation of how fashion was produced amongst a student population in rural America, Green, Lewis, and Jirousek (2013) reveal "the power of individuals to manipulate and appropriate the design and meaning(s) of fashion objects."[12] Such work reinforces the importance of reading, and thus re-defining, what is being worn, by whom, and why in America "against the grain" of accepted fashion knowledge and practices. It establishes ways of defining and thus investigating "fashion" more widely, and not just in America, but also elsewhere, by recognizing its creative and political significance in human lives more broadly than has often been discussed previously. The collaborative work of Green, Lewis, and Jirousek also reinforces the significance in doing this work in collaboration with interdisciplinary peers, as several of the authors in this volume do, to share and build upon their distinct and complementary expertise. Similarly, in the UK, Bide, Halbert, and Tregenza combined editorial responsibility for a recent anthology, which interprets "everyday fashion" through examinations of British clothing since 1600.[13]

## Approaches

The scholars who contribute to this book represent a variety of academic backgrounds, from fashion studies and fashion history to American studies, design studies, women's and gender studies, and professional practices of writing, teaching, criticism, and curation, that have brought them to an interest in fashion in American life. Race, gender, ethnicity, class, and colonialism are some of the critical perspectives through which they shed new light on how fashion might be defined and addressed within America (as a country, but not, in reality, as a series of United States). Though the book is organized into three distinct sections (discussed below) through their chapters, "red threads" emerge which the reader can identify and trace across and between the book. While it is in the final section that we focus specifically on methodologies, it should be noted that many of the chapters, by necessity, are multimethodological and transcend conventional disciplinary boundaries. Visual, historical, and archival research, ethnographic investigation, oral histories, and interviews inform and enliven the chapters. In their approaches, our authors not only add to our knowledge of what might be considered fashion in American life, but to the detailed and nuanced manner in which its investigation needs to be undertaken and presented. In that sense, this book is adding to a developing set of new approaches that are becoming evident for scholarly and general audiences.

In her book, *Fashion Before Plus-Size* (2023),[14] co-editor Lauren Downing Peters frames the fat female body as average rather than exceptional in America (or as ordinary, rather than extraordinary). Her study helps to broaden our understanding of what constitutes an "appropriately" American body, as well as the constraints (material and discursive) that have shaped (and hindered) American women's experiences of shopping and getting dressed in everyday life. The primary research that underpins this book, and our own edited volume, is essential to enable a re-thinking and re-definition of fashion in American life, both what it is and what it does. Shifts are taking place more widely in academic publishing and in exhibitions, although the changes are incremental, and perhaps can only be so, as a part of building on what already exists. A focus on the fashion system, and "fashion" as a noun, prevails, and with it the identification and celebration of previously unacknowledged designers. Several recent books and exhibitions come to mind.

Nancy Deihl's edited volume *The Hidden History of American Fashion: Rediscovering 20th Century Women Designers* (2018)[15] added substantially to our knowledge of some of the women who defined the American fashion system. Their contributions, from the rag trade of New York's Seventh Avenue to costumes for Hollywood and Broadway productions, are documented in sixteen wide-ranging chapters. One contributor, scholar and curator Elizabeth Way, applied a similar approach to her *Black Designers in American Fashion* (2021),[16] an edited volume that succeeded the *Black Fashion Designers* exhibition which she co-curated at the Museum at the Fashion Institute of Technology (FIT) in New York City in 2016/17. These were admirable pieces of work, which developed substantially our historical knowledge of designers whose activities had been obscured in part because of their gender and race. *Fashioning America: Grit to Glamour*, at the Crystal Bridges Museum of American Art, Arizona, in 2022/23, curated by Michelle Tolini Finamore, similarly emphasized "the work of designers who immigrated to America, Native American and Black designers, as well as iconic fashion brands and their impact on visual culture in every decade."[17] The book of the same title, edited by the curator, references indigenous fashion, westernwear, Black craftspeople, whiteness, racial plagiarism, and diversifying the future, as well as stories of erasure.

As distinct from scholarly publications, exhibitions tend to focus on what their known audiences are assumed to appreciate, and thus lean towards more clearly demarcated subjects and approaches. Even looking back over the last ten to fifteen years of exhibitions with perspectives on fashion in America, the work of named designers has predominated (even if some are only coming to wider attention). *In America: A Lexicon of Fashion,* held at the Costume Institute of The Metropolitan Museum of Art, New York, 2021/22 was a case-in-point. The exhibition aimed to develop a "revised vocabulary of American fashion, based on its expressive qualities"[18] and to reappraise the stereotypes of sportswear and ready-to-wear so clearly associated with the American fashion industry. The inspiration for the exhibition was the American patchwork quilt, presented as a metaphor for the country, its people, and their unique cultural identities. Nevertheless, the theme was explored through the presentation in the now all-too-familiar manner of showing individual, inevitably high fashion, pieces by named designers. (Some of whom, it should be noted, such as Christopher John Rogers, who launched his first collection in 2018, were young and had never shown their designs in a museum before.) While the convention of displaying the history of American fashion as a succession of silhouettes and designers is beginning to be challenged—as, for instance, in Emma McClendon and Lauren Downing Peters' Bard Graduate Center exhibition *(Re)Dressing American Fashion: Wear as Witness* (2025)[19]—it remains a standard curatorial tactic for a number of reasons. These include its easy digestibility and visual impact, even at the expense of blurring more complicated and uncomfortable (though truthful) histories.

Other exhibitions have taken a more regional approach in their exploration of American fashion history and its social and cultural impacts. For instance, the University of Sacramento's 2022 Library Gallery exhibition, *Dressing Sacramento:*

*120 Years of Fashion*, highlighted what local people wore from the 1860s. Garments in the Sacramento State Costume Collection were contextualized with photographs and captions, to highlight fashion's social impact.[20] Sonya Abrego's 2023 exhibition, *Crafting Denim*, which was on display at the John Cram Gallery in Asheville, North Carolina, and the Autrey Museum's 2022/23 exhibition *Dress Codes* took a similarly regional approach, focusing, respectively, on North Carolina's denim industry and the iconic dress of the American Southwest, over trying to define a singular "American fashion." These exhibitions' approaches are much closer to that of this book in their framing of American fashion through space, place, culture, society, history, politics, and human behavior.

Elsewhere, we can also note how indigenous Americans have rightfully begun to be acknowledged not just as wearers but *producers* of fashion, notably in the exhibition *Native Fashion Now*, which originated at the Peabody Essex Museum, Massachusetts in 2015, as well as in the Chicago Field Museum's recently-renovated Native North American Hall.[21] Such exhibitions as well as scholarship on indigenous dress practices on Turtle Island, including the journal *Fashion Studies*' recent an important volume on the topic, have begun to acknowledge indigenous peoples' many contributions to the fashion system while uplifting decolonized methods and approaches to fashion scholarship rooted in indigenous practice and knowledge.[22] Though there is still much work to be done on this topic, two authors in this volume make important, and valuable, inroads.

# Organization

The chapters in this book are organized into three sections, each with its own short introduction to contextualize the content and summarize the chapters, under the headings of "Refashioning," "Revisiting," and "Recovering the Everyday." While the first section, "Refashioning the Everyday," focuses on self-fashioning practices, and specifically how the dressed body functions as a site to variously uphold and upend ideals of American identity, the chapters in the second section, "Revisiting the Everyday," more expressly trouble the familiar narrative arc of twentieth century American fashion as a succession of designers and silhouettes. As noted above, the final section, "Recovering the Everyday," takes a somewhat different tack in its focus on sources and methods for recovering stories and histories that have been marginalized or forgotten.

These titles notwithstanding, the reader will note that there are overlaps and continuities between the approaches of the sections and their content—not least of which being their focus on "the everyday" as conceptualized by Lefebvre, de Certeau, and Highmore, and more specifically (with regard to fashion) by Buckley and Clark. This is inevitable, and reinforcing, especially in terms of methodologies. Sharing what we, and our authors, determine has to date been left over in American fashion (to borrow from Lefebvre's reference to everyday life),[23] has led to detailed and complex investigations. The outcomes, as the reader will recognize, enable us in this volume to demonstrate the significant and ongoing complexity of the role of fashion in American life, as well as the pathways and opportunities for ongoing and future research. The study of fashion in American everyday life is, without doubt, a significant work in progress.

## Notes

1 Angela Jansen, "Fashion and the Phantasmagoria of Modernity: An Introduction to Decolonial Fashion Discourse," *Fashion Theory* 24, Issue 6 (2020): 817, DOI: 10.1080/1362704X.2020.1802098
2 Ibid.: 816.
3 Stephen Greenblatt, *Renaissance Self-Fashioning: From More to Shakespeare* (Chicago: University of Chicago Press, 1980).
4 For further discussion, see Yasmin Ibraham, "The Dying Black Body in Repeat Mode: The Black 'Horrific' on a Loop," *Identities: Global Studies in Culture and Power* 29, no. 6 (2022): 711–20; Francesca Sobande, "Spectacularized and Branded Digital (Re)presentations of Black People and Blackness," *Television & New Media*, 22, no. 1 (2021): 131–46.
5 Nicky Wolf, "Urban Outfitters settles with Navajo Nation after illegally using tribes name," *The Guardian* (November 16, 2016), https://www.theguardian.com/us-news/2016/nov/18/urban-outfitters-navajo-nation-settlement
6 Nick Grant, "Is Fashion Relying too Much on Hip Hop to Stay Relevant?" *Fashionista* (November 15, 2017), https://fashionista.com/2017/09/hip-hop-fashion-relationship-relevance
7 Cheryl Buckley and Hazel Clark, *Fashion and Everyday Life: London and New York* (London: Bloomsbury, 2017).
8 Henri Lefebvre, *Critique of Everyday Life*, trans. John Moore (London: Verso, 1991); Michel de Certeau, *The Practice of Everyday Life*, tran. Steven Rendall (Berkeley, CA: University of California Press, 1984); Ben Highmore, ed., *The Everyday Life Reader* (London and New York: Routledge, 2002).
9 Carol Tulloch, "Style Activism: The Everyday Activist Wardrobe of the Black Panther Party and Rock Against Racism," in *Fashion and Politics*, ed. Djurdja Bartlett (New Haven and London: Yale University Press, 2019), 85–101.

10 See, for example, Christopher Breward and David Gilbert, eds., *Fashion's World Cities* (Oxford and New York: Berg, 2006).

11 Elizabeth Wilson, *Fashion and Everyday Life: London and New York, Fashion Theory* 23, Issue 4–5, (2019): 601–3, DOI: 10.1080/1362704X.2018.1429076

12 Denise Nicole Green, Van Dyk Lewis and Charlotte Jirousek, "Fashion Cultures in a Small Town: An Analysis of Fashion- and Place-making," *Critical Studies in Fashion & Beauty* vol. 4, nos 1 and 2, (2013): 72.

13 Bethan Bide, Jade Halbert, and Liz Tregenza, eds., *Everyday Fashion: Interpreting British Clothing Since 1600* (London and New York: Bloomsbury, 2023).

14 Lauren Downing Peters, *Fashion Before Plus-Size: Bodies, Bias, and the Birth of an Industry* (London and New York: Bloomsbury, 2023).

15 Nancy Deihl, ed., *The Hidden History of American Fashion: Rediscovering 20th Century Women Designers* (London and New York: Bloomsbury, 2018).

16 Elizabeth Way, ed., *Black Designers in American Fashion* (London and New York: Bloomsbury, 2021).

17 https://crystalbridges.org/calendar/fashioning-america-grit-to-glamour/

18 Andrew Bolton, Wendy Yu Curator in Charge of the Costume Institute https://www.metmuseum.org/exhibitions/in-america

19 This exhibition—which employs fifteen case study objects to examine how fashion and dress have been used to negotiate constructions of American identity and citizenship, and which bear visible signs of wear and handmaking—is accompanied by a catalog and digital humanities platform.

20 Jennifer K. Morita, "Library Gallery exhibit shows 120 years of how Sacramentans dressed—and fashion's social impact," Sacramento State University Newsroom (September 6, 2022), https://www.csus.edu/news/newsroom/stories/2022/9/dressing-sacramento-exhibit.html

21 Sarah Kuta, "Field Museum Confronts its Outdated, Insensitive Native American Exhibition," *Smithsonian Magazine* (May 26, 2022), https://www.smithsonianmag.com/smart-news/field-museum-confronts-outdated-insensitive-native-american-exhibition-180980148/

22 For a summary of this work, see the special issue of *Fashion Studies* co-edited by Riley Kucheran and Ben Barry in 2022.

23 See J. Seigworth and Michael J. Gardiner, "Rethinking Everyday Life: And Then Nothing Turns Itself Inside Out," *Cultural Studies* 18, no 2 (2004): 147.

# Bibliography

Bartlett, Djurdja, ed. *Fashion and Politics.* New Haven and London: Yale University Press, 2019.

Bide, Bethan Jade Halbert and Liz Tregenza, eds. *Everyday Fashion: Interpreting British Clothing Since 1600.* London and New York: Bloomsbury, 2023.

Buckley, Cheryl and Hazel Clark. *Fashion and Everyday Life: London and New York.* London: Bloomsbury, 2017.

de Certeau, Michel. *The Practice of Everyday Life.* Translated by Steven Rendall. Berkeley: University of California Press, 1984.

Deihl, Nancy, ed. *The Hidden History of American Fashion: Rediscovering 20th Century Women Designers.* London and New York: Bloomsbury, 2018.

Greenblatt, Stephen. *Renaissance Self-Fashioning: From More to Shakespeare.* Chicago: University of Chicago Press, 1980.

Highmore, Ben, ed. *The Everyday Life Reader.* London and New York: Routledge, 2002.

Lefebvre, Henri. *Critique of Everyday Life.* Translated by John Moore. London: Verso, 1991.

Peters, Lauren Downing. *Fashion Before Plus-Size: Bodies, Bias, and the Birth of an Industry.* London and New York: Bloomsbury, 2023.

Way, Elizabeth, ed. *Black Designers in American Fashion.* London and New York: Bloomsbury, 2021.

# Section One

# Refashioning the Everyday

Hazel Clark and Lauren Downing Peters

This section considers the ways that dress is employed as a tool for negotiating (and challenging) constructs of American identity. Practices and experiences of self-fashioning, or what historian Stephen Greenblatt has described as the self-conscious and deliberate act of taking images, references, and styles present within a culture and constructing an identity from them,[1] are central to the chapters in this section and shed light on the powerful role that dress plays in mediating American everyday life.

While the act of getting dressed is itself an ordinary, everyday practice that is more often than not undertaken in solitude—as, for instance, in one's bedroom or walk-in closet, or in the semi-privacy of a department store dressing room—the more ambivalent practice of self-fashioning is an inherently social, frequently political, and, as Greenblatt writes, often "artful," one.[2] Indeed, as Joanne Entwistle writes in *The Fashioned Body* (2000), the body is perceived in the West as "a project to be worked at, a project increasingly linked to a person's identity and self."[3] While consumer culture supplies no shortage of raw material from which to fashion identities—from clothing, to accessories, to beauty products—Americans (especially as knowledge of garment construction and repair have waned over the last century) are constrained both by what is available in the marketplace and by the complex of norms and ideals that govern what is considered "appropriate dress" in American society. As limiting in the options of self-fashioning may be in some contexts (e.g., in the workplace, at school, or in religious or ceremonial contexts), in others, expressive self-fashioning can be a tactic of resistance, subversion, and even survival.

Over the last two decades or so, a number of interdisciplinary fashion studies scholars have done much to re-center these important narratives. The queer aesthetics of "fabulousness" refined in New York's underground clubs and ballrooms and described by madison moore in *Fabulous: The Rise of the Beautiful Eccentric* (2018), for instance, are but one example of the myriad ways self-fashioning has been employed by America's most vulnerable and marginalized—not necessarily to carve out a space for themselves in the mainstream, but to cast off "norms that never had them in mind in the first place and respond to that suffering and exhausting by taking the risk to live exactly the way they see fit."[4] As in performances of fabulousness, the chapters in this section reveal the ways that dress can similarly be employed to challenge, upend, or radically reimagine constructions of indigeneity, race, gender, and bodily sovereignty in American life. Yet, whether performed in the service or in the subversion of a norm, American self-fashioning practices, as Michelle Tolini Finamore has observed, are never easily defined. A "matrix of converging and diverging narratives," they involve "stories of immigration, innovation, independence, hard work, and self-invention, of harmony and dissonance, [and] of difficulty and opportunity."[5] To phrase it differently, American self-fashioning is as diverse as the nation is large.

Some of these stories of self-fashioning are explored in this section, as, for instance, in Chapter 1, where Laura Allen investigates the local design iconographies of Northwest Coast peoples and the ways that they define the contours of kinship, wealth, and inherited rights. Melding her fieldwork with critical fashion theory, Allen both challenges scholarly definitions of "fashion" and, importantly, the legitimacy of settler national borders. Indeed, the decision to situate Allen's chapter as the first in this volume was intentional. Although there is a border separating Canada and the United States, Northwest lands and waters belong to Indigenous groups who are, among other things, united by bold sartorial iconographies. In addition to exploring the instability of the construct of American self-fashioning, Allen therefore also expands (and troubles) the geographical boundaries of "America."

In Chapter 2, Andrew Reilly frames an unlikely icon of American fashion—the cheerful Hawaiian shirt—as an important tool for negotiating ethnicity and belongingness on the remote island state of Hawai'i. Although it is the most ethnically diverse state in America, Reilly points out that residents typically fall into one of three groups: the Hawaiian, the local, or the haole. Focusing on haoles (a term locally assigned to white Hawaiians), Reilly explores the subtle ways in which the color and patterning on Hawaiian shirts are performatively employed to demonstrate cultural literacy, gain acceptance into local "in-groups," and to display ethnic solidarity. In doing so, he casts new light on a familiar, but frequently misinterpreted, garment.

Rebecca Jumper Matheson's contribution in Chapter 3 is a personal investigation into the construction of American femininity through dress in rural regions of West Texas. Drawing upon both archival sources and family oral histories, Matheson expands the definitions of American ready-to-wear and sportswear by discussing how women purchased, made, and wore the less frequently discussed categories of "country clothes" and "work clothes." What emerges is an important argument about the significance of continuity—or the way that an ordinary wardrobe organically grows and evolves over time, rather than in relation to fads and trends—and resourcefulness in American women's self-fashioning practices outside of the nation's bustling urban cores.

In the final chapter of this section, Chapter 4, Rikki Byrd broadens scholarly discussions of mourning attire to include garments made and worn by Black Americans as tools to respond to and cope with death within their families and communities. While frequently (and narrowly) associated with Queen Victoria's extensive wardrobe of black clothing amassed in the decades after Prince Albert's passing in 1861, Byrd argues that mourning attire has been no less important in the lives and self-fashioning practices of Black people. Adopting a case study approach, Byrd employs the work of Kerry James Marshall and a T-shirt designed by Kerby Jean Raymond to underscore the extraordinary fact that death has become an at once "peculiar and ordinary facet of Black life" in America.

# Notes

1 Stephen Greenblatt, *Renaissance Self-Fashioning: From More to Shakespeare* (Chicago: University of Chicago Press, 1980).
2 Ibid., 2.
3 Joanne Entwistle, *The Fashioned Body: Fashion, Dress and Modern Social Theory* (London: Polity Press, 2000), 19.
4 madison moore, *Fabulous: The Rise of the Beautiful Eccentric* (New Haven: Yale University Press, 2018), 5.
5 Michelle Tolini Finamore, "Introduction," in *Fashioning America: Grit to Glamour*, ed. Michelle Tolini Finamore (Fayetteville: The University of Arkansas Press, 2022), 15.

1

# Sovereignty Every Day

## Mobilizing Indigenous Fashion from the Northwest Coast

Laura J. Allen

"American fashion" is an unstable concept. Indigenous designers and wearers across the Americas disrupt and expand any definition of it. This chapter explores how Indigenous people in a localized context of dress and fashion—the North Pacific Coast of North America—strategically deploy clothes both historically and today to declare identity and sovereignty, and to "transform, accommodate, revise, and resist dominant structures."[1]

The region of focus stretches from what is now Southeast Alaska through Washington state, an area anthropologically characterized as the "Northwest Coast."[2] These lands and waters have belonged to numerous related Indigenous nations and individual communities since time immemorial. Thus, the region crosses and refutes US and Canadian national borders. In this region, Native "Northwest Coast style" usually refers to its bold iconography: the optically powerful, abstractly rendered figurative designs that are common on clothing here. These designs are recognizable to others in community, signaling family or tribal affiliation, familiar supernatural and ancestral beings, and/or local Indigeneity writ large. Within this aesthetic context, fashionable dress in this area—and I will visit terminology shortly—has always been a reflection of community ties both locally determined and globally engaged.

While drafting this chapter, I was invited to join an everyday moment of Northwest Coast fashion that took place in New York City (Lenape land), where I live as a non-Native curator and scholar. It was May 2022, and designer Yolonda Skelton was visiting from Vancouver to see her work in a museum exhibition. While traveling, she had learned that Nang K'uulas *Patrick Shannon*,[3] a Haida Gwaii-based photographer and co-founder of the groundbreaking all-Indigenous agency Supernaturals Modelling, was also in the city, as was Talaysay Campo, the agency's bright star. With a few hours free on a Saturday, the group

**Figure 1.1** Talaysay Campo modeling Yolonda Skelton's "Raven Transformation" dress. Brooklyn Bridge, Manhattan, May 14, 2022. Image © Patrick Shannon. Raven Transformation dress Yolonda Skelton/Sugiit Lukxs Designs © Yolonda Skelton, 2019. Reproduced with the permission of Patrick Shannon and Yolonda Skelton.

**Figure 1.2** Behind the scenes of figure 1.1, with Yolonda Skelton (left); Patrick Shannon (with camera); and onlookers. Image © Laura J. Allen. Raven Transformation dress by Yolonda Skelton/Sugiit Lukxs Designs © Yolonda Skelton, 2019. Reproduced with the permission of Laura J. Allen and Yolonda Skelton.

converged on the pedestrian lane of the Brooklyn Bridge to activate Skelton's designs in an impromptu photo shoot.

When I arrived, I noticed what they were wearing. Skelton wore a belt and shoulder bag adorned with bright, curvilinear forms depicting salmon heads that she drew and cut from Ultrasuede. Shannon was generously tattooed with his Indigenous family crests. Campo modeled a blue and black shift dress from Skelton's collection. As Campo expertly shifted positions for the photographer—arm up, hand on hip, leg bent—the dress' even rows of Ultrasuede feathers moved with her, catching the wind and mirroring the skyscraper windows above.

As we picked through the crowd together after finishing the shot, Skelton smiled at Campo with ease and familiarity. "I love you so much, Talaysay," she said. Then she turned to me. "We're here to uplift each other," she said.

On this occasion, a contingent of the Indigenous fashion system on the Northwest Coast both engaged with and challenged the continent's renowned fashion center, asserting their place within it. The fashion I have described—the dress, the accessories, the tattoos, and most importantly, the process—is shaped by their cultural values: Skelton is Gitxsan, Shannon is Haida, and Campo is shíshálh, each belonging to a distinct sovereign Indigenous nation of their Northwest region. Bringing their concepts of beauty, protocols for proper working relationships, and ethics about production and consumption to bear on the greater fashion system, this gathering was just one of the daily acts of sovereignty and self-determination that people from the Northwest Coast enact through the medium of fashion.

Throughout this chapter, I use the expansive definition of "fashion" articulated by non-Native scholars Abby Lillethun and Linda Welters: "changing styles of dress and appearance that are adopted by a group of people at any given time and place."[4] "Fashionable dress" is synonymous with the term "fashion." "Dress" is a broader term encompassing all modifications to the body by any group. Also expansive here is the notion of sovereignty. For this term, I turn to the theoretical work of Tuscarora scholar Jolene Rickard. She has developed "visual sovereignty" as a useful framework to interpret the work of Native artists.[5] She argues that from Indigenous perspectives, sovereignty is a broad concept, useful beyond its legal definition of political autonomy. It is "about self-defined renewal and resistance," a concept that seeks to honor "the understanding of power in Indigenous cultures," she writes.[6] Rickard urges that this interpretive lens focus on self-determination, "not just … assimilation, colonization, and identity politics."[7]

I argue that dress from the Northwest Coast—as both a mobile and mobilized form of self-fashioning—has been a key medium for social and political power both within and outside of Native communities, historically and today. Drawing from conversations with designers and wearers, object and image study, and observations of fashion contexts, this chapter is grounded in anthropological approaches that explore how clothing and other material culture mediate social relations.[8] It is written to emphasize those relations from both Native perspectives and my own, centering lived experience over Western theoretical constructs. Here, I am inspired by scholar and writer Leanne Betasamosake Simpson (Michi Saagiig Nishnaabeg),[9] who writes that Indigenous theory "is woven within kinetics, spiritual presence, and emotion. It is contextual and relational. It is intimate and personal with individuals themselves holding the responsibilities for finding and generating meaning within their own lives."[10] Further, Amanda J. Cobb-Greetham (Chickasaw) underscores that sovereignty manifests in everyday experiences: "After all, sovereignty really has practical meaning only as we experience it in the context of our relationships within our own nations and with other nations, including the United States," she writes. "… 'How' does sovereignty have meaning? In living."[11]

This frame—emphasizing everyday experience with the fashion that helps drive its relationality—dovetails with the construct of this book. While this chapter addresses the elaborate regalia (ceremonial dress) that is typically favored in scholarly analysis, it also locates quieter, more ordinary moments of dressing that are nonetheless contiguous with the power, principles, and agency that are embodied and enacted by regalia. These moments can be intimate, involving selection, assemblage, wearing, or observing dress. As anthropologist Daniel Miller argues, "The sensual and aesthetic—what cloth feels and looks like—is the source of its capacity to objectify myth, cosmology and also morality, power and values,"[12]—a perspective complimentary with the personalized theoretical approach that Betasamosake Simpson articulates.

With these approaches in mind, I have organized this chapter around case studies that highlight contemporary fashion practitioners as well as chiefly dress from both the late nineteenth century and today. When I drove Skelton to the airport to return to Vancouver after her visit, she noted how we each play a role in this fashion system: she's the designer, Shannon's the photographer, Campo's the model, and I am the writer, she said. For Northwest Coast fashion *centers* on its relationality: its activation in networks of relations between people, between human beings and more-than-human-beings (for example, animal kin and the supernaturals), and between people and place. The garments and their routine assertion of identity and power depend on these connections, and vice versa.

## Northwest Coast art and fashion

"In our world, it is understood that you cannot separate the land and water; they depend on each other to make the whole," writes Haida scholar Jisgang *Nika Collison*. "... In the same way, you cannot separate Haida art from our way of life, for without this context it has little meaning ... In its truest function, our art represents who we are and where we come from."[13] As one of the Northwest Coast's many art forms, fashionable dress reflects ways of life that have endured devastating upheavals due to colonialism—but also persist in profound ways. Historically, social life on the Northwest Coast revolved around structures of hierarchy and status, and it remains centered on key ideologies such as wealth and property (both tangible and intangible), reciprocity, and proper relations with the natural and supernatural worlds, as well as the practice of potlatching—the large feast events that still constitute the key social, economic, and political structure in Northwest Coast communities.

These cultural phenomena manifest in and require dress. "We put our culture on our sleeves, literally and metaphorically," Shannon told me after the Brooklyn Bridge shoot, pointing out the crest symbols tattooed on his skin that depict ravens. "My family has been on Haida Gwaii [the Haida homeland] for fourteen and a half thousand years … We're claiming our identities through this art, through these crests that belong to our lineages," he said.[14] Whether inked on the body or painted, appliquéd, woven into, or printed on worn objects, crests are usually designed using the region's best-known aesthetic approach. This approach is often called "formline" (coined by art historian Bill Holm) because of its codified, curving linear forms that make careful use of positive and negative space. Crests depict animals, objects, landscape or meteorological features, or other elements of the world and are rendered on material culture to indicate the lineage of the owner or wearer. These designs are derived from an ancestor's place-based encounters with the beings or features, and, as a result, project ongoing ties to both family and territory. Crests are highly valued as a kin group's collective property, and as such, protocol has long held that specific crests could only be utilized by a person if they had acquired the right to use them through inheritance or an owner's special permission.[15]

All that being said, Northwest Coast people and their art have long engaged in cross-cultural markets, which has shaped the look of these symbols and the decisions made on when and how to use them. For example, in precolonial times, communities vigorously traded with each other up and down the Pacific Coast as well as in the continental interior. Further, oral and written histories describe encounters with people from Asia and Hawai'i before and after Europeans arrived.[16] The intercultural conditions of life on the Northwest Coast rapidly escalated when Russian, British, and American people began to encroach in the late 1700s. At this time, Indigenous people drove the sociopolitical system and dictated trade relations here. Exchange with Euro/American mariners, naval officers, and merchants became robust, with crest-bearing carved, painted, and woven objects entering this market from family repositories as well as from artists making work specifically for new audiences and consumers.

Throughout the expansion of empire, the early fur trade period, the rise of the tourist industry, and resulting settler states, non-Natives have both appreciated and exploited the material and intellectual property of Northwest nations, for example, by appropriating and mass-reproducing their proprietary forms. At the same time, since these early markets, Native people in this region have made context-specific judgments of when local designs are acceptable for commercial use as a strategy for economic development, diplomatic outreach, expression of culture, and assertion of Indigeneity and sovereignty.

As a result of these factors, Northwest Coast design motifs are ubiquitous on commercial products in the region today, including tee shirts, jewelry, and high-end fashion.[17] Several designers in the twentieth century significantly advanced the development of the region's strong Indigenous fashion scene. For example, in the 1940s and 1950s, Ellen Neel, a Kwakwa̱ka'wakw woodcarver working in Vancouver, advocated for local Indigenous artists to enter commercial design. During this time of rampant appropriation of Native idioms by the dominant fashion and interior design worlds, Neel asserted Indigenous rights to their own imagery. In an important speech for the 1948 Conference on Native Indian Affairs, she said: "Our art continues to live . . . I believe it can be used to stunning effect on tapestry, textiles, sportswear, and in jewelry . . . We need only to have some sort of organization to which architects, builders and manufacturers could go to guarantee authentic products."[18] In subsequent years, Neel designed and sold a locally popular line of silk scarves, bags, and clothing with inherited crest designs that she had rights to use.[19]

In the 1980s and early 1990s, Dorothy Grant (Haida) and Himikalas Pamela Baker (Squamish/Kwakwa̱ka'wakw/Tlingit/Haida) began making, showing, and selling high-end fashion with their cultural aesthetics, a major turning point for regional Native fashion design.[20] Both continue to do so today. Skelton is among a new generation of designers who entered the field in the space they have created. From Hazelton, British Columbia (BC), Skelton had artistic and sewing talent since she was a teenager. After pursuing a psychology degree, she worked as a youth educator and counselor in several Native communities. In 2001, she began making regalia for community members and pieces to sell, supplementing her self-taught skills with technical courses and continuing to center youth empowerment in her work.[21]

In 2019, I visited Skelton's home studio then in Victoria, BC with my friend Henry Seaweed (Kwax̱itola).[22] Seaweed is a hereditary chief of a high-ranking family of the 'Nak'waxda'x̱w, a Kwakwa̱ka'wakw group. He is an elder, ceremonial leader, dancer, language instructor, and esteemed culture-bearer. In a playful moment from our visit, Seaweed modeled a short tie that Skelton created with a frog crest. Skelton's grandfather belonged to the Gitxsan frog clan, and the design represents her dear relative.

Seaweed held up the tie over his commercial T-shirt screen-printed with killer whales. Killer whales are one of Seaweed's most important crests, obtained by his lineage after two killer whales beached on the shore of Ba'as (Blunden Harbour) in 'Nak'waxda'x̱w territory. The whales transformed into a human husband and wife, and later into two islands that protect the people of Ba'as.

**Figure 1.3** Henry Seaweed and Yolonda Skelton in Skelton's studio. Victoria, B.C., September 7, 2019. Image © Laura J. Allen. "Grandpa's Frog Crest" by Yolonda Skelton/Sugiit Lukxs Designs © Yolonda Skelton, 2019. Reproduced with the permission of Laura J. Allen and Yolonda Skelton.

As dress scholar Joanne B. Eicher has noted, "ethnic dress helps to position an individual in time and place relationships."[23] Investigating aboriginally designed tee shirts among the Kwakwaka'wakw, anthropologist Aaron Glass argues that these garments not only communicate identity, but also are efficacious in forming and maintaining memories from specific relational contexts.[24] For example, Native families on the Northwest Coast frequently have T-shirts silkscreened as gifts for potlatch guests, marking collective participation at an event of importance to a particular family, community, and time. In Skelton's studio, the tie and T-shirt sustained the maker's and wearer's connections to relatives and ancestral land.

The visit also enabled important continuities within the local Indigenous fashion system, for example, collaborative patronage. Through my introduction, Seaweed met an artist from whom he could commission custom garments—say a tunic, vest, or robe with appliquéd designs—to depict his crests for ceremonial or other important occasions. Such patronage has been ongoing on the coast for centuries, involving regalia makers, carvers, jewelers, painters, and other producers, resulting from and generating intricate networks of family and friends. Skelton, for example, is developing a jacket for Patrick Shannon with appliquéd crests that match his tattoos in design and placement.

All fashion relies on human networks, but Indigenous fashion from the Northwest Coast rests on connections and design ideas that have unfolded over many centuries. These connections are made material as continuously adapted visual representations that are vital for identity projection within these "cultures of display."[25] The designed objects create and maintain regular opportunities for self-representation, group bonding, and furtherance of culture and territory: elements of the expansive definition of sovereignty that Rickard describes.

## Indigenizing American symbols

A distinctive red wool potlatch cape from the nineteenth century in the collection of the American Museum of Natural History (AMNH) demonstrates how fashion in this region has enacted sovereignty historically. This object shows how local designers chose to transform potent Euro-American symbols into Native ones to assert power against colonial interference. In the museum, this unusual cape is displayed alongside a more common robe style from the period called a "button blanket," made from a wool blanket.

Robes and capes are enduring local Indigenous silhouettes, yet these two examples of ceremonial regalia in the AMNH case would have been viewed as materially and aesthetically innovative at the time, made of imported trade textiles and mother-of-pearl buttons.[26] Both robes would have signaled the rank and esteem of their wearers.

The red robe, which features two large eagle crests appliquéd in navy blue wool and gleaming with rows of buttons, caught my attention when I was serving as a Curatorial Associate at the museum in 2017 and 2018. In the accession record, this cape is described as Tsimshian (from what is now northern British Columbia) and as "Chief's dress worn at feasts; modern in style and material." It was acquired by Israel W. Powell, the first Canadian Superintendent of Indian Affairs for British Columbia, likely in 1881. While many versions of formline eagles exist on late-nineteenth-century dress, the cape's eagles are distinctly American style: Each has wings outstretched and is grasping olive branches and arrows in its talons, as on the United States seal and American coinage, which

**Figure 1.4** Tsimshian cape (AMNH 16/360, left) in the Northwest Coast Hall, American Museum of Natural History, New York, N.Y., 2022. Image © D. Finnin/AMNH. Reproduced with the permission of AMNH.

circulated in British Columbia at the time. Art historian Kathryn Bunn-Marcuse has analyzed similar incorporations of American and European imagery for silver jewelry (which was fashioned from pounded coins), carved canes, and other works made by nineteenth and early twentieth-century Indigenous artists in the Northwest Coast market. The motifs include a range of American-style eagles, the lion and the unicorn of the British coat of arms, and scrollwork and floral designs from Victorian decorative objects.[27] Some artists, she writes, were "literally ... surrounded" by such imported imagery, and she argues that when it "is used to advance Indigenous meaning ... it becomes Indigenous."[28]

Also interesting is the fact that the robe's double-layered treatment seems inspired by European or American military greatcoats with overcapes.[29] Farther north, among the Unangax̂ (Aleut) of Southwest Alaska, artists would sometimes adapt the local waterproof gutskin parka, made of processed marine mammal intestines, for non-Native traders and officers by fashioning the material into a similar double-caped style. These gutskin capes could be gifted to high-ranking captains and dignitaries as part of diplomacy.³⁰ In addition, the scarlet color and ermine trimming of the AMNH cape resemble styles of English coronation robes. While both red wool and ermine fur have long been locally popular on chiefly headdresses and other regalia on the Northwest Coast, the robe's overall approach to design appears to be influenced by numerous foreign styles that signal wealth, status, and leadership. Thus, this "modern" piece is particularly responsive to new design ideas: it is fashionable. Its maker and owner were marking their participation in a modernity that is Indigenously determined.

Even without knowing the lived experience of the individual(s) who commissioned or owned this robe, it is clear that the symbolic choices to project power and progressiveness would have been effective in their sociocultural context. It is likely that Powell obtained the robe in the largely Coast Tsimshian community of approximately 1,200 people at Port Simpson, known today as Lax Kw'alaams.³¹ Here, the British Hudson's Bay Company had established the Fort Simpson fur trading post in 1834. After several devastating smallpox epidemics, by the time Powell visited in 1881, the community was an outgrowth of a significant relocation of multiple Indigenous villages to the fort area. By the late nineteenth century, the region shifted away from a Native subsistence and trade economy to a colonially imposed wage labor system that was economically tied to both the American West and Canada. Through this upheaval, the former social order and prestige system of local chiefs was disturbed, and more ethnic complexity prevailed.³²

At the same time, colonial agents and missionaries were increasingly pressuring Native people to give up ceremonial practice and its regalia as part of assimilation policy. The Canadian government made potlatching illegal in 1884, three years after this robe was collected. The use of American eagles and other foreign design ideas could be read as an act of assimilation or patriotism: adopting the symbols of an oppressor as a strategic bid of allegiance. I suggest instead that the maker and/or owner of the cape were Indigenizing these symbols as a power play, an act of sovereign resistance. Comparative are the American flags in Plains beadwork in the late nineteenth and early twentieth century, when Native religious ceremonies were also outlawed by the US government. Douglas Schmittou and Michael Logan write that "this profound artistic innovation was borne from incredibly harsh interethnic relations, in which ... Plains Indian tribes used material culture and the flag motif as a highly visible element within a larger strategy for survival as sovereign nations."³³

Given the repressive colonial regimes on the Northwest Coast around the same time, the Tsimshian robe embodies complex local power exchanges. In donning this robe at a potlatch, the chiefly wearer knew that its flamboyant style would motivate Tsimshian social recognition of their claims in a bid for, or maintenance of, a sovereign position, especially given the instability of high-ranking potlatch positions due to mass death and migration. The owner may have sought to elevate their position in this sociopolitical context by invoking visual connections to colonial power. As Daniel Miller has noted of dress, "... power exists in larger measure to the degree to which it can take a form—a form that reconfigures the authority of the past with that of the present."[34] This "modern style" cape enabled the wearer to assert and maintain their customary clan-based authority systems within a new social and political economy, visually negotiating the rising influence of colonial authorities.

Further, the very act of conducting a ceremonial, publicly or privately, at this time would have flouted colonial dominance given the developing potlatch ban. Non-Natives may have witnessed this cape while worn—perhaps even Powell himself, a Canadian government authority figure. Adopting this fashionable style with symbols and silhouettes recognizable to both Native people and Euro-Canadians/Americans likely aided the wearer's navigation of shifting social relations. Such double coding of iconography, theorized by art historian Ruth B. Phillips as "dual signification," offers semiotic ambiguity in cross-cultural spaces. The multiple meanings of the cape's symbology appear both assertive and protective in a context of colonial oppression.[35] With its Indigenization of the most candid symbols of colonizing forces, this cape can be read as an act of resistance that strategically engages with Americanness, fully "grounded in local cultural and political agendas."[36]

## Dressing sovereign

The dress choices of leaders remain critical to compel political action within and outside of Native communities. The wardrobe of Marilyn Slett [K̓áwáził], who is Haíłzaqv (Heiltsuk) from the central coast, is a case in point. Slett has been the elected chief councilor of the Heiltsuk Nation since 2008. Her leadership roles include serving as president of Coastal First Nations, an alliance to protect one of the planet's largest remaining temperate coastal rainforest systems through conservation-based economic development. She is also a former board member of the British Columbia Assembly of First Nations. Given Slett's diplomatic responsibilities, unique, compelling clothes that demonstrate her cultural and family affiliations are of vital importance. "As an Indigenous leader, I always think it's a responsibility to wear clothing that represents me as a Heiltsuk person, whether it is meeting with ministers, governments, or dignitaries," she explained to me.[37]

To achieve her look, Slett works frequently with Indigenous designers, as well as with Wendy Van Riesen, who is of European descent. Van Riesen creates gauzy clothes with hand-designed prints in small batches or one-offs in her home studio a few hours north of Vancouver. For sustainability, her signature material is repurposed polyester curtain sheers—the unused rolls and roll ends from home goods manufacturers. These environmental values appeal to Slett as much as Van Riesen's aesthetics. For a number of years Van Riesen collaborated with a friend, the Haida artist Reg Davidson, on a ready-to-wear line called *Yáahl, Gúud, Tsai*, which featured his formline designs. This collection became popular among Native wearers across the coast and has inspired special commissions from Indigenous clients such as Slett, for whom Van Riesen will co-develop and print pieces to order.[38]

For example, Van Riesen created a number of blouses that prominently feature the official symbol of the Heiltsuk Nation, a copper, whose design Slett supplied to Van Riesen for this series. Coppers are shieldlike objects that are among the most valued items owned by families on the Northwest Coast. In this case, the blouses—which Slett and other Haíłzaqv people wear proudly—are a direct depiction of national sovereignty. Other custom prints developed together represent life-changing events for the leader, a process not dissimilar to how new crest designs emerge. For example, on a jacket that Van Riesen made for Slett (not shown), the designer printed black drips on the kimono sleeves that represent fuel oil. On the front, she printed Slett's ancestral name (Ḵáwáził), her great-great-grandfather's name, and the name of their ancestral village. The design references a significant oil spill from the American tug-barge *Nathan E. Stewart* in 2016. The boat ran aground in an important Haíłzaqv food harvesting and cultural site, releasing 112,200 liters of diesel fuel and lubricants into coastal waters. Slett has been instrumental in coordinating the nation's response, which remains ongoing. "[The Heiltsuk Nation] did a lot of proactive work as a result," she explained. "We created a spill investigation report, a traditional laws adjudication report of the breaches of our laws, and we designed an Indigenous marine spill response center." Besides reflecting Haíłzaqv protection of territory, the clothes were healing during this traumatic experience. "There were times I couldn't talk about [the spill] without crying, there was so much grief," Slett said. Commissioning and wearing a blouse or jacket that invoked her ancestors, her nation, and her own identity helped ground and embolden her for the press

**Figure 1.5** Wendy Van Riesen/Dahlia Drive "Big Blouses" commissioned by Chief Marilyn Slett. They are printed with the symbol of the Heiltsuk Nation, a copper. Images © Wendy Van Riesen, 2021. Copper logo by Shirl Hall © Heiltsuk Nation. Reproduced with the permission of Wendy Van Riesen and Marilyn Slett.

conferences and dialogues needed to carry forth the nation's demands, and provided a visual reference of lived experience.[39]

For an event of historic importance to the Heiltsuk Nation in October 2019, Slett assembled a complex outfit that integrated a new, innovative piece co-developed with Van Riesen with cherished items from Slett's wardrobe. That month, the Heiltsuk Nation dedicated their first big house—a type of customary architecture—since the 1884 potlatch ban, erected in their main community of Bella Bella. "People came adorned in their best. How we were going to dress was a big thing," Slett told me, with emotion, while sitting in the cedar-planked building during our phone interview. "It was really important to us, that we ... were paying respect to who we are, the big house [and our ancestors]."[40]

Slett's outfit, which is mostly visible in figure 1.6, testifies to the complex relationality of Indigenous fashion. The button robe and dance apron belonged to Slett's grandmother, made after the potlatch ban was dropped from Canada's Indian Act in 1951. That was when women in her community again felt able to sew and wear visibly "cultural" dress without risk of arrest. The robe was made by her grandmother's sister Lillian, and the apron by Lillian's daughter. Lillian's son designed both crests. Slett commissioned her moccasins from a married couple who are Cree and Nisga'a; the moccasins' painted eagle and killer whale crests were designed by a Haiłzaqv artist. A Haida artist crafted the copper head ring,

*Sovereignty Every Day* 31

**Figure 1.6** Chief Marilyn Slett [Ḱáwázil̓] (center, in red and black button blanket and beige apron) at the opening of the Heiltsuk Nation Big House, Bella Bella, BC, October 2019. Image © Jeremy Williams/River Voices. Reproduced with the permission of Jeremy Williams.

while another Haíɫzaqv artist made the cedar and fur headpiece inside.[41] Van Riesen's contributions are the sheer brown cape beneath the button blanket and over the apron, as well as the purple polka-dotted dress peeking out from under these layers.

I focus here on the sheer cape, which is a unique dress item that remixes generations of local aesthetics and meanings. Given the physical activity of the five days of opening ceremonies—lots of moving, sitting, standing, and speaking—Slett wanted a lighter weight robe as an alternative to her wool button blanket, which can be heavy. She also wanted to reference customary clothing made of harvested and processed cedar bark, a material still used for regalia items today and visible on the woman standing to Slett's left in Figure 1.6. At Slett's request, Van Reisen custom-printed a pattern that resembled woven cedar bark on the sheer polyester for the cape, invoking deep relations with the plant world. Slett also requested a detachable fur collar. The one she chose, which was actually Van Riesen's grandmother's, is made of ermine. As seen on the red Tsimshian cape, this fur is spiritually potent and a symbol of esteem and chiefly status.

Through this material and aesthetic experimentation and creative assemblage with older pieces, the new cape maintains values held since time immemorial. It represents a complex range of interpersonal, intercultural, and interspecies relations as well as ties to the ancestral lands and waters that the Heiltsuk Nation actively stewards. Slett's ensemble visually supports her nation's sovereignty: their right to determine their future as they see fit. "For us, Indigenous sovereignty as a community is really important," she remarked. "You can see it in the imagery of the big house."[42] As part of Haíłzaqv resurgence, creating the big house was a decades-long effort that directly confronts the losses wrought by the colonial government and intense missionization on the central coast.

The Haíłzaqv's regalia actively refuse centuries of colonialism and assert ancestral title for lands and waters that are theirs to steward according to their cultural tenets. When Slett wears Van Riesen's pieces, she identifies herself as not just Haíłzaqv, but also as a driver of the nation's anticolonial work. These clothes embody the ideologies, materialities, and relations that carry the Haíłzaqv forward for the generations ahead.

## We uplift each other

As these case studies have endeavored to show, Indigenous fashion from the Northwest Coast strongly projects identity in a way that can disturb and dismantle legacies of colonization. Its relational aspects are central to this activity. As with Native fashion more broadly, practitioners on the Northwest Coast today tend to center community-based processes, such as collaboration, hiring Indigenous staff, training in technical practices, and youth empowerment. In this way as well, the work is an act of self-determination, one way to preserve, support, and advance Native nations both on and off their ancestral territories. As Skelton put it to me: "As Indigenous fashion designers we can have an influence and show a different way of being. It's not about me. It's about us. We have a collective ideology. That's what we bring."[43]

This collective, relational approach was once again obvious to me a few days after Skelton left New York to return to Vancouver. Shannon met up with designer Korina Emmerich (Puyallup) in her Brooklyn apartment studio for another impromptu shoot. Originally from Oregon, Emmerich often features Pendleton blanket patterns and focuses on social and environmental justice with her line EMME. On the walls, photocopied pages of Puyallup language terms—for clothes, for colors, for time—were taped up near formline screenprints and a poster with activist designer Céline Semaan's comment that "Everything you make returns to the Earth as food or poison." During the afternoon, Indigenous friends came by to help model bright blue and red pieces from her new collection, with plenty of spontaneous dancing to a Spotify playlist, laughing, and love throughout the afternoon. "Just another day as an Indigenous creative," I heard Shannon say. As I left the building, another friend was entering. She wore a baseball cap I've seen sold at REI, embroidered with "You Are on Native Land." It's a fitting final word on Indigenous fashion as a mode of sovereignty. These clothes embody the right to govern lands and waters, to care for them, and for each other, as Native people see fit—from time immemorial, and for a forever future.

## Acknowledgments

I extend my deep gratitude to all the colleagues in this chapter who graciously accommodated me for interviews, site visits, and multiple conversations for preparation and review of the content. I also thank Amanda Thompson, Aaron Glass, Anna Conlan, and Alexandra Dumont for reading drafts and offering incisive commentary that strengthened the text.

## Notes

1. Sascha T. Scott and Amy Lonetree, "The Past and the Future Are Now," *Arts* 9, no. 3 (September 2020): 77, 2.
2. Some characterize the Northwest Coast culture area as extending to the northern California border.
3. In this chapter, a person's Native name is included alongside their name in English according to preference, or in square brackets. The convention of the Haida Nation (to which Shannon belongs) is to follow Haida names with English names in italics.
4. Linda Welters and Abby Lillethun, eds., *The Fashion Reader*, 2nd edn. (Oxford and New York: Berg, 2011), xxvii.
5. Jolene Rickard, "Art, Visual Sovereignty and Pushing Perceptions," in *The Routledge Companion to Indigenous Art Histories in the United States and Canada*, eds. Heather L. Igloliorte and Carla Taunton, Routledge Companions, (New York: Routledge, Taylor & Francis Group, 2023), 21–9.
6. Jolene Rickard, "Visualizing Sovereignty in the Time of Biometric Sensors," *South Atlantic Quarterly* 110, no. 2 (April 1, 2011): 467, 468.
7. Jolene Rickard, "Sovereignty: A Line in the Sand," *Aperture* no. 139 (1995): 51.
8. E.g. Daniel Miller, "Style and Ontology," in *Consumption and Identity*, ed. Jonathan Friedman (Chur: Harwood Academic Publishers, 1994), 71–96; Daniel Miller, "Introduction," in *Clothing as Material Culture*, eds. Susanne Küchler and Daniel

Miller (Oxford: Berg, 2005), 1–19; Aaron Glass, ed., *Objects of Exchange: Social and Material Transformation on the Late Nineteenth-Century Northwest Coast* (New York: Bard Graduate Center, 2011).

9   Words in parenthesis that follow a person's name(s) indicate their tribal affiliation or heritage.

10  Leanne Betasamosake Simpson, *As We Have Always Done: Indigenous Freedom Through Radical Resistance* (Minneapolis: University of Minnesota Press, 2017), 151.

11  Amanda J. Cobb, "Understanding Tribal Sovereignty: Definitions, Conceptualizations, and Interpretations," *American Studies* 46, no. 3/4 (2005): 124, 125.

12  Miller, "Introduction," 1.

13  Nika Collison, "Everything Depends on Everything Else," in *Raven Traveling: Two Centuries of Haida Art*, ed. Daina Augaitis (Vancouver, BC: Vancouver Art Gallery, 2006), 57. For an art-historical overview see Aldona Jonaitis, *Art of the Northwest Coast*, 2nd edn. (Seattle: University of Washington Press, 2021).

14  Patrick Shannon, interview by Laura Allen, Brooklyn, NY, May 16, 2022.

15  Not all designs from the Northwest Coast represent crests. For example, Coast Salish figures may depict ancestors, spirits, or other important beings, but are not considered inherited symbols that stand for a specific kinship group. See Jonaitis, *Art of the Northwest Coast*, 57–88.

16  Collison, "Everything Depends on Everything Else," 58; William W. Fitzhugh and Aron Crowell, eds., *Crossroads of Continents: Cultures of Siberia and Alaska* (Washington, DC: Smithsonian Institution Press, 1988), 312.

17  Solen Roth, *Incorporating Culture: How Indigenous People Are Reshaping the Northwest Coast Art Industry* (Vancouver, BC: University of British Columbia Press, 2018).

18  Cited in Phil Nuytten, *The Totem Carvers: Charlie James, Ellen Neel, and Mungo Martin* (Vancouver, BC: Panorama Publications, 1982), 50.

19  Lou-ann Ika'wega Neel, "Ellen Neel and Carving on the Coast," in *Unsettling Native Art Histories on the Northwest Coast*, eds. Kathryn Bunn-Marcuse and Aldona Jonaitis (Seattle: University of Washington Press, 2020), 140–1 and Carolyn Butler Palmer, ed., *Ellen Neel: The First Woman Totem Pole Carver* (Victoria, BC: flask, 2021). See also Roth, *Incorporating Culture*, 52–4.

20  Pamela Baker, interview by Laura Allen, North Vancouver, BC, September 9, 2019; Dorothy Grant, interview by Laura Allen, Tsawwassen, BC, September 9, 2019.

21  Yolonda Skelton, interview by Laura Allen, Victoria, BC, September 7, 2019; email to author, September 28, 2022.

22  See note 3.

23  Joanne B. Eicher, ed., *Dress and Ethnicity: Change Across Space and Time*, Berg Ethnic Identities Series (Oxford: Berg, 1995), 4.

24  Aaron Glass, "Crests on Cotton: 'Souvenir' T-Shirts and the Materiality of Remembrance Among the Kwakwaka'wakw of British Columbia," *Museum Anthropology* 31, no. 1 (May 1, 2008), 3.

25 Glass, "Crests on Cotton," 2.
26 Mother-of-pearl buttons became available in the 1820s, becoming a favored alternative to locally sourced shell beads and other embellishments.
27 Kathryn Bunn-Marcuse, "Bracelets of Exchange," in Glass, *Objects of Exchange*, 61–9; Kathryn Bunn-Marcuse, "Eagles and Elephants: Cross-Cultural Influences in the Time of Charles Edenshaw," in *Charles Edenshaw*, eds. Robin K. Wright and Daina Augaitis (London: Black Dog Publishing, 2013), 175–87.
28 Bunn-Marcuse, "Eagles and Elephants," 182.
29 The shoulder cape's shape is also not dissimilar to historical cedar-bark capelets from the region, but the tiered approach is unusual.
30 Fitzhugh and Crowell, *Crossroads of Continents*, 57.
31 In 1881, Powell visited the Tsimshianic locales of Fort/Port Simpson/Lax Kw'alaams, nearby Metlakatla, villages on the upper Nass River, and Kitkatla on the Skeena River: see "Annual Report of the Department of Indian Affairs for the Year Ended 31st December 1881" (Ottawa: Maclean, Roger & Co., 1882), 147–54. The AMNH exhibition label indicates acquisition in 1881 at Lax Kw'alaams.
32 Louis Allaire, "A Native Mental Map of Coast Tsimshian Villages," in *The Tsimshian: Images of the Past, Views for the Present*, ed. Margaret Seguin (Vancouver: University of British Columbia Press, 1984), 82–98, 97.
33 Douglas A Schmittou and Michael H Logan, "Fluidity of Meaning: Flag Imagery in Plains Indian Art," *The American Indian Quarterly* 26, no. 4 (2002): 559–604, 580.
34 Miller, "Introduction," 12.
35 Ruth B. Phillips, *Trading Identities: The Souvenir in Native North American Art from the Northeast, 1700–1900* (Seattle: University of Washington Press; Montreal: McGill-Queen's University Press, 1998), 19–20.
36 Nicholas Thomas, *Entangled Objects: Exchange, Material Culture, and Colonialism in the Pacific* (Cambridge, MA: Harvard University Press, 1991), 88.
37 Marilyn Slett, interview by Laura Allen, telephone, November 26, 2019.
38 Wendy Van Riesen, interview by Laura Allen, North Vancouver, BC, September 8, 2019.
39 Slett, interview.
40 Slett, interview.
41 Marilyn Slett, email to author, December 13, 2019.
42 Slett, interview.
43 Skelton, interview.

## Bibliography

Allaire, Louis. "A Native Mental Map of Coast Tsimshian Villages." In *The Tsimshian: Images of the Past, Views for the Present*, edited by Margaret Seguin, 82–98. Vancouver, BC: University of British Columbia Press, 1984.

"Annual Report of the Department of Indian Affairs for the Year Ended 31st December 1881." Ottawa: Maclean, Roger & Co., 1882.

Bunn-Marcuse, Kathryn. "Bracelets of Exchange." In *Objects of Exchange: Social and Material Transformation on the Late Nineteenth-Century Northwest Coast*, edited by Aaron Glass, 61–9. New York: Bard Graduate Center, 2011.

Bunn-Marcuse, Kathryn. "Eagles and Elephants: Cross-Cultural Influences in the Time of Charles Edenshaw." In *Charles Edenshaw*, edited by Robin K. Wright and Daina Augaitis, 175–87. London: Black Dog Publishing, 2013.

Butler Palmer, Carolyn, ed. *Ellen Neel: The First Woman Totem Pole Carver*. Victoria, BC: flask, 2021.

Cobb, Amanda J. "Understanding Tribal Sovereignty: Definitions, Conceptualizations, and Interpretations." *American Studies* 46, no. 3/4 (2005): 115–32.

Collison, Nika. "Everything Depends on Everything Else." In *Raven Traveling: Two Centuries of Haida Art*, edited by Daina Augaitis, 56–64. Vancouver, BC: Vancouver Art Gallery, 2006.

Eicher, Joanne B. ed. *Dress and Ethnicity: Change Across Space and Time*. Berg Ethnic Identities Series. Oxford: Berg, 1995.

Fitzhugh, William W. and Aron Crowell eds. *Crossroads of Continents: Cultures of Siberia and Alaska*. Washington, DC: Smithsonian Institution Press, 1988.

Glass, Aaron. "Crests on Cotton: 'Souvenir' T-Shirts and the Materiality of Remembrance Among the Kwakwa̱ka'wakw of British Columbia." *Museum Anthropology* 31, no. 1 (May 1, 2008): 1–18.

Glass, Aaron, ed. *Objects of Exchange: Social and Material Transformation on the Late Nineteenth-Century Northwest Coast*. New York: Bard Graduate Center, 2011.

Jonaitis, Aldona. *Art of the Northwest Coast*. 2nd edn. Seattle: University of Washington Press, 2021.

Miller, Daniel. "Style and Ontology." In *Consumption and Identity*, edited by Jonathan Friedman, 71–96. Chur: Harwood Academic Publishers, 1994.

Miller, Daniel. "Introduction." In *Clothing as Material Culture*, edited by Susanne Küchler and Daniel Miller, 1–19. Oxford: Berg, 2005.

Neel, Lou-ann Ika'wega. "Ellen Neel and Carving on the Coast." In *Unsettling Native Art Histories on the Northwest Coast*, edited by Kathryn Bunn-Marcuse and Aldona Jonaitis, 133–49. Seattle: University of Washington Press, 2020.

Nuytten, Phil. *The Totem Carvers: Charlie James, Ellen Neel, and Mungo Martin*. Vancouver, BC: Panorama Publications, 1982.

Phillips, Ruth B. *Trading Identities: The Souvenir in Native North American Art from the Northeast, 1700–1900*. Seattle: Montreal, Quebec: University of Washington Press; McGill-Queen's University Press, 1998.

Rickard, Jolene. "Sovereignty: A Line in the Sand." *Aperture* no. 139 (1995): 50–9.

Rickard, Jolene. "Visualizing Sovereignty in the Time of Biometric Sensors." *South Atlantic Quarterly* 110, no. 2 (April 1, 2011): 465–86.

Rickard, Jolene. "Art, Visual Sovereignty and Pushing Perceptions." In *The Routledge Companion to Indigenous Art Histories in the United States and Canada*, edited by Heather L. Igloliorte and Carla Taunton, 21–9. Routledge Companions. New York: Routledge, Taylor & Francis Group, 2023.

Roth, Solen. *Incorporating Culture: How Indigenous People Are Reshaping the Northwest Coast Art Industry*. Vancouver, BC: University of British Columbia Press, 2018.

Schmittou, Douglas A. and Michael H. Logan. "Fluidity of Meaning: Flag Imagery in Plains Indian Art." *The American Indian Quarterly* 26, no. 4 (2002): 559–604.

Scott, Sascha T. and Amy Lonetree. "The Past and the Future Are Now." *Arts* 9, no. 3 (September 2020): 77.

Simpson, Leanne Betasamosake. *As We Have Always Done: Indigenous Freedom through Radical Resistance*. Minneapolis: University of Minnesota Press, 2017.

Thomas, Nicholas. *Entangled Objects: Exchange, Material Culture, and Colonialism in the Pacific*. Cambridge, MA: Harvard University Press, 1991.

Welters, Linda and Abby Lillethun, eds. *The Fashion Reader*. 2nd edn. Oxford and New York: Berg, 2011.

2

# Haoles in Hawaiian Shirts

Andy Reilly

Not only is Hawai'i[1] the most ethnically-diverse state in the United States of America, it is also one of the most ethnically-diverse places in the world.[2] The US Census Bureau identifies the state's diverse population using racial categories of American Indian/Alaskan Native, Asian American, Black or African American, Hawaiian/Pacific Islander, and White. However, those who call the Islands home generally use ethnicity to categorize people into one of three groups: Hawaiian (i.e., those whose claim indigenous ancestry), local (i.e., descendants of early immigrants), or haole (i.e., white, pronounced how-lee). One site in which ethnicity and belongingness are expressed in Hawai'i is played out in the Hawaiian shirt.

Little academic attention has been given to how residents of Hawai'i select their Hawaiian shirts other than what tourists *do not* wear. Kaiser and Green note descriptions of binary identity oppositions—who one is and is not "cannot capture how power works; they cannot explain complex interactions and influences through which people negotiate, regulate, and appropriate style-fashion-dress."[3] Tulloch defines style-fashion-dress as a combination of style (via agency through developing an aesthetic image that is reflective of one's true self); fashion (incorporation of a trend); and dress (assemblage of body modifications as defined by Roach-Higgins and Eicher).[4] Kaiser and Green propose *(k)nots*[5] as a means to explore the complexity and entanglement of identity:

> The knot metaphor of fashion allows us to consider how some truths can be covered over temporarily, only to be revealed as a knot is loosened. Hence, truth is partial and contingent, according to issues of time, space, and power relations. The three-dimensional surface of a knot both reveals a temporary prominence and conceals portions of the threads underneath. In the process, self-other relations emerged as entangled, rather than binary.[6]

This chapter examines the aesthetic preferences of residents vis-à-vis identity using the (k)nots metaphor through interviews with Hawaiian, local, and haole men. The chapter notes how haole men navigate their whiteness and sartorial style to align with the concept of the *good haole* (as opposed to the *dumb haole* or the *fucking haole*) through the lens of social identity theory. Tajfel and Turner's seminal work on social identity posits that in-group versus out-group behavior is an outcome of status and an individual's identification with a group.[7] They theorize that social identity is established through a process of categorization, identification, and social comparison. Categorization occurs when groups of people are classified together according to a common characteristic (e.g., ethnicity, geographic region). Identification occurs when a person aligns with a group based on that common characteristic. And social comparison—that is evaluating one group to another—results in positive (one group is viewed as better than the other) or negative (one group is viewed as worse than the other) distinctiveness.[8] Those who are part of the in-group are given more preferential treatment than those outside the group (in-group bias). Negative distinctiveness can be reduced or eliminated by minimizing differences. Haoles may turn to the Hawaiian shirt to minimize differences as an outsider.

## Locals and haoles

People had been inhabiting what today are known as the Hawaiian Islands since the eighth century AD in relative isolation. Contact with British explorer Captain James Cook on January 18, 1778, brought trade to the Islands and among the items traded were Hawaiian sandalwood and sugar for European clothing and Asian textiles; opportunities for trade and commodities also heralded the arrival of people from other lands to the Islands.[9] By the middle of the nineteenth century, plantations were established to grow agricultural crops and between 1850 and 1950 various immigrant groups were sought for labor; although the plantation owners could recruit from one country, recruiting from many allowed for labor control and the dominance of Euro-Americans over other ethnic groups. For example, the practice of allocating jobs and pay by ethnicity ensured ethnic divisiveness. As the Honorable William L. Lee, President of the Royal Agricultural Society, advised:

> To all those planters who can afford it, I would say, procure as many laborers as you can, and work them by themselves, as far as possible separate from the natives, and you will find that, if well managed, their example will have a stimulating effect upon the Hawaiian, who is naturally jealous of the coolie and ambitious to outdo him.[10]

Between 1850 and 1950 nearly 400,000 immigrants arrived in waves from China, Japan, Okinawa, Philippines, Portugal, Azores, Madeira Islands, Korea, Puerto Rico, Spain, Germany, Pacific Islands, and Russia.[11]

The US had a fervent interest in the Hawaiian Islands for military purposes and American businessmen had an interest in the Hawaiian Islands for economic purposes. Missionaries, politicians, and businessmen began to influence Hawaiian Kingdom politics and forced changes within the system, including altering the land tenure system to allow for private ownership and combining the Hawaiian legal system with Euro-American-style laws. The Hawaiian League (composed mostly of non-Hawaiians) drafted a new constitution which it forced King Kalākaua to sign in 1887. This became known as the Bayonet Constitution and stripped the Hawaiian monarchy of much of its power. The Hawaiian Kingdom was overthrown in 1893 when Queen Liliʻuokalani was forced to abdicate under threat of military action against the Hawaiian people.[12] This made way for the US to annex Hawaiʻi which became a territory in 1898 and a state in 1959.

*Local* is a term used by residents of Hawaiʻi to describe people of mixed ethnicities who grew up in the Hawaiian Islands and are descendants of early immigrants. When New England missionaries arrived in 1820 concerted efforts were made to change Hawaiian values, beliefs, and society, with the result that it became a culture which combined both Hawaiian and American values.[13] Local identity incorporates "certain elements of Hawaiian culture and resistance to haole hegemony."[14] For example, respect for the land, reverence of family and ancestors, and exhibiting aloha, or love, gratitude, and compassion in daily life. However, it was not until the 1930s that local identity was solidified due to the Massie case.[15] In September 1931, Thalia Massie, a white woman who was married to a white US Naval officer, accused five young men of rape. The police gathered five men whom she identified as her assailants, two were Hawaiian, two Japanese American, and one was Hawaiian/Chinese. Conflicting accounts of what happened that night, questionable evidence, and an inconsistent timeline resulted in a mistrial. Two of the accused men were subsequently kidnapped; one was beaten and the other shot and killed when he would not confess to the alleged crime. Thalia's mother, husband, and two naval friends were charged with the kidnapping and murder and the subsequent murder trial (with the accused defended by Clarence Darrow) led to manslaughter convictions and 10 years in prison. However, immediately after, the Governor commuted their sentences to one day and the convicted left the Islands.[16] Rosa argues that the Massie Case reinforced local oppression and created a collective identity.[17] After the trial, local ethnic newspapers criticized haole leaders of the US Territory of Hawai'i as traitors and emphasized the difference between haole and other ethnic groups against a background of class and power. "'Local' signifies a historical relationship based on a commonality among working class-people of color and their differences from whites."[18]

When white people move to Hawai'i they experience their whiteness differently than how they experience it on the mainland US where white is the majority racial group. The colonial history of the US, the multi-ethnic population of the Hawaiian Islands, and the categorization of people as Hawaiian, local, or haole combine to create a tension with regard to ethnicity and how it is embodied and performed on the Islands. The word haole in Hawaiian means foreign but has come to mean white person, or as Rohrer argues, acting white: "Local constructions of haole also emphasize performative haoleness or acting haole, the exhibiting of attitudes and actions that run counter to local and Hawaiian social values."[19] These attitudes and actions reinforce the colonizing history by foreigners in the Hawaiian Islands who "civilized the natives" and demonstrate disregard for Hawaiian culture and history. Rohrer identifies three classifications of haole: the *dumb haole* or white person who is unaware of local customs, but not necessarily mean-spirited; the *fucking haole* or white person who displays conscious disrespect/contempt for Hawaiian people and culture; and the *good haole* or white person who embraces local culture and learns about the complex history of the Islands. White people may turn to the Hawaiian shirt to demonstrate they are a *good haole*.

## The Hawaiian shirt

The Hawaiian shirt emerged in the 1930s and a rich diversity of ethnic groups contributed to the development of the shirt.[20] Fundaburk argues a combination of tourism, industry prospects, developments in textiles, and artists led to the development of the shirt. It was made from Asian textiles using Euro-American tailoring methods by Chinese and Japanese immigrants.[21] It may have been influenced by the barong tagalog worn by Filipino men and palaka shirts (i.e., plantation frocks) worn by plantation laborers. Hope notes one story of the origin of the shirt is attributed to a Japanese immigrant tailor named Koichiro Miyamoto (known as Musa-Shiya) in 1933 or 1934 when a customer ordered a shirt made of Japanese yukata cloth cut in the Western style.[22] Marketing guru George Mellen helped market him by writing Musa-Shiya's newspaper

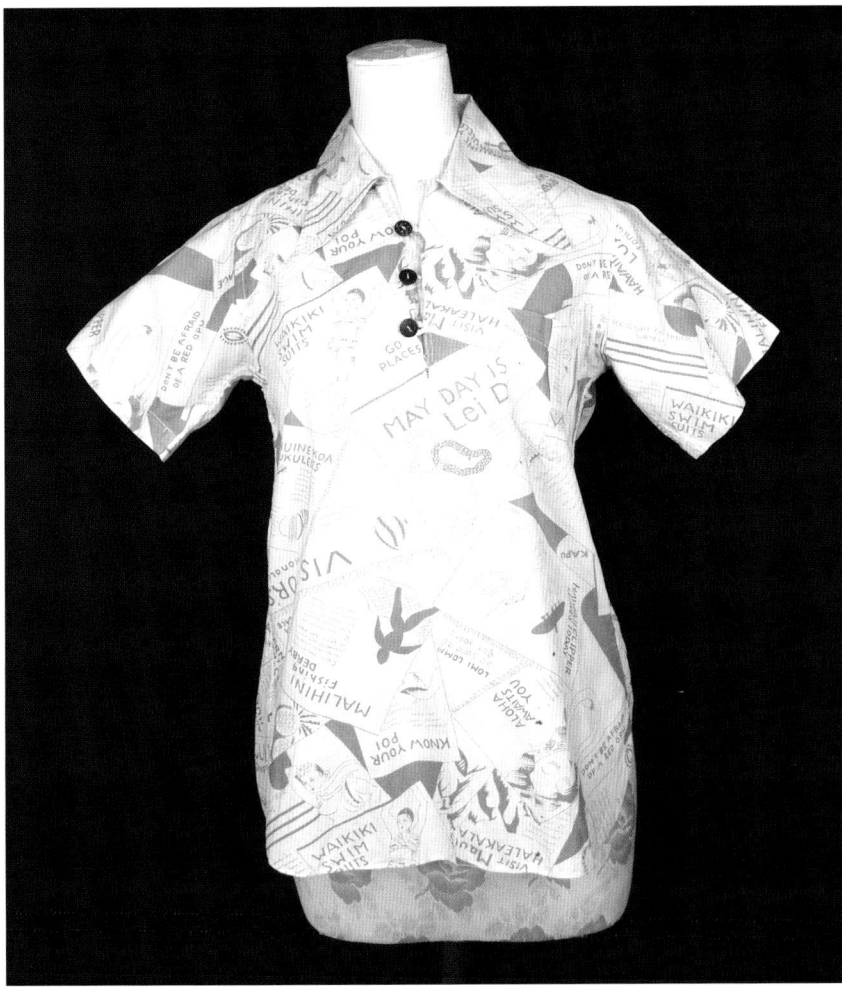

**Figure 2.1** 1930s Hawaiian shirt with images of postcards. University of Hawai'i Historic Costume Collection.

advertisements in broken English and ghost-writing a book *How Musa-Shiya the Shirtmaker Broke into Print*. Imai contends this gave Musa-Shiya an air of "Oriental authenticity" that appealed to haole consumers during a time of anti-Japanese sentiment in Honolulu and helped to transform his shop into a tourist destination.[23]

Residents had little interest in the Hawaiian shirt which was viewed as a tourist commodity. Indeed, Hawaiian shirt manufacturers marketed the shirts to tourists but wanted to gain a foothold among resident consumers which led them to lobby the legislature. In 1947, the city and county employees were allowed to wear Hawaiian shirts to work and the legislature designated "Aloha Week" (later a month) to promote local apparel businesses. However, Hawaiian shirts were controversial in businesses outside of tourist-dense Waikiki and it took efforts like Aloha Wednesdays (1948), legislative endorsement (1962), Aloha Fridays (1965), an endorsement from the Hawaiian Chamber of Commerce (1969), and change in the design (1960s), to shift local perception of the shirt as appropriate local attire. However, what type of shirt to wear was a matter of taste and identity. Arthur argues that "by the 1960s 'local' identity was well-entrenched and at the time the aloha shirt followed two design paths, one for 'locals' and the other for tourists and other outsiders."[24] The reverse shirt, made with the "back" side of the fabric facing out, emerged in the early 1960s and became a marker of local identity. Reverse shirts gave the shirt a faded, muted look, similar to one that had been worn in the sun for years which appealed to local consumers.[25]

## Methods

Grounded Theory methods were used to guide this study.[26] I interviewed Hawaiian, local, and haole men in 2021–2 to examine how they navigate identity through the Hawaiian shirt. Participants were recruited through word-of-mouth and interviews were held in person or via Zoom. In total, eighteen men were interviewed (five identified as Hawaiian, five as local, and eight as haole). They ranged in age from thirty to their seventies. Interviews were semi-structured, and I asked participants to explain how they show or display their identity through the Hawaiian shirt and their thoughts in general on the Hawaiian shirt. I asked them to provide their general thoughts on the Hawaiian shirt, if they have a favorite Hawaiian shirt, occasions they wear Hawaiian shirts, and aesthetics or styles they prefer. I then asked how their choices in aesthetics reflect their ethnic identity and if their choices have changed over time. Responses often lead to further questions for clarification. Some participants brought their own Hawaiian shirts to the interview and discussed the attributes they preferred. In general, Hawaiian and local participants drew a distinction between the types of shirts they preferred versus haoles. Haoles noted how their preferences changed over time and how they learned about the unspoken codes or rules of wearing Hawaiian shirts in Hawai'i. I took notes during the interview, summarized them afterward, and asked the interviewee to review them for accuracy. Participants were given the choice of using their real name or a pseudonym. This method was approved by the IRB of the University of Hawai'i, Mānoa. The interviews were analyzed using an iterative, deductive method where I systematically and repeatedly read interviews looking for similar themes across participants and grouping responses into clusters.

## Results and discussion

Interviews with Hawaiian and local men about their shirt preferences support Tajfel and Turner's thesis of categorization and identification in that reverse shirts are used to identify one as Hawaiian or local.[27] Specifically, they noted how reverse shirts are common features of daily life in Hawai'i and are only worn by Hawaiians or locals, and are desirable because they look bleached or faded in comparison to other Hawaiian shirts and therefore do not make one stand out from the crowd. Daniel (local) shared that reverse shirts are "synonymous with local shirts"[28] and Doug (Hawaiian) said reverse shirts were the norm for him when growing up: "When it came to aloha shirts it was the reversible type, that's all I knew."[29] Ethan (Hawaiian) shared, "I like it because it's dimmed"[30] while Amador (Hawaiian) shared, "They look better inside out because they are not so bright."[31] Bryant (local) noted he loves to find Hawaiian shirts in thrift stores because "they already have the faded look."[32] And John (Hawaiian) discussed the reason for his preferences because of the "subtle colors, not too bright, not standing out. Blending in, I don't want to stand out."[33] This element of not standing out is an important feature of Hawaiian and local culture in Hawai'i.

Also, in line with social identity theory, Hawaiian and local men noted how the Hawaiian shirt is a means of group identification. Specifically, they noted how the Hawaiian shirt is a tool used to communicate their ethnic identity (as Hawaiian or as local) due to the hues, motifs, general symbolism, and geographic origin of the shirt. They discussed how the aesthetics need to relate culturally to the Hawaiian Islands and help to identify them as truly from Hawai'i. For Ethan (Hawaiian), the shirt is a means to show ethnic pride: "It's like a Hawaiian flag for me. I can wear it ... and people know where I'm from. It expresses the Hawaiian side of me and makes me feel happy. I enjoy wearing them. I'm happy in my own ethnicity and happy to wear them."[34] Doug (Hawaiian) also discussed his ethnicity in relation to Hawaiian shirts: "I like prints that tell a story, a mo'olelo [story/shared narrative]. I like the uniqueness of the story they want to tell through their print. Definitely want to wear that, to represent our Hawaiian

**Figure 2.2** This David Shepard shirt tells a moʻoelo. Photo courtesy of the author.

culture ... The motif has to represent something cultural or nature. Color tones are more earth tones, the browns, the greens, black, blues."[35] Likewise, John (Hawaiian) noted he wears Hawaiian shirts for anything that "requires a collar" and prefers "some type of local print, shows Hawaiian things, things found in Hawaiʻi, like art, fish, or something from Hawaiʻi, Polynesian prints. They are more true to what Hawaiʻi is."[36] Likewise, Amador (Hawaiian) looks for brands or shirts that represent the island, such Micah Kamohoaliri and Pili, or feature images of local flowers, fauna, or Hawaiian tattoos.[37]

Local and Hawaiian men also prefer using motifs that represent the accuracy and uniqueness of Hawai'i to show their local identity. Shawn (local) identifies as local, "a mixed poi dog [slang for mixed]."[38] He prefers "simple colors, not flashy, with a strong and nice pattern, and simple print" and likes Polynesian tattoo motifs and reverse shirts from the brand Reyn Spooner and prefers something that is "not as loud." Similarly, Daniel (local) shows his local identity through Polynesian motifs, woodblock type of prints (e.g., Reyn Spooner), and fish ("everyone fishes here").[39] Lyle (local) has worked at Hawaiian shirt retail stores Rix and Kahala Sportswear and has amassed a large collection.[40] During his collection's height, he could wear a different shirt each day of the year. To show localness Lyle wears "Polynesian prints, dark blues, blacks, dark green, some reds."[41] Likewise, Andrew (local) noted how subtlety and non-stereotypical depictions of Hawai'i are important to his choice in shirts: "Being local, I didn't want to be too obvious. I don't like to stand out. I generally prefer earth tones, greens, and browns. I stay away from prints like surfing, tiki, flowers. I go for leafy or kapa designs. Both show I'm local and not a tourist."[42] Reinforcing the idea of subtle, muted colors preferred as a marker of Hawaiian and local identity, Bryant[43] (local) referenced a classic, popular design: "Like Reyn Spooner and reverse flag shirts. So simple. It doesn't stand out but you know it. Everyone's seen it."[44] The shirt Bryant references, the Lahaina Sailor print, is a classic design from Reyn Spooner and includes the Hawaiian state flag, state bird (the nene goose), and state flower (hibiscus).

Contrary to the aesthetics of Hawaiians and locals in their choices of shirts, tourists are generally categorized as sartorial clods, especially in their choices in Hawaiian shirts, and are assumed to wear stereotypical Hawaiian prints and vivid colors.[45] Both Hawaiian and local men noted an abhorrence for "touristy" shirts and made judgments based on comparisons between shirts worn by the in-group (locals and Hawaiians) versus the out-group (tourists and haoles). For example, John (Hawaiian) does not wear touristy shirts: "Touristy kine [pidgin meaning kind or type], wouldn't wear them. Colors, prints, I think they represent more what people from the mainland see Hawai'i is. They will wear that because that's what they think is Hawai'i."[46] Shawn (local) observes that haoles prefer Tommy Bahama shirts but "it doesn't seem Hawaiian."[47] Tommy Bahama is not a local or Hawaiian brand and therefore it is viewed as not authentic; that is, someone who does not know the codes would opt for a Tommy Bahama shirt.

ABC is a popular convenience store in tourist-laden Waikiki, and among the car dashboard hula dancers, tiki mugs, and plastic flower lei they sell are

**Figure 2.3** Paul wears the "Lahaina Sailor" shirt from Reyn Spooner. Photo courtesy of the author.

Hawaiian shirts. Haoles new to the Islands are perceived as preferring the stereotypical Hawaiian shirts mostly associated with tourism marketing: bright colors, softer fabrics, and large floral motifs, and these shirts are often referenced when talking about the style of shirt preferred by tourists. As Lyle (local) said, "When you see a person in ABC shirts you know this person is not from here."[48]

**Figure 2.4** A typical shirt sold at ABC and seen on tourists in Waikiki. Photo courtesy the author.

Amador (Hawaiian) observed,

Tourists start with ABC stores. You know what ABC means? All Bright Colors ...A haole friend from the mainland asked me to send him a Hawaiian shirt and sent me to the ABC store. He said they have the best designs and colors. He liked the brightness and boldness. If you want to most floral, brightest, boldest you go to ABC.[49]

Daniel (local) also shared his observation that haoles prefer shirts sold in ABC:

> Anyone who visits the islands has a certain view from watching Elvis Presley in *Blue Hawaii* or other movies and when they get here, they find out it's different. One guy thought we all lived in grass shacks and was surprised how developed it is here.[50]

Local and Hawaiian men typically described their preferences for Hawaiian shirts in binary terms, pointing to the difference between their aesthetic and those of tourists, and not uncommonly suggesting that the tourist aesthetic is undesirable—a further binary emphasis. On the other hand, haole descriptions appear more complex, as their responses more generally involve descriptions of negotiating identity, rather than simply preferring one aesthetic over an alternative. Haoles born and raised in Hawai'i are known as *kama'āina haole* (Hawaiian, "person of the land," used to denote someone who has lived in Hawai'i a long time) and are attuned to Hawai'i's history with foreigners. They have different experiences to those of Hawaiians and locals when growing up. According to Matt (kama'āina haole):

> There is more of noticing the haole strata. You're haole, local haole, which is what I was, and then there's fucking haole, which is a white guy acting poorly. You have the different frame of haole. And dumb haole, that's another haole categorization. I'm local haole. My mom and dad went to UH and they were born here, my aunt's here.[51]

Matt understands the codes of Hawaiian shirts and appropriateness, especially the subtle details. He prefers the vintage, faded style of Hawaiian shirts, a feature that aligns himself with the in-group. He shares a story that emphasized the further complexities of Hawaiian shirt codes:

> I was with a friend one time and were going somewhere and I was wearing an aloha shirt and my friend just turns to me and says, 'Brah, that shirt's so Punahou [a private school].' And I just died laughing and I looked and he was right. It was a Punahou shirt. More of like bankers wearing aloha shirt, not as floral, smaller repetition print, more of a dress shirt. I always like the inside-out look. Don't get too *high maka maka* [stuck-up, pretentious], right?[52]

Matt's comparison of his shirt to Punahou and *high maka maka* can be understood in the class differences in Hawai'i. While Punahou has students of all socio-economic classes, its reputation is that of an elite, private school and is known for its distinctive alumni. Clark (kama'āina haole) noted a similar experience. He "never wore ABC shirts ever," and rarely wears Hawaiian shirts now, but he did recall an early memory of wearing a Hawaiian shirt for picture day in elementary school. "My mom would make me wear a Hawaiian shirt. I had a pink one, it was like a surf company and it had writing all over it and I remember the collar buttoned to itself and I didn't understand why the collar would button to itself. So haole!"[53] His equation of the button-down collar on Hawaiian shirts reveals another distinction of class and ethnicity; as originally produced in the 1930s Hawaiian shirts were made with a flat, camp collar, but as more people began to wear Hawaiian shirts in professional settings, the stand-up, button down collar was used which is perceived to be foreign. This distinction aligns with Matt's observation of the Punahou-looking shirt and emphasizes that different Hawaiian shirts are perceived by class and ethnicity. They also highlight Kaiser and Green's (k)nots proposition that self/other relationships are entangled and dependent on time, space, and power relationships.[54]

Matt and Clark were born and raised in Hawai'i and learning the codes was part of their upbringing. However, for *malihini* (newcomer) there is a learning curve to being haole in Hawai'i and understanding the messages embedded in the aesthetics of Hawaiian shirts. Bryant (local) shared: "You see it on TV—the stereotypical sunsets in bright orange but that's not what we wear here. You move here—you wear that—someone will pull you aside and tell you that's not what we wear. It's definitely a rite of passage, a turning point."[55] Will (haole) was told early on what types of Hawaiian shirts are appropriate to wear: "When I moved to Hawai'i I bought the ABC shirts but was told really quick not to wear those shirts. I still like color but now have to think if it is okay to wear since I'm a resident and not a tourist."[56] But, he wears colorful shirts when on the mainland US, which supports one facet of the (k)not metaphor—that truth is sometimes covered over and is contingent of time and space and context.

Similarly, Georges (haole) remembered, "I didn't know haole identity existed. You know about European and other ethnicities but eventually learned about haole and when it is appropriate to use the word. I didn't want to be that person, typical white person." One of the methods he used to be a *good haole* is through his choice in Hawaiian shirts:

> As you pick up on cues, you arrive and you're a tourist and you associate Hawai'i with cheesy signals, then once you realize the that Hawai'i is cultural or environment, is not like this romanticized idea of Waikiki—used to be a swamp and not white sand beaches—it's now all an artifice. Concurrently, I negotiated my haole-identity dress. For me it was a professional identity to some extent. It [the shirt] helped negotiate educational, business, social realms in Hawai'i as a haole; yes, I'm a white person but I sort of have developed some cultural sensitives of the issues that plague Hawai'i on occasion.[57]

Fritz (haole) also negotiated his haole identity. When he moved to Hawai'i he bought shirts for the "kitsch, the mainland idea of Hawaiian shirts. Then I was exposed to other professionals and saw more fitted, tailored cuts."[58] He noted his change was due to identifying a resident (not "local") in Hawai'i. He explored many locally-produced brands when selecting his wardrobe, which now includes Kahala, Tori Richard, Sig Zane, and Ari South. He likes different brands for different reasons, from the fabric itself to the quality to the fit, but he is always conscious that whatever he buys it needs to be "local appropriate."

Likewise, Adam (haole) remarked that he knew little of Hawai'i before he moved other than the stereotypes of a fantasy paradise. "Obviously, growing up one learns there is the really gaudy, obnoxious aloha shirts . . . my sense or what I thought was that I knew that's not what people wore here in any formal sense. So, I knew I wasn't going to get anything like that, bright colors." He relied on someone who was living in Hawai'i who provided him with rules:

> I didn't like pullovers, but she taught me I can do pullover buttons, patterns that were not too unrelated or too garish. The one rule that I've taken most to heart for quality is that the pocket patterns need to line up with the pattern of the shirt. I really believe in that to this day, that is an important distinction . . . That's a measure of craft, that's someone saying they want it to look really nice, that this is a formal thing and it should have that.[59]

He also looks for the Made in Hawai'i label: "How can you have an aloha shirt that isn't designed or made locally?"

Like other haoles, Vaughn (haole) learned about codes through longtime residents of Hawai'i. His preference is for faded, subtle designs in pastel blues and greens, that button up, with a standing collar. The collar is similar to what he wore growing up in England and also is aesthetically appealing—he said his long neck would be emphasized with a camp collar. "I like the [Polynesian], classic patterns. I like reverse shirts." When he married a *kama'āina haole* she bought shirts for him and told him the dos and don'ts of Hawaiian shirts. He learned about brands and where to buy shirts from colleagues. "The more you learn the more it's intimidating. It's like drinking wine and learning the wine you like is the tip of the iceberg and there is so much more to learn . . . You go to Macy's and there is a whole department, a whole floor, dedicated to aloha shirts. It's far more sophisticated than what you believe." He likens the coding of aloha shirts to the coding of dress in England. He was born into a working-class background and learned what is acceptable in forms of dress (collars, ties, cuffs, buttons, shirt pockets, etc.) for working versus middle class and for those pursuing middle-upper-class careers. "It's a rite of passage because in London you learn what is appropriate and you do the same in Hawai'i. It's a uniform."[60]

Similarly, Paul (haole) described Hawaiian shirts as a uniform. When he moved to Honolulu, he purchased a Hilo Hattie brand shirt: "It was fun, loud colors, but I don't wear it anymore. They are out of place here. I want a shirt that ordinary people wear."[61] He now wears Reyn Spooner shirts which he describes as the typical downtown Honolulu businessman's uniform.

As the (k)not is loosened, the Hawaiian shirt becomes a site for identity creation for haoles in Hawai'i, revealing truths about race, space, time, history, and culture. Stories shared by participants demonstrated how haoles moved from the well-intentioned but clueless dumb haole to the good haole. Doug[62] (Hawaiian) illustrated this in his observation of how malihini change their preferences over time: "It's kind of like there's an entry level aloha attire and then premier. Those who come here for a short stay, they get the ABC shirt ... Those who embrace the culture, it's almost a rite of passage to be able to wear beyond entry level shirts. It shows you are embracing the culture, you kind of earn your localness."

## Haoles in Hawaiian shirts

The Hawaiian shirt is the de facto uniform of Hawai'i, both literally (as in the case of tourist personnel) and figuratively (for dress, professional, and casual attire). The complexity of Hawai'i's history with colonization and militarization has resulted in a site of tension in the types of shirts that are selected by residents. For the in-group, the codes are a natural part of everyday living, learned and understood early in life, in a land that is both tourist destination and home. For the out-group, the codes are a new learning experience for people who have seen Hawai'i mostly in Hollywood movies and tourist brochures.

Through the colonization of Hawai'i by the United States and the mixture of ethnic groups in the Islands, Hawaiian shirts have become a marker of identity and a (k)not of ethnicity, culture, and aesthetics. Aesthetics of the shirt are used to not only differentiate in-group versus out-group members[63] but also to establish one's unique identity within the complexity of the history and culture of Hawai'i. For haoles, the process of moving from out-group to in-group is facilitated by the Hawaiian shirt. The coded language of the shirt—motif, color saturation, brand—establishes identity as Hawaiian or local or haole, but it is more than *not the other*. It is an aesthetic choice that represents one's identity by selecting brands and designs that tell a moʻoelo, display Hawaiian tattoo patterns, are made locally, or demonstrate one's understanding of, and respect for, Hawaiian and local values.

Arthur argues, "In Hawaiʻi, it appears that the ritual use of aloha attire[64] is a means of group identification and ethnic solidarity."[65] She notes how aloha attire is used in rites of passage by residents—baby luau, May Day (Lei Day), graduation, weddings, and funerals. The comments of Hawaiian, local, and haole men support the idea that Hawaiian shirts are used as a means of ethnic affiliation as well as a rite of passage for malihini. When haoles move to Hawaiʻi, learning this code not only helps diminish negative difference but also move from the *dumb haole* into, and create an identity as, the *good haole*.

# Notes

1 The official spelling includes the ʻokina (ʻ), which was not commonly used until the 1990s. The mark was seldomly used prior and is rarely used today by non-local writers. It is not used in the word Hawaiian.
2 Mychael Schnell, "Hawaii is the Most Diverse State in the US" (*The Hill*: https://thehill.com/homenews/state-watch/567625-hawaii-california-and-nevada-are-most-diverse-states-in-the-us-census/, August 12, 2021). "Hawaii Ethnicity" (ToHawaii.com, https://www.to-hawaii.com/ethnicity.php#:~:text=Hawaii%20is%20one%20of%20the,is%20Alaska%20with%207.3%25, *c*. 2010).
3 Susan B. Kaiser and Denise N. Green, *Fashion and Cultural Studies*, 2nd edn. (London: Bloomsbury, 2021).
4 Carol Tulloch, "Style-Fashion-Dress: From Black to post-Black," *Fashion Theory* 14, no. 3 (2010): 273–303. Mary Ellen Roach-Higgins and Joanne B. Eicher, "Dress and Identity," *Clothing and Textiles Research Journal* 10, no. 4 (1992): 1–8, https://doi.org/10.1177/0887302X9201000401
5 *(K)nots* refers to both the knot as metaphor but also that dress is used to create who one is and who one is not.
6 Kaiser and Green, *Fashion and Cultural Studies*, 43.
7 Henry Tajfel and John C. Turner, "An Integrative Theory of Intergroup Conflict," in *The Social Psychology of Intergroup Relations*, eds. William G. Austin and Stephen Worchel (Monterey, CA: Brooks/Cole Publishing, 1979), 33–7.
8 Leon Festinger, "A Theory of Social Comparison Processes," *Human Relations* 7 (1954): 117–40.
9 Gavan Daws, *Shoal of Time: The History of the Hawaiian Islands* (Honolulu, Hawaiʻi: University of Hawaiʻi Press, 1968).

10 Wm. L. Lee, *The Transactions of the Royal Hawaiian Agricultural Society*, vol. 1, no. 3 (Honolulu, Hawai'i: Government Press, 1852, https://evols.library.manoa.hawaii.edu/bitstream/10524/2020/RHAS-v1n3-1852.pdf), 6–7.

11 Andrew W. Lind, *Hawaii's People*, 4th edn. (Honolulu, Hawai'i: The University Press of Hawai'i, 1980).

12 Ralph Kuykendall, *The Hawaiian Kingdom*, vol. 3 (Honolulu, Hawai'i: University of Hawai'i Press, 1967). Daws, *Shoal of Time*.

13 Jonathan Y. Okamura, "Aloha Kanaka Me Ke Aloha 'Aina: Local Culture and Society in Hawaii," *Amerasia* 7, no. 2 (1980): 119–37.

14 Judy Rohrer, *Haoles in Hawai'i* (Honolulu, Hawai'i: University of Hawai'i Press, 2010): 33.

15 Lind, *Hawaii's People*.

16 David E. Stannard, *Honor Killing: Race, Rape, and Clarence Darrow's Spectacular Last Case.* (New York City: Penguin Books, 2006).

17 John P. Rosa, "Local Story: The Massie Case Narrative and the Cultural Production of Local Identity in Hawai'i," *Amerasia Journal* 26, no. 2 (2000): 93–115.

18 Rosa, "Local Story," 98–9.

19 Rohrer, *Haoles in Hawai'i*, 35

20 Arthur, "The Aloha Shirt and Ethnicity in Hawai'i."

21 Emma Lyla Fundaburk, *The Garment Manufacturing Industry of Hawaii*, part 1, vol. 2 (Honolulu, Hawai'i: Economic Research Center, University of Hawai'i, 1965).

22 Dale Hope, *The Aloha Shirt* (Hillsboro, OR: Beyond Words Publishing, Inc., 2000).

23 Shiho Imai, *Creating the Nisei Market. Race and Citizenship in Hawaii's Japanese American Consumer Culture* (Honolulu, Hawai'i: University of Hawai'i Press, 2020).

24 Arthur, "The Aloha Shirt and Ethnicity in Hawai'i," 27.

25 Hope, *The Aloha Shirt*.

26 Barney Glaser and Anselm Strauss, *The Discovery of Grounded Theory: Strategies for Qualitative Research* (Chicago: Aldine, 1967).

27 Tajfel and Turner, "An Integrative Theory of Intergroup Conflict."

28 Interview by author, Honolulu, Hawai'i, February 26, 2022.

29 Interview by author, Honolulu, Hawai'i, March 4, 2022.

30 Interview by author, Honolulu, Hawai'i, March 2, 2022.

31 Interview by author, Honolulu, Hawai'i, Mach 14, 2022.

32 Interview by author, Honolulu, Hawai'i, March 12, 2022.

33 Interview by author, Honolulu, Hawai'i, March 15, 2022.

34 Interview by author, Honolulu, Hawai'i, March 2, 2022.

35 Interview by author, Honolulu, Hawai'i, March 4, 2022.

36 Interview by author, Honolulu, Hawai'i, March 15, 2022.

37 Interview by author, Honolulu, Hawai'i, March 15, 2022.

38 Interview by author, Honolulu, Hawai'i, February 26, 2022.

39 Interview by author, Honolulu, Hawaiʻi, February 26, 2022.
40 Interview by author, Honolulu, Hawaiʻi, March 5, 2022.
41 Interview by author, Honolulu, Hawaiʻi, March 5, 2022.
42 Interview by author, Honolulu, Hawaiʻi, March 17, 2022.
43 Interview by author, Honolulu, Hawaiʻi, March 12, 2022.
44 Interview by author, Honolulu, Hawaiʻi, March 17, 2022.
45 Marcia A. Morgado and Andrew Reilly, "Funny Kine Clothes: The Hawaiian Shirt as Popular Culture," *Paideusis* 6 (2012): 1–24.
46 Interview by author, Honolulu, Hawaiʻi, March 2, 2022.
47 Interview by author, Honolulu, Hawaiʻi, February 26, 2022.
48 Interview by author, Honolulu, Hawaiʻi, March 5, 2022.
49 Interview by author, Honolulu, Hawaiʻi, March 14, 2022.
50 Interview by author, Honolulu, Hawaiʻi, February 26, 2022.
51 Interview by author, Honolulu, Hawaiʻi, March 10, 2021.
52 Interview by author, Honolulu, Hawaiʻi, March 10, 2021.
53 Interview by author, Honolulu, Hawaiʻi, March 1, 2021.
54 Kaiser and Green, *Fashion and Cultural Studies*.
55 Interview by author, Honolulu, Hawaiʻi, March 12, 2022.
56 Interview by author, Honolulu, Hawaiʻi, March 4, 2022.
57 Interview by author, Honolulu, Hawaiʻi, February 26, 2021.
58 Interview by author, Honolulu, Hawaiʻi, March 1, 2021.
59 Interview by author, Honolulu, Hawaiʻi, March 3, 2021.
60 Interview by author, Honolulu, Hawaiʻi, March 14, 2022.
61 Interview by author, Honolulu, Hawaiʻi, June 25, 2022.
62 Interview by author, Honolulu, Hawaiʻi, March 4, 2022.
63 Tajfel and Turner, "An Integrative Theory of Intergroup Conflict."
64 Aloha attire is a style of dressing unique to the Hawaiian Islands due to its textiles and prints.
65 Linda B. Arthur, "Aloha Attire and Rites of Passage in Hawaiʻi": 1996: n.p.

# Bibliography

Arthur, Linda B. "Aloha Attire and Rites of Passage in Hawaiʻi." Paper given at the Costume Society of America, May 31, 1996.

Arthur, Linda B. "The Aloha Shirt and Ethnicity in Hawaiʻi." *Textile* 4, no. 1 (2006): 8–35.

Daws, Gavan. *Shoal of Time: The History of the Hawaiian Islands*. Honolulu, Hawaiʻi: University of Hawaiʻi Press, 1968.

Festinger, Leon. "A Theory of Social Comparison Processes." *Human Relations* 7 (1954): 117–40.

Fundaburk, Emma Lyla. *The Garment Manufacturing Industry of Hawaii*, part 1, vol. 2. Honolulu, Hawai'i: University of Hawaii, 1965.

Glaser, Barney and Anselm Strauss. *The Discovery of Grounded Theory: Strategies for Qualitative Research*. Chicago: Aldine, 1967.

Hope, Dale. *The Aloha Shirt*. Hillsboro, OR: Beyond Words Publishing, Inc., 2000.

Imai, Shiho. *Creating the Nisei Market. Race and Citizenship in Hawaii's Japanese American Consumer Culture*. Honolulu, Hawai'i: University of Hawai'i Press, 2020.

Kaiser, Susan. B. and Denise N. Green. *Fashion and Cultural Studies*, 2nd edn. London: Bloomsbury, 2021.

Kuykendall, Ralph, *The Hawaiian Kingdom*, vol. 3. Honolulu, Hawai'i: University of Hawai'i Press, 1967.

Lee, Wm. L. *The Transactions of the Royal Hawaiian Agricultural Society*, vol. 1, no. 3. Honolulu, Hawai'i: Government Press, 1852, https://evols.library.manoa.hawaii.edu/bitstream/10524/2020/RHAS-v1n3-1852.pdf

Lind, Andrew W. *Hawaii's People*, 4th edn. Honolulu, Hawai'i: University Press of Hawai'i, 1980.

Morgado, Marcia A. "From Kitsch to Chic: The Transformation of Hawaiian Shirt Aesthetics." *Clothing and Textiles Research Journal* 21, No. 2 (2003): 75–88.

Okamura, Jonathan Y. "Aloha Kanaka Me Ke Aloha 'Aina: Local Culture and Society in Hawaii." *Amerasia* 7, No. 2 (1980): 119–37.

Roach-Higgins, Mary Ellen and Joanne B. Eicher. "Dress and Identity." *Clothing and Textiles Research Journal* 10, No. 4 (1992): 1–8, https://doi.org/10.1177/0887302X9201000401

Rohrer, Judy, *Haoles in Hawai'i*. Honolulu, Hawai'i: University of Hawai'i Press, 2010.

Rosa, John P. "Local Story. The Massie Case Narrative and the Cultural Production of Local Identity in Hawai'i." *Amerasia Journal* 26, No. 2 (2000): 93–115.

Schnell, Mychael. "Hawaii is the most diverse state in the US." *The Hill* (2021). https://thehill.com/homenews/state-watch/567625-hawaii-california-and-nevada-are-most-diverse-states-in-the-us-census/

Stannard, David E. *Honor Killing: Race, Rape, and Clarence Darrow's Spectacular Last Case*. New York City: Penguin Books, 2006.

Tajfel, Henri and John C. Turner. "An Integrative Theory of Intergroup Conflict." In *The Social Psychology of Intergroup Relations*, edited by William G. Austin and Stephen Worchel, 33–7. Monterey, CA: Brooks/Cole Publishing, 1979.

To Hawaii.com (n.d., *c.* 2010). "Hawaii Ethnicity," https://www.to-hawaii.com/ethnicity.php#:~:text=Hawaii%20is%20one%20of%20the,is%20Alaska%20with%207.3%25)

Tulloch, Carol. "Style-Fashion-Dress: From Black to post-Black." *Fashion Theory* 14, no. 3 (2010): 273–303.

3

# "Smart Togs for Action"

Everyday Clothes for Rural Women in Texas in the 1950s

Rebecca Jumper Matheson

In 1914, one of American author Edna Ferber's characters noted, "[W]e are apt to forget that those [fashionable] types form only a thin upper crust, and that down beneath there are millions and millions of regular, everyday women doing regular everyday things in regular everyday clothes."[1] In the 1950s, the consumer group of everyday American women looked to a range of sources for their everyday dress choices, and developed fashion practices that had been cultivated in previous decades. As Cheryl Buckley and Hazel Clark argue in *Fashion and Everyday Life: London and New York*, in everyday wardrobes both new and old garments hang side-by-side.[2] Similarly, within the wardrobes of American women of the 1950s, new formal dresses co-existed with seemingly incongruous everyday items such as old housedresses.

This chapter will explore aspects of American women's everyday fashion of the 1950s, with a focus on rural areas of Texas, and particularly East Texas. Postwar Texas was a newly majority-urban state in the midst of major demographic and cultural change, as many farm workers who had migrated to cities for industrial work during the Second World War did not return to agriculture when the war ended.[3] Contrary to popular imagery of Texas as an arid landscape, the Pineywoods of East Texas is a land of lush forests, and in the 1950s, timber and oil and their associated industries allowed many East Texans to remain in rural areas even if they no longer farmed for a living.[4]

Throughout this chapter, I am utilizing Buckley and Clark's definition of everyday fashion as practice-focused, or indicative of, "the ordinary and mundane practices of wearing, where items are drawn from the personal wardrobe in a routine manner," alongside definitions of fashionable behavior not limited to youthful, wealthy, or avant garde wearers.[5] The chapter will consider what women in the countryside and small towns of Texas chose to wear for everyday activities, such as housework and outdoor chores, and how these women obtained clothing in spaces other than large urban department stores. Everyday fashions in the 1950s included sportswear separates, long a staple of American fashion, marketed for country and suburban lifestyles, with the idea of collecting pieces that defied the swift pace of seasonal fashion change. Rural Texas women purchased clothing in local stores, bought through mail order catalogs, and sewed clothes at home, allowing for customization according to individual taste, and encouraging an appreciation for both the fabric and labor involved in the creation of garments. Everyday clothing was one means through which women both embraced and contested post-war narratives of consumption in fashion, adding new pieces to their wardrobes while also retaining elements from the past.

Buckley and Clark propose utilizing "theories of everyday life so as to explore the routine elements of fashion," and "understanding fashion as a manifestation of routine daily lives that remains with people over time . . . disruptive of fashion's structures and systems as well as its visual codes and norms of consumption."[6] The goal of considering everyday fashion is to bring to light fashion practices beyond the traditionally more visible manifestations of Parisian or high fashion. Fashion historian Lourdes M. Font defines high fashion as "luxury and novelty combined into an irresistible force."[7] In conjunction with Buckley and Clark's theory of everyday fashion, which draws in part upon the work of Henri Lefebvre, I add elements from the Edna Ferber quotation above. While the Ferber quotation was originally intended as fictional dialogue rather than fashion theory, I argue that Ferber—however unintentionally—offers a helpful three-part theory of the everyday with regard to clothing: a kind of "found theory."

Ferber's context was a fictional traveling petticoat saleswoman of the 1910s, who knew the fashion needs of small-town American women who rejected the extreme styles of urban modernity, including youthful tango fashions. For Ferber, writing specifically in an American context (albeit earlier in the century), everyday clothes are those worn by most women who are not clients of haute couture or expensive ready-to-wear. They are middle class, working class, or poor—anyone who does not form part of the most fashionable "thin upper crust." According to Ferber, these everyday women need clothes for their everyday activities, as they are women who "[w]ash on Monday, and iron on Tuesday."[8] And finally, Ferber notes, they wear "regular everyday clothes": I interpret this as the kinds of basics that form the backbone of a wardrobe, rather than the standout or ceremonial pieces that so often find their way into museum collections. While Ferber's fiction was written decades before the 1950s, I think her insights remain applicable to that later period in US history as well. This chapter will seek to explore some of the ways that some consumer groups of American women of the 1950s clothed themselves and their families in day-to-day life in the 1950s, bearing in mind Ferber's framework.

## Methods: Finding everyday togs

Approaches for this research include visual analysis of snapshots, oral history, and textual analysis of print sources such as newspapers, magazines, and home economics textbooks. The materials I have consulted are eclectic, and often ephemeral, due to the nature of my research goals. As Buckley and Clark have noted, when studying everyday fashion "[t]he methodological challenge ... is to find the means to research those things, people and ideas that have remained unobserved, to locate and interpret the intimate ..."[9] In investigating the unobserved and intimate, a scholar must consider access. I grew up in rural Angelina County, East Texas, and this region is a place to which I have ongoing connections. In trying to discover more about American women's everyday fashion in the 1950s, I turned to many primary sources relating to rural Texas, including visual sources from Central and South Texas, but especially East Texas.

One means of researching everyday fashion is to consult archives that are less typically employed by fashion historians, such as collections with a focus on regional history and genealogy. For this project, the East Texas Research Center (ETRC) at Stephen F. Austin State University, and, to a lesser extent, the Library of Congress were important sources for archival photographs. The photographs I have used include both images that are part of the university's archives and community-sourced snapshots that have been digitized through the East Texas Digital Archives.

Another important approach is oral history.[10] My interest in this method dates to my high school years when I planned a small oral history project and read compilations of *Foxfire* and our local counterpart, *Loblolly*.[11] In 2004, I included oral history as a key methodology in my master's thesis, which investigated why some women in the United States wore sunbonnets throughout the twentieth century. I recruited narrators among the older women in my own family and friends. One of the advantages of oral history is that the focus remains on the narrator and the story that person desires to tell. My sunbonnet narrators shared quite a bit of information that was not directly related to sunbonnets, and

**Figure 3.1** Dana Rusk (later Jumper), about age ten, with her mother, Louise Jenkins Rusk. *c.* 1956. Author's collection.

now in researching 1950s everyday fashion I have turned again to the published interview transcripts which yielded helpful information.

I also asked my mother, Dana Rusk Jumper (1946–2022), to share her memories of everyday fashion in East Texas in the 1950s, and she wrote down in longhand her memories of clothing practices, including everyday tasks such as how her mother, Louise Jenkins Rusk (1912–2008) did laundry.

These are exactly the types of everyday fashion practices that can remain "stubbornly invisible" even in alternative sources such as diaries and letters.[12] Consulting narrators' memories makes the "invisible" aspects of everyday fashion reappear, like invisible ink held over a flame.

## Country clothes

Much American sportswear sold through stores was ready-to-wear produced under principles of mass manufacturing. Mass manufactured clothing designs were one way to reach a broader audience of "regular, everyday women" within the context of a culture of mass consumption. Concurrently, some designers of American sportswear defied the pace of change normally associated with high fashion, creating separates that could be worn for many years. Many of the sportswear garments produced were designed for everyday, mundane tasks of life, or even special events like church attendance, rather than the grand occasions that called for the spectacular expressions of high fashion. In 1950, only 26.8 percent of women in Texas worked outside the home, so clothing for home-centered activities would have been an important part of their wardrobes.[13]

The concept of ongoing wardrobe building was important in American sportswear of the 1950s, especially in the category of "country clothes." Country clothes were sportswear pieces intended for wear in suburban or rural areas. Generally, garments of this type did not change dramatically from year to year.[14] Many of the clothes shown in a 1960s *Vogue* article still appear "classic" today: polo shirts, wrap skirts, capri pants, and cable-knit cardigans.[15] American women who purchased the country clothes type of sportswear were addressed as "collectors" by both fashion editors and advertisers.[16] For example, a 1954 *Vogue* "Shop Hound" promotion described a Phelps Associates ensemble of cotton shirt and wrap skirt with a leather belt as, "For the Phelps collectors—three more casual jewels."[17] The metaphor of jewelry implies artistic and intrinsic value and the assumption in the text is that pieces were added to the wearer's collection each year, while the old garments from previous seasons were not discarded. When *Vogue* editors wrote of country clothes, they imagined these garments worn by women who divided their time between urban and suburban or country living. Yet similar garments were also worn by women who spent most, if not all, of their time outside major urban centers.

## Sportswear separates

Sportswear items such as shirtdresses, skirts, and blouses were also worn by women in rural Texas. The photograph of my mother and grandmother in Figure 3.1 shows a middle-aged, white, working-class East Texas woman's sportswear ensemble from about 1956. My grandmother, Louise Jenkins Rusk, wears a light-colored cotton gingham blouse that buttons down the front and is tucked into a front-wrapping skirt, her waist accentuated by a leather belt with a brass buckle. Dana Rusk Jumper, about age ten in the photo, recalled later, "Mother ... wore straight skirts and blouses. The blouse was tucked into the skirt and a belt was a common accessory. Mother loved pretty clothes ..."[18] Louise's straight skirt contrasts with the width of Dana's taffeta skirt, which relied on starched petticoats underneath for its fullness. Dana remembered wearing "skirts with petticoats under them to school" (although the taffeta fabric indicates this was a special occasion not a regular school day), and also stated that, "Sweater sets were popular to wear with our skirts, full skirts for younger girls, while older girls wore both full and straight skirts."[19]

Both Louise's skirt and blouse are neatly ironed, and only slight creases from sitting down can be seen on the skirt front. Dana recalled later, "Mother spent hours ironing our clothes. We would not have even considered that any garment could be worn in public without it being starched and ironed."[20] Ironing is an ephemeral craft that has not received enough attention in fashion history. Louise had the skills to iron with either an electric iron or the non-electric variety. Dana wrote, "I have a memory of Mother using the heavy flat irons that she heated on the stove. The electric iron must have needed repair. Irons were repaired, not replaced."[21] Dana carried the detailed ironing skills that Louise taught her throughout her life; she could make each tiny pleat in a baby's dress a study in geometrical precision. The practice of ironing was also imbued with ideas about neatness in grooming; one might not have much money to spend on clothes but one could at least make them neat and clean. Dana also continued to hold her beliefs about the importance of ironing long after it became less important in fashion. My younger sister and I both recall Dana prompting us to iron items such as T-shirts and jeans when we were in high school in the 1990s.

A 1958 photograph from the East Texas Research Center shows three members of a white family from rural East Texas. Figure 3.2. The woman on the right—probably a visitor who has arrived in the automobile beyond the fence—wears a lightweight printed cotton dress with three-quarter-length sleeves and a Peter Pan collar and dangles her metal framed handbag from the crook of her elbow. The woman on the left is slightly more casually dressed in a solid cotton blouse that buttons down the front, with the sleeves cuffed to just above the elbows, and a slightly full skirt. As in the photo of Louise Jenkins Rusk in Figure 3.1, the blouse and skirt combination seems to have been a look favored by middle-aged women.

**Figure 3.2** Everyday rural East Texas fashions, 1958. The Spivey family. The East Texas Research Center, R. W. Steen Library, Stephen F. Austin State University, Nacogdoches, Texas.

Younger East Texas women sometimes opted for separates including skirt and blouse combinations, such as in a photograph of the Stephen F. Austin State University bookstore. Figure 3.3. In this photo, two women, shown seated and perusing books on the right, both wear light-colored woven sleeveless blouses, probably of cotton. The climate of East Texas is sub tropical humid, and while many public buildings were airconditioned in the 1950s, 69.7 percent of Texas homes were still not airconditioned at the end of the decade.[22] Therefore, women embraced styles that suited the climate, such as the sleeveless styles worn by the students in the photo.

Skirt and sweater combinations were also worn by young matrons like Frances Maxine (Rose) Leaphart, who was photographed holding her young daughter Rebecca, c. 1956, in the Central Texas town of Brownwood. Figure 3.4.

Leaphart's hair is cut short at the sides and curled on the top. She is hatless and appears to be holding a yellow bonnet that matches her young daughter's coat. Leaphart's main garments consist of an off-white, short sleeved knit sweater, and a purple tweed skirt with pleats at the back hem. She has accessorized the ensemble with a double strand of beads that look gray in the photo but may be light purple to coordinate with the skirt. In addition, she wears earrings and bright red lipstick. Her black Mary Jane-style flats allow her to stand comfortably on the grassy lawn without the heels sinking into the grass.

**Figure 3.3** "Interior shot of the Stephen F. Austin State College bookstore when it was located off East College," July 29, 1952. The East Texas Research Center, R. W. Steen Library. Stephen F. Austin State University, Nacogdoches, Texas.

The items of sportswear shown in these photographs could have remained in the wearer's wardrobe for multiple years. Home economist Bess V. Oerke wrote in a 1956 high school economics textbook, *Dress*, which was adopted for use in the Texas public school system, "Few of us ever have an opportunity to select an entirely new wardrobe, but it is possible for each of us to have a complete wardrobe... *if we make plans*. Start with the clothes you have on hand, using them as a basis for your wardrobe."[23] Oerke suggested that clothes be repaired, then remodeled or altered before finally being given away.[24] She also noted that the vast majority (86 percent) of high school girls had ten to thirty wearable garments in their wardrobes.[25]

## Wash dresses and other work clothes

Many items of sportswear and other everyday garments that entered American women's wardrobes were made in fabrics that were easy to care for. These items tended to be made in less formal fabrics, from less formal fibers—washable, woven cottons for example—rather than those that were higher on what dress historian

**Figure 3.4** Frances Maxine (Rose) Leaphart holding daughter Becky, *c.* 1956, Brownwood, Texas. Courtesy of Audrey Young.

Lou Taylor has termed the hierarchy of textiles.[26] While washing machine ownership rose quickly in the immediate post-war period, about 37 percent of American households did not own washing machines in 1950.[27] Dana Rusk Jumper remembered that in the early 1950s her mother washed clothes in a galvanized tub set up on a table in the back yard, using a rub board to scrub the clothes, and rinsing them in a second tub.[28] Beatrice Upshaw, who grew up in a Nacogdoches County Freedom Colony (a place settled by formerly enslaved Black Texans following Emancipation) called County Line, recalled that into the 1960s, "This was before the days of automatic washing machines—not that they had not been invented yet, just that no one in our community had one."[29] Upshaw and her family members boiled their laundry in an iron pot, using either a commercial detergent like Tide or homemade lye soap.³⁰ The strenuous nature of doing laundry without an automatic machine meant that clothes that were sturdy and simple to wash were popular. Consumer demand for this type of garment was catered to by the American "wash dress" industry, composed of manufacturers of inexpensive women's ready-to-wear dresses made of washable fibers like cotton.³¹

An American woman's wardrobe of the 1950s usually contained at least some clothing meant for housework or at-home wear. One popular garment for housework was the housedress, which was a subcategory of the wash dress industry. Bess V. Oerke's textbook, *Dress*, offered a sample budget for a rural farming family that called for the purchase of two housedresses per year for the mother of the family. In contrast, the suggested budget recommended only purchasing one wool dress and one summer (i.e., cotton) dress over a two-year period. This budget allowed for the housedresses to cost three to four dollars each.³²

Interestingly, Oerke, while acknowledging that women were still purchasing housedresses, argued that for 1950s homemakers, "The popular housedress of the last decade no longer serves her needs. Substitutes for it include jeans, shorts, slacks, coveralls, and dainty washable cotton frocks."³³ A *Life* magazine article profiled fashion designer Elizabeth Phelps' "new substitutes for the monotonous house dress [which] consist of slacks with narrow, tapering legs and, since she like many people does not approve of bulging slacks on women, of concealing apron skirts or tunics as well. All are of plain, practical work fabrics like denim, poplin or sailcloth."³⁴ The housedress was an item of everyday clothing considered so ordinary that it is dismissed as monotonous by the *Life* magazine journalist (probably fashion editor Sally Kirkland). Elizabeth Phelps' designs, on the other hand, exemplified an intentional engagement between the everyday and high fashion similar to that of Claire McCardell's Popover dress of a few years prior: modernist ideals such as simplicity joined with design principles of functionality in a way that seemed fresh and new but could easily take their place within a woman's wardrobe of everyday clothes.

While adult women did not usually wear trousers for public activities in town, such as shopping, trousers were an option for outdoor work and at-home wear. A *c.* 1951–4 photograph portrays a Mexican American South Texas family, the Ramirezes, who were being relocated due to the United States/Mexico Falcon Dam project on the Rio Grande River. Figure 3.5.

This photo shows two women wearing trouser and shirt ensembles. The woman on the left wears a dark western-style shirt, with pockets on the chest, with her trousers. The woman on the right wears hoop earrings, a light-colored button-front shirt, trousers, and tasseled loafers. The woman on the right also

**Figure 3.5** United States Information Agency, "Manuel Ramirez and members of his family in front of their home in Texas will be relocated as a result of the joint US-Mexico Falcon Dam construction project on the Rio Grande River," c. 1951–4. Library of Congress, Prints and Photographs Division.

demonstrates that the way women wore garments could be as important as the garments themselves and shows some elements of customization that add flair to the basic shirt: firstly, she has rolled the sleeves to above the elbow. Rolling was an example element of everyday styling, for both men and women, allowing the end user to give a fashionable touch to an item of basic sportswear. As seen on the woman on the right, tying the front ends of the shirt, rather than tucking it in, was another means of personalizing a mass manufactured garment.

## Continuity and consumption

One important theme in the study of everyday clothing is the concept of continuity. A woman's relationship with clothing was not just shaped by consumerist messaging from 1950s fashion media, advertising, and promotion, but also by her lived experiences of the past and the demands of the present. Her wardrobe was therefore a set of objects maintained in an ongoing set of practices including shopping, sewing, repairing, and retaining or discarding.[35]

Rural women obtained everyday clothing in several ways, including mail order catalogs, local and chain stores in small towns, and home sewing. Mail order catalogs enabled women to purchase ready-to-wear clothing without traveling to town. For example, housedresses could be purchased ready-made for less than $2 in the Fall 1949 Sears catalog.[36] A 1950 *Women's Wear Daily* article noted that mail order houses served a principally rural population who wanted their house dresses cut differently than those purchased by shoppers in larger metropolitan areas.[37] This may point to practical considerations, perhaps because rural women did more outdoor work in their house dresses.

Small towns of the 1950s offered both local department stores and chain stores such as J. C. Penney. J. C. (James Cash) Penney had begun his empire of department stores by intentionally targeting smaller towns of 1,000 to 3,000 people, claiming, "I know how to run a store of our type—the sort of store that appeals to small-town people."[38] Dana Rusk Jumper recalled shopping with her mother at the local Penney's store: "I loved that store because there were stairs to climb to get to the ladies' and children's clothing area."[39] Small town stores offered a convenient shopping experience with an advantage over mail order catalogs in that shoppers were able to see, touch, and try on clothing before purchasing—at least for some shoppers.[40] Department store shopping was, however, typically mediated through the "saleslady" who could make the consumer experience positive or negative. Historian Susan Porter Benson argues that in department stores that did not have self-service schemes, "salespeople controlled the customer's access to the merchandise and actively influenced the course of a sales transaction."[41] Benson notes that department stores began implementing self-service during the Second World War, but Dana recalls that the salesperson remained crucial to small town department store shopping in East Texas in the 1950s:

> The salesladies were always there to help the customers choose clothing, take the selected clothing to the dressing rooms, help you with buttons, zippers, etc., take more clothing in and out of the dressing rooms, and give suggestions and opinions (often unsolicited) on the clothing. Depending on the personality and the character of the saleslady, the constant attention given to a customer could be a real help or a real annoyance.[42]

Saleswomen's advice and persuasiveness were by no means the only factors in the final sale, however. Customers also used their knowledge of garment construction to inform their decision-making process. Dana noted, "Whenever we shopped for 'readymade' clothes, we always looked at the inside of the garment. We looked at how the seams were finished and the depth of the hem, along with the evenness of the stitching."[43] By looking at the garment's interior, the shopper could assess the quality of the item. This was especially important for rural East Texas women like Louise who expected their clothing to wear well and last for a long time.

In the 1950s, home sewing offered a budget-friendly option for increasing the size and variety of an American woman's wardrobe. Buckley and Clark cite the sewing machine, paper patterns for home sewing, "ready-to-wear systems, and improved methods of distribution, dissemination and retailing" as prompts for fashion assuming a new ubiquity in everyday lives in the twentieth century.[44] While many of these technologies had begun transforming the relationship of ordinary Americans to fashion in the nineteenth century, in the mid-twentieth century they became even more affordable. Oerke gives an example of a college woman of the 1950s who sewed seventeen garments for her wardrobe. Purchased ready-to-wear, the items would have cost $184, but she was able to make them for a cost of $91.75. Despite the 157 hours spent in working to sew the garments, this student was satisfied with her savings of 58 cents per hour.[45] In the 1950s, there was wide consumer sewing literacy, bolstered by a combination of knowledge passed down within families, home economics curricula in schools and colleges, and commercial sewing centers such as those run by the Singer sewing machine company.[46] This was confirmed by Dana who recalled, "Many of the ladies in our community had sewing machines and made some of the clothing for their families. Several ladies made a bit of extra money sewing for customers."[47]

Some of the everyday dress items that women sewed at home included housedresses and other clothes for housework. Women's service magazine *Woman's Day* offered its own line of sewing patterns, which coordinated with articles in the magazine. Journalist Margaret Parker Gary argued that women of 1950 wanted "work-about clothes as attractive and functional as her modern household"; specifically, this meant clothes that were easy to put on, launder, and move in, while also looking "smart and becoming."[48] Three years later, Gary produced an article and pattern featuring Elizabeth Phelps' designs for housework, "Smart Togs for Action," which centered around a coverall with two different length skirts for layering.[49] The emphasis was on providing home sewers with an opportunity to create housekeeping clothes that were both practical and fashionable.

## Resourcefulness

Some home sewing practices that continued among rural East Texas women of the 1950s were a direct continuation of fashion practices from more economically challenging times. Design historian Pat Kirkham discovered in her oral histories of British women that beauty practices originating in the scarcities of the Second World War were sometimes continued even in later years.[50] In my own research, I also found that fashion practices that were learned early in women's lives became embedded in their relationship to clothing. Dana recalled that her mother, always economical, eschewed clothing like housedresses intended for housework and simply wore "dresses that were older and worn that were no longer suitable for wearing when going shopping or visiting friends."[51] Additionally, in the 1950s some rural East Texas women continued sewing practices such as cutting down old garments to remake them into new ones, and sourcing new fabrics from specially-printed flour sacks to be made into items of clothing. Dana remembered an example of remaking an old garment:

> Mother would also use old clothes, salvage the "good" fabric ... One top she made was a bold red and blue stripe. In its early life, the fabric was part of Daddy's pajamas. I wasn't so sure about wanting to wear it. I felt better about it when our kindly mail carrier Mr. Haley told me how much he liked it.[52]

Dana's ambivalence about a remodeled garment demonstrates that even children of the 1950s could feel the pressure to purchase something brand new, yet her mother's choices as a homemaker included careful conservation of textile resources in keeping with the practices, household economics, and accessibility of fabric of earlier decades of the twentieth century.

Flour sacks are known to have provided a similar opportunity for home sewers to inexpensively make something new. Fashion historian Loris Connolly notes that flour and grain sacks had been used for clothing since the nineteenth century, but it was in the 1930s that cloth bag manufacturers diversified their offerings with colorful dyed or printed materials.[53] For example, Louise had used these sacks as a source of fabric for clothing including sunbonnets as a young matron of the 1930s, and continued to use sacking for home sewing in the 1950s, even though she was able to afford other fabrics.

However, some women felt there was a stigma attached to using these materials. Another narrator, Faye McClain Rusk (1914–2004), stated that, "... I didn't have to have it, but during the Depression, people would make things out of food or flour sacks ... Kids would come to school wearing it, and I'd recognize the flour sacks ... because we bought the same flour! ... We never did wear the flour sack dresses."[54] With improving economic conditions in the 1950s, rural women who felt the stigma that Faye Rusk pointed out were probably quick to abandon the practice of using flour sacking, while thrifty homemakers continued the careful economy they had learned during hard times. Connolly found that in a 1960 survey of rural homemakers, 56 percent were still recycling cotton bag material in their home sewing, and Connelly argues that it was actually the increased cost of cotton versus paper packaging, rather than a decline in consumer demand, that led bag manufacturers to discontinue bags intended as dress goods.[55]

## Conclusion

Everyday 1950s fashions of women in rural Texas included sportswear elements like the country clothes of their suburban peers, and many of these sportswear pieces were meant to be kept in a wardrobe long term. Rural East Texas women's everyday fashion included practices such as careful ironing and dressing for the climate. Women's wardrobes also contained items of everyday at-home clothing such as housedresses and trousers—wardrobe elements that might not be socially acceptable for women to wear "in town." Rural East Texas women's practices of obtaining clothing included ordering from mail order catalogues and shopping at small town stores, and these retailers targeted the rural customer with specific merchandise, including garment cuts aimed at rural women's preferences. Rural women's wardrobes also showed an ongoing dialogue of continuity and consumption, as they participated in home sewing and resourceful practices, including remodeling garments and making new garments from cotton sacking. My research has also indicated that women who adopted certain fashion practices at an early age—from meticulous ironing to economical repurposing of textiles—continued these practices throughout their lives. While the decade of the 1950s in the United States is often associated with a consumerist shift, many rural women of Texas continued everyday clothing practices that they had employed over time, which emphasized a careful and conserving attitude toward textiles and clothing.

## Acknowledgments

I want to thank a number of people who made this research possible, including the Spivey family, for kind permission to publish their photo from the East Texas Research Center digital collection, Stephen F. Austin State University; Kyle Ainsworth, Special Collections Librarian, East Texas Research Center, Stephen F. Austin State University; Audrey Young, for kind permission to publish her photo of Frances Maxine (Rose) Leaphart and Becky Leaphart; as well as others who generously shared photos or memories of everyday East Texas fashions of the 1950s including the late Dana Rusk Jumper, Rachel Jumper Kimbrell, Len Medford, Belinda Smith, and Rosemary Varsey.

## Notes

1  Edna Ferber, *Personality Plus* (Urbana and Chicago, IL: University of Illinois Press, [1914] 2002), 82.
2  Cheryl Buckley and Hazel Clark, *Fashion and Everyday Life: London and New York* (London and New York: Bloomsbury, 2017), 7.
3  Robert A. Calvert, "Texas Post World War II," rev. by Sean P. Cunningham, in Texas State Historical Association, *Handbook of Texas* Online, https://www.tshaonline.org/handbook/entries/texas-post-world-war-ii, accessed September 7, 2022.
4  Bob Bowman, *Pitser: The Rise of a Native Son* (Lufkin, TX: Best of East Texas, 2000), 101, 132; Howard Walker, *Memoirs of Howard Walker and Other Trivia* (Lufkin, TX: Lufkin Kiwanis Club, 1992), 106.
5  Cheryl Buckley and Hazel Clark, "Conceptualizing Fashion in Everyday Lives," *Design Issues* 28, no. 4 (Autumn 2012): 19.
6  Buckley and Clark, *Fashion and Everyday Life*, 4.
7  Lourdes M. Font and Trudie A. Grace, *The Gilded Age: High Fashion and Society in the Hudson Highlands, 1865–1914* (Cold Spring, NY: Putnam County Historical Society & Foundry School Museum, 2006), 26.
8  Ibid.
9  Buckley and Clark, *Fashion and Everyday Life*, 16.
10 Dress historian Lou Taylor notes that oral history is especially helpful for sharing voices that might be left out of "big history." Lou Taylor, *The Study of Dress History* (Manchester and New York: Manchester University Press, 2002), 242.
11 Eliot Wigginton, ed., *Foxfire 3: Animal Care, Banjos and Dulcimers, Hide Tanning, Summer and Fall Wild Plant Foods, Butter Churns, Ginseng, and Still More Affairs of Plain Living* (Garden City, NY: Anchor Press/Doubleday, 1975); Thad Sitton, ed., *The*

*Loblolly Book: Water Witching, Wild Hog Hunting, Home Remedies, Grandma's Moral Tales and Other Affairs of Plain Texas Living* (Austin, TX: Texas Monthly Press, 1983).

12  Buckley and Clark, *Fashion and Everyday Life*, 9.
13  Calvert, "Texas Post World War II."
14  "Permanent Week-end Clothes-list," *Vogue*, May 1, 1960: 169.
15  Ibid., 168,170, 173.
16  "Shop Hound," *Vogue*, October 15, 1954: 65; "Permanent Week-end Clothes-list," *Vogue*: 169, 171.
17  "Shop Hound," 65.
18  Dana Rusk Jumper, letter to author, May 14, 2022: 1.
19  Ibid., 2, 4.
20  Ibid., 4.
21  Ibid., 2.
22  Raymond Arsenault, "The End of the Long Hot Summer: Air Conditioning and Southern Culture," *The Journal of Southern History* 50, no. 4 (November 1984): 610–11.
23  Bess V. Oerke, *Dress* (Peoria, IL: Chas. A. Bennett, 1956), 77.
24  Ibid., 79.
25  Ibid., 90.
26  Lou Taylor, "De-coding the Hierarchy of Fashion Textiles," in *The Textile Reader*, ed. Jessica Hemmings (London: Bloomsbury, 2012), 420–1.
27  Thomas R. Tibbetts, "Expanding Ownership of Household Equipment," *Monthly Labor Review* vol. 87, 10 (October 1964): 1134.
28  Dana Rusk Jumper, letter to author, May 22, 2022: 1.
29  Beatrice Upshaw, *A Biscuit for Your Shoe: A Memoir of County Line, a Texas Freedom Colony* (Denton, TX: University of North Texas Press, 2020), 219.
30  Ibid.
31  "Wash Dress Industry—In Statistics," *Women's Wear Daily*, January 23, 1941: 23.
32  Oerke, *Dress*, 92.
33  Ibid., 538.
34  "Work Clothes: New Substitutes for House Dress Are Rugged, Trim, and Tailored," *Life*, February 7, 1949: 89.
35  See Buckley and Clark, "Conceptualizing Fashion in Everyday Lives," 19.
36  Sears, Roebuck, *Fall/Winter 1948–1949 Catalog*: 193.
37  Harry Birse, "HDI Offers to Confer with Mail Order Group on Sizing," *Women's Wear Daily*, February 27, 1950: 27.
38  Norman Beasley, *Main Street Merchant: The Story of the J. C. Penney Company* (New York: Whittlesey House, 1948), 73.
39  Dana Rusk Jumper, letter to author, May 14, 2022: 6.
40  Afro-American Studies scholar Traci Parker observes that African American customers were both welcomed and treated unequally in large urban department

stores; this was likely true in smaller towns as well. Traci Parker, *Department Stores and the Black Freedom Movement* (Chapel Hill, NC: The University of North Carolina Press, 2019), 3.
41  Susan Porter Benson, *Counter Cultures: Saleswomen, Manager, and Customers in American Department Stores, 1890–1940* (Urbana and Chicago, IL: University of Illinois Press, 1986), 125.
42  Dana Rusk Jumper, letter to author, May 14, 2022: 6.
43  Ibid., 7.
44  Buckley and Clark, *Fashion and Everyday Life*, 4.
45  Oerke, *Dress*, 87.
46  In 1948, a Singer Sewing Centers brochure advertised classes in home dressmaking and home decoration, as well as classes specifically for teenage girls ages twelve to seventeen. Singer Sewing Machine Company, *The Secret of Beautiful Clothes and a Beautified Home* (n.p.: Singer Manufacturing Co., 1948), 4.
47  Dana Rusk Jumper, letter to author, May 14, 2022: 7.
48  Margaret Parker Gary, "Dressed for the Job," *Woman's Day*, January 1950: 50–1.
49  Margaret Parker Gary, "Smart Togs for Action," *Woman's Day*, January 1953: 18–20, 82.
50  Pat Kirkham, "Beauty and Duty," in *War Culture: Social Change and Changing Experience in World War Two*, eds. Pat Kirkham and David Thoms (London: Lawrence & Wishart, 1995), 16.
51  Dana Rusk Jumper, letter to author, May 22, 2022: 3.
52  Dana Rusk Jumper, letter to author, May 14, 2022: 3.
53  Loris Connolly, "Recycling Feed Sacks and Flour Bags: Thrifty Housewives or Marketing Success Story?" *Dress* 19 (1992): 22–4.
54  Rebecca Jumper Matheson, *The Sunbonnet: An American Icon in Texas* (Lubbock, TX: Texas Tech University Press, 2009), 159.
55  Connolly, "Recycling Feed Sacks and Flour Bags," 31.

# Bibliography

Arsenault, Raymond. "The End of the Long Hot Summer: Air Conditioning and Southern Culture." *The Journal of Southern History* 50, no. 4 (November 1984): 597–628.

Beasley, Norman. *Main Street Merchant: The Story of the J. C. Penney Company*. New York: Whittlesey House, 1948.

Benson, Susan Porter. *Counter Cultures: Saleswomen, Manager, and Customers in American Department Stores, 1890–1940*. Urbana and Chicago, IL: University of Illinois Press, 1986.

Bowman, Bob. *Pitser: The Rise of a Native Son*. Lufkin, TX: Best of East Texas, 2000.

Buckley, Cheryl and Hazel Clark. "Conceptualizing Fashion in Everyday Lives." *Design Issues* 28, no. 4 (Autumn 2012): 18–28.

Buckley, Cheryl and Hazel Clark. *Fashion and Everyday Life: London and New York*. London and New York: Bloomsbury, 2017.

Calvert, Robert A. "Texas Post World War II." Rev. by Sean P. Cunningham. In Texas State Historical Association, *Handbook of Texas* Online, https://www.tshaonline.org/handbook/entries/texas-post-world-war-ii, accessed 7 September 2022.

Connolly, Loris. "Recycling Feed Sacks and Flour Bags: Thrifty Housewives or Marketing Success Story?" *Dress* 19 (1992): 17–36.

Ferber, Edna. *Personality Plus*. Urbana and Chicago, IL: University of Illinois Press, [1914] 2002.

Font, Lourdes M. and Trudie A. Grace, *The Gilded Age: High Fashion and Society in the Hudson Highlands, 1865–1914*. Cold Spring, NY: Putnam County Historical Society & Foundry School Museum, 2006.

Gary, Margaret Parker. "Dressed for the Job." *Woman's Day*. January 1950: 50–1, 74.

Gary, Margaret Parker. "Smart Togs for Action." *Woman's Day*, January 1953: 18–20, 82.

Kirkham, Pat. "Beauty and Duty." In *War Culture: Social Change and Changing Experience in World War Two*, edited by Pat Kirkham and David Thoms. London: Lawrence & Wishart, 1995.

Matheson, Rebecca Jumper. *The Sunbonnet: An American Icon in Texas*. Lubbock, TX: Texas Tech University Press, 2009.

Oerke, Bess V. *Dress*. Peoria, IL: Chas. A. Bennett, 1956.

Parker, Traci. *Department Stores and the Black Freedom Movement*. Chapel Hill, NC: University of North Carolina Press, 2019.

"Permanent Week end Clothes-list." *Vogue*. May 1, 1960: 168–77, 226.

"Shop Hound." *Vogue*. October 15, 1954: 64–5.

Singer Sewing Machine Company. *The Secret of Beautiful Clothes and a Beautified Home*. n.p.: Singer Manufacturing Co., 1948.

Sitton, Thad, ed. *The Loblolly Book: Water Witching, Wild Hog Hunting, Home Remedies, Grandma's Moral Tales and Other Affairs of Plain Texas Living*. Austin, TX: Texas Monthly Press, 1983.

Taylor, Lou. *The Study of Dress History*. Manchester and New York: Manchester University Press, 2002.

Taylor, Lou. "De-coding the Hierarchy of Fashion Textiles." In *The Textile Reader*, edited by Jessica Hemmings. London: Bloomsbury, 2012.

Tibbets, Thomas R. "Expanding Ownership of Household Equipment." *Monthly Labor Review*. Vol. 87, 10 (October 1964): 1131–7.

Upshaw, Beatrice. *A Biscuit for Your Shoe: A Memoir of County Line, a Texas Freedom Colony*. Denton, TX: University of North Texas Press, 2020.

Walker, Howard. *Memoirs of Howard Walker and Other Trivia*. Lufkin, TX: Lufkin Kiwanis Club, 1992.

Wigginton, Eliot, ed. *Foxfire 3: Animal Care, Banjos and Dulcimers, Hide Tanning, Summer and Fall Wild Plant Foods, Butter Churns, Ginseng, and Still More Affairs of Plain Living*. Garden City, NY: Anchor Press/Doubleday, 1975.

*Women's Wear Daily*. 1941–59.

"Work Clothes: New Substitutes for House Dress Are Rugged, Trim and Tailored." *Life*. February 7, 1949, 88–90.

4

# Examining the Ordinary

## Mourning Adornment and Black Death

Rikki Byrd

In 2014, I visited the exhibition "Death Becomes Her: A Century of Mourning Attire" at the Anna Wintour Costume Institute at the Metropolitan Museum of Art. The exhibition's title was blocked onto a white wall and made evident by white raised letters in all caps that were circumscribed by a white oval. From the left, the leaves and branches of a gray and black weeping willow tree tipped over into the oval inching their way toward some of the letters. The exhibition was organized under the leadership of then Curator-in-Charge Harold Koda and Assistant Curator Jessica Regan, who chose mourning as a fitting topic to explore "the evolution of the silhouette in woman's attire."[1] It was the Costume Institute's first fall exhibition in seven years and its first under its new name, which bore the prefix of the esteemed American *Vogue* editor. Covering mourning attire from the nineteenth and early twentieth century—a period that saw mourning dress move from a sartorial practice of the upper class to a mode that proliferated across lower classes—"Death Becomes Her" cast an ensemble of mannequins outfitted in mostly black against a stark white backdrop, illuminating the history of a trend that was equally modish as it was somber.

Across the field of fashion studies, research on mourning often highlights the sartorial legacies of the wealthy, a particular classed and gendered analysis that has long defined the field. In *Fashion and Everyday Life: London and New York*, fashion studies scholars Hazel Clark and Cheryl Buckley bring to the fore the field's preoccupation with the extraordinary, which is typically denoted by a focus on luxury, the upper class, and the mainstream. To expand the field's focus on styling practices not often centered, Clark and Buckley encourage a turn to the ordinary to elucidate fashion objects and people's experiences with dress that are overlooked based on the people that wear them and the places they are most frequently worn:

The ordinary escapes notice because it fails to stand out; here again fashion provides an exemplar. The clothes worn by most people going about their daily lives have been typically a synthesis of new and old, bold and mundane. This perception that the everyday is hard to locate, difficult to know and outside of traditional fields of knowledge demands an alternative approach when dealing with a subject such as fashion so as to sidestep fashion's 'distinct, superior, specialized, structured activities'...Indeed, we argue that fashion was embedded and contingent in the practices of people's daily lives, and it was located in some familiar spaces such as the street, although not only the major thoroughfares of the modern city but also its margins and back streets. It took shape in some intimate places: the wardrobe or the sewing box as well as in the rituals and commonplace social interactions of weddings, going out on the town or to the dance.[2]

It is no longer a secret that the canon of fashion has been in crisis not only because of the absence of the ordinary, but also because of systemic issues that it has perpetuated. Like many archives and histories, fashion has long been narrativized from a singular perspective, and often diminished or erased the experiences of Black people and people of color and the several conditions that they have lived under in the United States; conditions that have both produced a particular advent of design, a shift in production or a popularized mode of style, while also producing violent conditions that oppressed marginalized people.[3] Returning to mourning attire, at preeminent fashion archives and in fashion exhibitions in major fashion capitals, such as London and New York, these issues of singularity persist, focusing on white, upper-class experiences with mourning as if grief has a color line.[4] I call attention to such privileging to tease out the lengths of erasure when certain histories are not valued.

For example, "Death Becomes Her" covered time periods marked by the entrance of the Gilded Age, which saw an influx of wealth particularly on Fifth Avenue, when and where the Metropolitan Museum opened and continues to stand today. While curators of the exhibition note that the time period covered was one marked by high mortality rates (across racial groups), especially during childbirth and among infants, it was also one of racial terror, marked by a succession of proclamations and amendments created to legally end slavery, a brief stint of Reconstruction, and the entrance of slavery's new form known as Jim Crow. My point here is not to argue that "Death Becomes Her" should have dedicated a great deal of time to the entirety of the time period, but to think through Clark and Buckley's suggestion of the ordinary and expand it to think through its complexity. Indeed, high mortality rates were a part of ordinary life during this time period, so often that, as the curators show, a fashionable trend developed as a response to this.

Yet, these rates were significantly higher for Black people so much so that as Karla FC Holloway writes, "we worked this experience into the culture's iconography and included it as an aspect of black cultural sensibility."[5] Such examples are illustrated by Deborah McDowell's discussion of the popularity of post-mortem photography during the period that was often commissioned in memoriam for a grieving family. She notes a mid-twentieth century series by famed Harlem Renaissance photographer James Van Der Zee titled *Harlem Book of the Dead (1978)*. In step with his oeuvre, which often focused on Black social mobility in Harlem, his series of post-mortem photographs featured images of Black people adorned in their mourning attire as they grieved those they had lost or the deceased themselves.[6] McDowell traces these disproportionate Black deaths and the Black aesthetic practices that followed through the end of the twentieth century, analyzing the way the media documented Black death in the late 1990s to the lengths that it turned the Black body, even in death, into a spectacle, an occurrence not wholly different than media representations of Black death in the twenty-first century. This is perhaps most cogently illustrated by the accumulation of Black people murdered by police and the social media circulation of videos and images of them today.

"Death Becomes Her" opened three months after Eric Garner was killed in Staten Island, New York and two months after Michael Brown was killed by a police officer in Ferguson, Missouri—deaths that further catalyzed the #blacklivesmatter hashtag created in 2013 after the acquittal of George Zimmeran who murdered Trayvon Martin. The hashtag ushered in a contemporary Black freedom struggle that continues to call for, among several policy changes and community resources, police reform and abolition. While an exhibition held inside an esteemed fashion institution on New York's Fifth Avenue chronicled mourning dress of the elite, protests were organized along the same avenue calling for justice in the wake of a jury decision to not indict the police officer who killed Garner.[7] In addition to these organized efforts, from 2012 to present day, activists, entertainers, politicians, among several others have expressed their alignment with the movement through everyday fashion objects, such as the hoodie (which Martin was wearing the day of his death) and T-shirts with images and names of people who had been killed by police.

It is only now that I am thinking of this symmetry—an exhibition examining the sartorial history of mourning attire opening against the backdrop of Black deaths that connected a country's violent past with its violent present and elucidated how long death has interrupted Black people's lives.[8] It is in this interstice that this chapter unfolds as I bring into conversation the study of mourning attire and the study of Black death to think through the ways that

Black people have long experienced death as ordinary in this country, and how they have used everyday adornment practices to respond to this reality. In this chapter, I draw on Clark and Buckley's scholarly explication and exploration of the ordinary to explore the term in two ways: first, in step with the ways that Clark and Buckley use a case study approach to pull back the everyday experiences with dress not often prioritized in fashion; and second, to think through death as a peculiar and ordinary facet of Black life, and how Black people engage with this through adornment. For the latter portion, I draw on Christina Sharpe's prominent text *In the Wake: On Blackness and Being*, in which she explores the reverberations of slavery that conditions Black life in the contemporary. She puts forth a meditation and reflection for ways that Black people continue to live in what she calls "the wake of slavery." More specifically, I draw on Sharpe's invocation of "an ordinary note of care" to hold space for the possibility of Black life:

> In what I am calling the weather, antiblackness is pervasive as climate. The weather necessitates changeability and improvisation; it is the atmospheric condition of time and place; it produces new ecologies...the weather trans*forms Black being. But the shipped, the held, and those in the wake also produce out of the weather their own ecologies. When the only certainty is the weather that produces a pervasive climate of anti-blackness, what must we know in order to move through these environments in which the push is always toward Black death?[9]

To explore the ordinariness of fashion and the ordinariness of Black death in the United States, this chapter examines two objects: First, the artwork *Heirlooms and Accessories* (2002) by the artist Kerry James Marshall, a triptych in which the artist uses the history of mourning jewelry to reflect on the murder of Thomas Shipp and Albert Smith, two men killed by a white lynch mob in 1930. Second, I turn to a T-shirt created by fashion designer Kerby Jean-Raymond in the wake of Black people slain by police, who were named and uplifted in the Movement for Black Lives. Both artist and designer find utility in everyday clothing and accessories and draw on them to amplify the manifestation of Black death, their closeness to it, and how, in its accumulation it is actually quite extraordinary.

## Adorning a Spectacle: Kerry James Marshall's Signifyin(g) in *Heirlooms and Accessories* (2002)

In *Heirlooms and Accessories* (2002) American artist Kerry James Marshall appropriates a 1930 black-and-white photograph of the lynching of Thomas

**Figure 4.1** Kerry James Marshall, *Heirlooms and Accessories* (triptych), 2002, Ink-jet prints on paper in wooden artist's frames with rhinestones, 51 x 46 inches © Kerry James Marshall, Courtesy of the artist and Jack Shainman Gallery, New York.

Shipp and Abram Smith. In the original photograph, taken by studio photographer Lawrence Henry Beitler, the entire spectacle is rendered, including Shipp and Smith's murder and a fragment of the mob that was estimated at more than 5,000 spectators which had gathered in the yard of Marion, Indiana's courthouse. Marshall reproduces the image as a triptych and manipulates the photo in such a way that it almost completely whites out the original scene, though yellow outlines remain of figures and objects in the image. However, Marshall maintains isolated portraits of three women in each of his images, all of which stare back at Beitler's camera. Marshall has adorned each woman's face with lockets suspended from chains, mirroring the now opaque lynching in the background. It is through this use of adornment that Marshall indicts the women as "'accessories' to the crime" of Shipp and Smith's murders and interrogates how the women are inheritors and arbiters of whiteness and the absolution of responsibility of antiblack violence.[10] Not only this, curator Anna Katz writes that in *Heirlooms and Accessories* "Marshall strategically responds to ethical and historical requirements: the technique enables him to resist spectacularizing murderous brutality while still uncompromisingly portraying the extent to which that same murderous brutality was, in point fact, a spectacle and an ordinary, leisurely one at that."[11]

In her study of the role of photography in Black freedom struggles, visual culture scholar Leigh Raiford discusses the dual power of lynching photography during what she regards as the apex of lynching between 1882 and 1930. On the one hand, lynching photography was a perpetuation of the desire to maintain white supremacy in a post-Emancipation society. On the other, it became a critical tool for antilynching activists to advance their cause for civil rights by calling attention to the heinous brutality shaped by the "afterlives of slavery".[12]

Despite such egregious violence, Raiford brings attention to the ordinariness of lynching during the period, writing:

> Lynching also needs to be considered a leisure activity deeply embedded in the rise of consumer culture in the South in the late nineteenth and early twentieth centuries. As historian Grace Hale has argued, lynchings helped ease white anxiety about a new culture of consumption that exposed holes in the blanket segregation of the New South. This new mass society signaled a "raceless" consumer culture, one in which any person, of any race, gender, or class, could purchase goods in any number of mixed public spaces. Not only did lynchings "reverse the decommodification of black bodies begun with emancipation," writes Hale, but they enforced a segregated consumer society, a commodity culture in which only whites could experience or consume the "amusement" of lynching, and only blacks could be lynched and consumed, often literally by fire.[13]

Raiford's articulation of a consumer culture shaped briefly by desegregation during Reconstruction invites a reflection on fashion's role in commodity culture during the time period, which included technological advances in manufacturing, the proliferation of styles through the launch of fashion publications such as *Vogue*, and a workforce inclusive of women.[14] Additionally, mourning attire proliferated across social classes during the nineteenth century, due in part to fashion publications, which allowed readers to learn and adopt modish styles. In her extensive study of mourning dress, costume historian Lou Taylor notes "By the 1860s and 1870s, elegant mourning dress was a firmly established fact in the United States of America as well as in Europe," with dresses made of vast amounts of fabric, such as silk and crape.[15] Mourning attire also included forms of adornment beyond clothing, such as mourning jewelry "worn as a souvenir of the deceased." Taylor cites examples such as locks of hair fastened into lockets common in the Victorian era and the use of bones and teeth among Indigenous cultures in Australia and Taranaki.[16] Writing of mourning jewelry across cultures more generally, Taylor notes its three basic functions:

> First, it acted as a souvenir of the deceased, seen in some churches as an open reassurance to the departed spirit that it had not been forgotten. Secondly, it was made as a memento mori—a reminder to the living of the inevitability of death. The third function, always present, but subtly unstated in mourning etiquette, was that of status symbol dressing.[17]

Before the nineteenth century, portraits were painted into lockets making them an expensive form of adornment thus relegated to the wealthy. By the mid-1800s, Taylor notes the advent of a new trend in mourning jewelry, in which photographs were mounted into lockets and other accessories due to the invention the daguerreotype, named after Louis Daguerre who is credited with inventing photography. This new technological advancement not only allowed lockets to become more accessible (on par with the movement of fashionable trends across social status), but it also enhanced the circulation and commodification of images as photography evolved. An early illustration of this is the 1850s invention and popularization of carte de visites, which were small albumen prints affixed to cards and often shared widely for various purposes. Yet, for Black people, whose lives and images have been warped by a history that always categorized us as the Other across several mediums, photography further illustrated how "the field of representation (how we see ourselves, how others see us) is a site of ongoing struggle."[18] One early and notable example of this period is photographer Joseph T. Zealy's daguerreotypes of seven enslaved people taken in 1850. Zealy was commissioned by Harvard professor Louis Agassiz, who wanted to study and prove the superiority of white people, further perpetuating scientific racism. In contrast, the infamously titled image "The Scourged Back" taken in 1863 served a different purpose, though was no less spectacularizing. Widely circulated in the Civil War era to aid in abolitionist efforts, the image features a Black man with his back turned toward the camera revealing a scarred back caused by being whipped during his time in slavery.

These notable examples do not obfuscate the ways Black people utilized the camera for their own purposes, politically, professionally, and leisurely.[19] Black feminist scholar bell hooks writes of the role of photography in Black life, noting the ways images taken and displayed by Black people "rebelled against all those photographic practices that reinscribed colonial ways of looking and capturing the images of the black 'other.'"[20] Specifically discussing the commemorative displays of portraits in Black homes, hooks attests to how these practices that shape our relationship to domestic places also shape our relationship to the visual. To illustrate this, she cites a scene in Toni Morrison's 1992 novel *Jazz*, in which a photograph of a deceased girl sits on the mantel in the main character's parlor. Morrison was inspired to write the novel after encountering a photograph taken by James Van Der Zee of a deceased Black woman in her coffin; the woman had been killed by her lover. The photograph is a part of Van Der Zee's aforementioned *Harlem Book of the Dead*. The book reads as an alternative archive to the history of lynching photography in the twentieth century, as well as a rebuke of the years of antiblack violence that was imaged in the centuries earlier. While images of disfigured bodies circulated for contrasting effects during the period marked by Raiford, images in Van Der Zee's book show deceased Black people in coffins dressed in their Sunday Best or images of them superimposed with images of their loved ones still living. Through his photographic methods and ethics, Van Der Zee imaged his subjects, living and dead, with dignity against a backdrop of mediums that had long denigrated Black life.

Kerry James Marshall puts forth similar methods and ethics in *Heirlooms and Accessories*. Moving beyond his oeuvre, defined mostly by painting, Marshall's turn to the medium of photography and other digital methods bring to the fore not only an indictment of the women who he has isolated in the photograph, and by turn, whiteness, but he also posits a critical intervention when we read for the ways in which the history of mourning attire and photography converge within his frames. Marshall's triptych not only appropriates the original image in the art historical sense, but he also employs "signifyin(g)" on the history and popularity of mourning dress, and more specifically mourning jewelry. Here, I borrow from historian Henry Louis Gates and literary and fashion scholar Eric Darnell Pritchard, who writes:

> Through signifying, a person or object disrupts an assigned meaning to symbols, words, phrases, images or gestures (signification), thereby creating and circulating some other meaning than what was originally intended (signifying) by suggesting a point of view through slightly obscured or stealth tactics. Subsequently, signifying gives a word, an object, or an event, an entirely new orientation—a remix. Signifying is thus a practice that illuminates the agency of the communicator.[21]

Not only within the image does Marshall carry out this performance of flipping the script, he also does so in the frame of each image in his triptych, by outfitting it in rhinestones, which are constructed to suggest a jewel box holding accessories/heirlooms. Through his interrogation of the spectacularizing of Black death and the perniciousness of whiteness, there is also a question of value. Read through the context of a capitalistic art market, Katz suggests that Marshall's use of the rhinestones in the frame:

> ... is another such pendant or charm, one that hangs around the neck of the museum... In an interview, Marshall addressed this point in terms of a "white power elite" that builds institutions, codifies definitions, and creates markets, retaining exclusive purchase on determining "who is good and what is best in art; delegitimizing the creative achievements of African American artists; and essentially bequeathing "heirlooms" to successive generations of white cultural financial brokers."[22]

Additionally, by detailing the harrowing mementos that white spectators took with them after lynchings, Raiford brings further attention to Marshall's signifyin(g). Not only were images such as Shipp and Smith's widely circulated as souvenirs of the murderous event; those who were present often walked away with objects from the victim, such as pieces of clothing, locks of hair and, at times, body parts. Writing of the lynching of Shipp and Smith, Raiford signals to a section in a framed photograph of the lynching where a tuft of hair is attached to a matte board. Listing instances such as these, among others, Raiford concludes that:

> The collection of relics as religious fetishes is a practice that dates back to ancient and medieval times, when the devoted would gather, trade, and keep close the remnants of saints' lives or their bodies. Indeed, in a complex manner lynching incorporated elements of ancient traditions and antebellum nostalgia.[23]

While Taylor draws attention to the bodily fragments of deceased loved ones fashioned into a memento mori for those left behind to mourn their loss, Raiford complicates this by analyzing such acts of memorialization alongside antiblack violence.

According to the trend and intent of mourning jewelry detailed by Taylor above, one might presume that the bodies of Shipp and Smith are what should be adorned by the lockets in Marshall's triptych. However, in step with Raiford's explication of commodity culture and blackness during the time period in which the photograph was taken, Marshall not only returns the gaze to the white women staring back at the camera, he also, though not explicitly stated, situates the three women as commodities, souvenirs themselves. They are not only accessories to murder, as Katz notes in her analysis of the work, Marshall's own annotation of the image, turns them into souvenirs that act as a reminder of their role in the event.[24]

This is not to say that Marshall's only concern is with the white women in the photograph, or whiteness more generally. Indeed, in whiting out much of the details from the original image, including Shipp and Smith's bodies, Marshall attempts to tend to Shipp and Smith via his refusal to repeat the imaged violence, sounding Sharpe's "ordinary note of care." We might read this work then as a form of Black redaction and annotation, as formulated by Sharpe, who writes of these methods:

> I am interested in ways of seeing and imagining responses to the terror visited on Black life and the ways we inhabit it, are inhabited by it, and refuse it. I am interested in the ways we live in and despite that terror. By considering that relationship between imaging and imagining in the registers of Black annotation and Black redaction, I want to think about what these images call forth. And I want to think through what they call on us to do, think, feel in the wake of slavery—which is to say, in an ongoing present of subjection and resistance.[25]

Within this formulation, the duality of Marshall's triptych comes into stark relief. Indeed, the whiteness called out stands in contrast to his oeuvre which focuses primarily on Black figures and involves an in-depth interrogation of the variations of black, which "mark the historical absence of black bodies in the Western canon of painting." However, his turn to photography to explore the lynching of Shipp and Smith should not be read as a complete departure. Instead, what becomes clear across his practice, whether through painting or photography, figuration or abstraction, is Marshall's stated engagement with "the dialectic of absence and presence."[26] While in works such as *Black Painting* (2003–6), the abundance of black renders the intricately decorated scene almost invisible, *Heirlooms and Accessories* leans into invisibility to both call attention to whiteness and also protect Shipp and Smith. In this way, Marshall's work is situated within a genealogy of activists, artists, and other creative practitioners, who have drawn on adornment to remark upon antiblack violence, critique an industry (fashion and art) that erases and commodifies blackness, Black people and their bodies, and attempt to honor, memorialize, and protect those no longer with us.[27]

## A Troubling Object: Pyer Moss's "They Have Names" T-shirt

Within the fashion industry contemporary practitioners are also engaging mourning adornment to comment on antiblack violence. In 2019, during New York Fashion Week, model and actress Indya Moore attended the Daily Front Row Fashion Media Awards, where they were honored with the Cover of the Year Award for appearing on the cover of the June 2019 issue of *Elle* magazine. Moore was the first trans person to be featured on the cover of the publication. Wearing a red Oscar de la Renta gown, Moore complemented their look with lengthy earrings designed by Areeayl Yoseefaw. Cascading down their torso, the earrings were made of gold frames that each held an image of a Black trans woman who had been killed that year. Altogether the frames and images equaled sixteen; in preparation for the event, another trans woman was killed, whom Moore chose to remember by carrying a framed image of them throughout the event.

Like Marshall, Moore's engagement with mourning jewelry is palpable, bringing to the fore again Taylor's discussion of the history of lockets that people wore to remember those who have passed. Moore's decision to utilize their own body as a means to call attention to antiblack and transphobic violence amplified the abundant silences that reverberate in an industry that has benefitted from the aesthetic practices cultivated by Black trans women. Furthermore, their adornment that evening also presents a political act, though this time not within the museum or the art market, but within the fashion industry—an industry that had only recently begun to contend with the accumulated deaths of Black people who had been killed by police, but also the years of discrimination, exclusion, and appropriation that had long existed on runways, in fashion editorials, across staffing and more.

This political shift is most notably reflected in Bethann Hardison's 2013 letters to fashion councils such as the Council of the Fashion Designers of America, and those in Paris, London, and Milan, which Hardison accused of upholding a history of racism.[28] In the following years, articles across popular media began to document the number of models of color who appeared on the runways or fashion publications, and an uptick in conversations around cultural appropriation began to abound. By 2015, following the 2012 murder of Trayvon Martin, as well as the 2014 murders of Eric Garner, Michael Brown, and Tamir Rice, designers such as Kerby Jean-Raymond addressed the industry directly on the runway.

For his Spring/Summer 2015 show during the New York Fashion Week presentation for his clothing brand Pyer Moss, Jean-Raymond wore a white T-shirt that he titled "They Have Names," which in black font on the back of the shirt listed the names of Black men and boys who had been murdered by police between 1999 and 2014. Within the context of mourning attire, we might read Jean-Raymond's shirt less as one associated within a lineage of modish styles originating with the elite and trickling down the class ladder, as Taylor explicates. Instead, Jean-Raymond's T-shirt is more aligned with Rest in Peace T-shirts which bear the images and names of loved ones who have passed, a mourning aesthetic that is commonplace within Black working-class communities. Literary scholar Robin Brooks situates shirts like Jean-Raymond's within the lineage of naming shirts that proliferated in the wake of the aforementioned murders. Writing that these T-shirts are just as integral a mode of awareness as that of hashtags, Brooks argues:

> ... memorial shirts, or what I call the "shirts of the movement," operate as a form of visual life writing; the shirts collectively (in reference to the larger movement) and individually (in reference to the deceased person) tell a story. I discuss how shirts of the movement preserve memories *and* call for action. More specifically, I contend that these shirts are not only symbols of grief, expressions of empathy, and coping mechanisms but are also a public stance against racial injustice and anti-Black racial terror.[29]

While Brooks analyzes the precarious history and personal and political function of shirts that both memorialize the lives taken by state-sanctioned violence, she also elucidates notable tensions. She brings attention to the ways these murders both engender aesthetic forms of mourning that also become gendered, This chasm is apparent in Pyer Moss's decision to create a separate shirt with a list of Black women who were murdered by police. Brooks also calls attention to commodity culture, which Raiford brings to our attention regarding lynching.[30] In her discussion of the ethics of shirts from creation to an accumulated profit, Brooks writes:

> ... the selling of these cotton memorial shirts creates a profit, and a large market exists for them. Not everyone at demonstrations across the nation purchases memorial shirts via campaigns with a known history. Some purchase them online, which makes me wonder who profits from the shirts and who are the people and companies that have received money for the shirts...Some see the memorial shirt business as exploitative and another form of commodifying Black death and grief. Some activists have pushed back against families who attempt to trademark the name and image of their deceased family member as well. In response, families often explain that they are not trying to profit; rather, their aim is to protect the legacy of their loved one.[31]

Originally, Jean-Raymond created the shirts for his design team to wear during the show, but after inquiries about the sale of the shirts, he moved forward with reproducing them, donating the proceeds to the American Civil Liberties Union (ACLU). Despite the end of its production, the T-shirt has continued to circulate across mediums. In 2017, Colin Kaepernick, the former quarterback for the San Francisco 49ers, whose refusal to stand during the national anthem gained him national attention, wore a custom "They Have Names" shirt in an editorial for the December issue of *GQ* magazine (he also appeared on the cover of that month's issue). That T-shirt now titled "Even More Names," listed names of Black men and women such as Charleena Lyles, Sandra Bland, and Freddie Gray. And in 2019, the original "They Have Names" shirt was displayed in a section on resistance dressing in the fashion exhibition *Power Mode: The Force of Fashion* at the Museum at the Fashion Institute of Technology. Among the objects shown in this section was a T-shirt that read "I Can't Breathe" referencing Eric Garner's last words, a Women's March T-shirt, and a Dior T-shirt that read "We Should All Be Feminists."

Read alongside Katz's suggestion that Marshall's frames imply an indictment of an art market that has simultaneously delegitimized Black history and Black lived experiences while also commodifying blackness for profit, T-shirts such as Jean-Raymond's indict the fashion industry while also functioning as a troubling object itself. The T-shirt, caught in the throes of an institution that perpetuates and thrives from capitalism, presents the challenges and desires to produce an object so undeniably and unapologetically connected to a life constantly conditioned by mourning,[32] which also brings its share of profit and popularity for its maker.

## Conclusion

In this chapter, I have attempted to situate the history of mourning attire alongside the ways in which Black artists and designers have drawn on adornment and clothing to address antiblack violence in their respective works. This encourages not only a more expansive analysis of the many histories of mourning attire, and the social and cultural contexts in which they function, but also illustrates the potential of reading objects "against the bias grain" as posited by historian Marissa Fuentes. In her discussion of Black women and slavery, Fuentes describes such a methodological approach through a definition that lends itself to fashion discourse. As she states in an interview:

> By "bias grain" I was thinking about creating elasticity when one cuts fabric on the bias, particularly linen. It stretches and gives while maintaining the function of the material…Reading along the bias grain was also to push the concept of reading against the grain a little further–from reading 'between the lines' to reading what is not between the lines at all.[33]

Not only have I attempted to perform an analysis that looks at objects not wholly invested in an interrogation or analysis of adornment such as Marshall's *Heirlooms and Accessories*, but I have also attempted to return to sites where fashion is explicitly the object of focus and mode of representation and interrogation. In this way, I build on visual studies scholar Nicole Fleetwood's inquiry: "How do we return to what we already know with curiosity and openness so that new forms of knowing and recognition emerge?"[34] Such inquiries have helped me formulate a host of other queries that present opportunities for further exploration regarding the intersection of fashion and mourning, and more specifically fashion and Black lived experiences as they relate to mourning. Such inquiries include those speculative and others that are at times pronounced, and others offer a hum under the more evident analyses (a kind of honoring of those who have passed on and whose stories were not documented): Who dressed the upper echelons of society, fixed their food, drove their carriages, tended their children on an everyday basis, but also when they mourned? How did the people who performed these tasks mourn in brief given moments and stolen ones? What are the rituals, refusals, and remembrances they held close even when they could not have the time or space to mourn like those that they served? These questions bring to the fore what I consider to be an intersection of ordinary life, often shaped by our experiences with clothing, and with the ordinariness of antiblackness, often shaped by the ways Black people's lives have been conditioned in such a way that always brings them close to death.

# Notes

1 Sam Roberts, "Exploring the Culture of Mourning," *The New York Times*, October 4, 2014, https://www.nytimes.com/2014/10/26/arts/artsspecial/death-and-grief-influence-new-york-exhibitions.html.
2 Cheryl Buckley and Hazel Clark, *Fashion and Everyday Life: London and New York* (London: Bloomsbury Publishing Place, 2017), 9.
3 I name the United States specifically here due to this book's focus on fashion in America, however such conditions have also shaped the lives of Black people and people of color globally.
4 I, of course, borrow this notable phrasing from W. E. B. Du Bois' most celebrated text *The Souls of Black Folk*, in which he argues in his opening line that "the problem of the Twentieth Century is the problem of the color line." *The Souls of Black Folk* (Mineola, New York: Dover Publications Inc., 1994).
5 Karla FC Holloway, *Passed On: African American Mourning Stories* (Durham, NC: Duke University Press, 2002), 6.
6 Deborah McDowell, "Viewing the Remains: Death, Spectacle and the [Black] Family," in *The Familial Gaze*, ed. Marianne Hirsch (Lebanon, PA: University Press of New England, 1999).
7 See, "Protests Continue in New York City on Friday," *The New York Times*, December 5, 2014, https://www.nytimes.com/2014/12/06/nyregion/eric-garner-protests-new-york-city.html.
8 Holloway, *Passed On*, 6.
9 Christina Sharpe, *In the Wake: On Blackness and Being* (Durham, NC: Duke University Press, 2016), 106.
10 Anna Katz, "Souvenirs and Heirlooms," *Kerry James Marshall: Mastry*, ed. Helen Anne Molesworth (Chicago: Museum of Contemporary Art Chicago, 2016), 150.
11 Ibid.
12 Saidiya Hartman, Lose Your Mother: A Journey Along the Atlantic Slave Route (New York: Macmillan Publishers, 2008).
13 Leigh Raiford, *Imprisoned in a Luminous Glare: Photography and the African American Freedom Struggle* (Chapel Hill, NC: University of North Carolina Press, 2011), 36.
14 See, Phyllis G. Tortora and Sara B. Marcketti, *Survey of Historic Costume*, 6th ed. (London: Fairchild Books; Bloomsbury Publishing, 2015).
15 Lou Taylor, *Mourning Dress: A Costume and Social History* (London: Allen and Unwin, 1983), 132.
15 Ibid, 224.
16 Ibid., 224–5.
17 Ibid, 224.
18 bell hooks, "In All Our Glory: Photography and Black Life," *Art on My Mind: Visual Politics* (New York: New Press, 1995), 57.

19 For example, in 2021, the Smithsonian American Art Museum acquired an archive of daguerreotypes taken by some of the earliest Black photographers, some of which made mourning jewelry. See "Smithsonian Acquires Rare Antique Portraits by First Black Photographers," NPR.com, August 29, 2021, https://www.npr.org/sections/pictureshow/2021/08/29/1031703142/smithsonian-acquires-rare-antique-portraits-from-first-black-photographers.
20 hooks, "In All Our Glory: Photography and Black Life," 62.
21 Eric Darnell Pritchard, "Sex, Sexuality, and Signifying: Patrick Kelly's Queer Enterprise," in *Patrick Kelly Runway of Love*, ed. Laura Camerlengo (San Francisco: Fine Arts Museums; New Haven: Yale University Press, 2021), 39.
22 Katz, "Souvenirs and Heirlooms," 150–1.
23 Ibid, 37.
24 Katz draws an apt comparison between *Heirlooms and Accessories* and Marshall's *Souvenir* series created between 1997 and 1998, in which an anonymous Black figure tends to a parlor. Images of figures such as Martin Luther King Jr., Malcolm X, and John F. Kennedy, among others, appear in the work as a way of memorializing them. Putting these works into conversation, Katz writes: "if *Heirlooms and Accessories* is implicational, *Souvenir I* is invitational. Both interfere with the habitual viewing mode of contemplation in the form of women, who, with their gaze, point the finger," 151.
25 Sharpe, *In the Wake*, 116.
26 Dieter Roelstraete, Kerry James Marshall, "An Argument for Something Else," *Kerry James Marshall: Painting and Other Stuff* (Brussels: Ludion, 2013), 22.
27 For a robust exploration of the way visual artists have addressed antiblack violence in their work see *Grief and Grievance: Art and Mourning in America* (London and New York: Phaidon, 2020); *Site of Struggle: American Art Against Anti-Black Violence* (Princeton, NJ: Princeton University Press, 2022).
28 See Allie Jones, "Former Model Calls Out Designers for Racism," *The Atlantic*, September 6, 2013, https://www.theatlantic.com/culture/archive/2013/09/former-model-calls-out-designers-racism/311367.
29 Robin Brooks, "R.I.P. Shirts or Shirts of the Movement," *Biography* 41, no. 4 (Fall 2018): 807.
30 It should be noted that the murders of those memorialized and mobilized within movements such as the Movement for Black Lives are also situated within this history of lynching.
31 Brooks, "R.I.P. Shirts or Shirts of the Movement," 813.
32 I adopt this phrasing from Claudia Rankine's 2015 *New York Times* article, "The Condition of Black Life is One of Mourning," https://www.nytimes.com/2015/06/22/magazine/the-condition-of-black-life-is-one-of-mourning.html.
33 "Q&A Marisa Fuentes, Dispossessed Lives," The Junto: A Group Blog on Early American History, May 15, 2017, https://earlyamericanists.com/2017/05/15/qa-marisa-fuentes-dispossessed-lives.

34 Nicole Fleetwood, *Troubling Vision: Performance, Visuality, and Blackness* (Chicago: University of Chicago Press, 2010), 7.

# Bibliography

Brooks, Robin. "R.I.P. Shirts or Shirts of the Movement." *Biography* 41, no. 4 (Fall 2018): 807–30.

Buckley, Cheryl and Hazel Clark. *Fashion and Everyday Life: London and New York*. London: Bloomsbury Academic, 2017.

Du Bois. W.E.B. The Souls of Black Folk. Mineola, New York: Dover Publications Inc., 1994.

Fleetwood, Nicole. *Troubling Vision: Performance, Visuality, and Blackness*. Chicago: University of Chicago Press, 2010.

Hartman, Saidiya. Lose Your Mother: A Journey Along the Atlantic Slave Route. New York: Macmillan Publishers, 2008.

Holloway, Karla FC. *Passed On: African American Mourning Stories*. Durham, NC: Duke University Press, 2003.

hooks, bell. "In All Our Glory." *Art on My Mind: Visual Politics*. New York: New Press, 1995.

Katz, Anna. "Souvenirs and Heirlooms." In *Kerry James Marshall: Mastry*, edited by Helen Anne Molesworth. Chicago: Museum of Contemporary Art Chicago, 2016.

McDowell, Deborah. "Viewing the Remains: Death, Spectacle and the [Black] Family." In *The Familial Gaze*, edited by Marianne Hirsch. Lebanon, PA: University Press of New England, 1999.

Pritchard, Eric Darnell. "Sex, Sexuality, and Signifying: Patrick Kelly's Queer Enterprise." In *Patrick Kelly Runway of Love*, edited by Laura Camerlengo. San Francisco: Fine Arts Museums; New Haven: Yale University Press, 2021.

"Q&A Marisa Fuentes, Dispossessed Lives." The Junto: A Group Blog on Early American History. May 15, 2017. https://earlyamericanists.com/2017/05/15/qa-marisa-fuentes-dispossessed-lives.

Raiford, Leigh. *Imprisoned in a Luminous Glare: Photography and the African American Freedom Struggle*. Chapel Hill, NC: University of North Carolina Press, 2011.

Roberts, Sam. "Exploring the Culture of Mourning." *The New York Times*. October 4, 2014. https://www.nytimes.com/2014/10/26/arts/artsspecial/death-and-grief-influence-new-york-exhibitions.html.

Roelstraete, Dieter and Kerry James Marshall. "An Argument for Something Else." *Kerry James Marshall: Painting and Other Stuff*. Brussels: Ludion, 2013.

Sharpe, Christina. *In the Wake: On Blackness and Being*. Durham, NC: Duke University Press, 2016.

Taylor, Lou. *Mourning Dress: A Costume and Social History*. London: Allen and Unwin, 1983.

# Section Two

# Revisiting the Everyday

Hazel Clark and Lauren Downing Peters

This section focuses on histories of American fashion that have been forgotten, marginalized, or which have simply gone untold. Each of the authors in this section "revisit" the canon of American fashion and, in doing so, expand, trouble, and redefine it. By-and-large, this canon has been shaped, on the one hand, by iconic objects—from the shirtwaist to denim jeans—and, on the other, by the contributions of notable designers. Central, too, to the story of American fashion are the entangled histories of mass manufacturing the rise of New York as a fashion capital, and Americans' embrace of ready-to-wear in the late nineteenth century. Simple, functional, affordable, and hardwearing, American ready-to-wear, as Nancy Green has written, has been "defined and defended by American industrial discourse."[1] Christopher Breward has similarly remarked upon the "clean lines, simple construction, and disarming functionality" that endow ready-to-wear with "a strange blankness [and] a characterless transparency of meaning."[2] Others have interpreted the simplicity and functionality of ready-to-wear as a byproduct of the democratic ideals that have underpinned American fashion manufacturing since its inception in the nineteenth century. Indeed, Claudia Kidwell and Margaret Christman have written that "the common quality of American dress has served to obliterate ethnic origins and blur social distinctions," thereby upholding—or perhaps *fashioning*—the mythology of America as a great melting pot.[3]

In many ways, American fashion is as much a response to the fussiness of French *haute couture* and to the rigidity of English tailoring, as it is a tool that has been used to develop a unifying national character.[4] American dress *is* everyday dress, but in the writing of this narrative much has been embellished, left out, and glossed over. The contributions of Black designers and women designers, for instance, have only recently been redressed.[5] Missing, too, from many histories of American fashion are perspectives that shed light on the vast amount of cheap, immigrant labor that has long served as the engine of domestic mass manufacturing.[6] The homogenizing mythology of American fashion has obscured stories and experiences that are untidy and uncomfortable, but which are essential to understanding the true breadth and diversity of dress as it is experienced by ordinary people in the context of everyday life. The authors in this section read (and in some cases re-read) the history of American fashion and dress "against the grain." That is, they expand the canon beyond iconic objects and notable designers to focus on, among other things, practices of appropriation, the alternative fashion press, and the political language of dress.

In her contribution to this section, Laura McLaws Helms recounts in Chapter 5 the brief history of the countercultural fashion magazine *Rags*. Running for only thirteen issues in 1970 and 1971, *Rags* chronicled the personal style of ordinary Americans in some of the first documented "on the street" fashion photographs. *Rags* was unique within the landscape of the countercultural press to the extent that it framed ordinary dress as something worthy of analysis and discussion. Its influence, however, reached far beyond the independent press and, in many ways, was ahead of its time. Today, we are so completely familiar with street style "candids" or "outfit of the day" (OOTD) posts on social media. As McLaws Helms argues in this chapter, however, it was the editors at *Rags* who first recognized that it's "out in the streets where it's all happening."

In Chapter 6, Amanda Thompson analyzes the ways that dress has been employed as a "political language" both by Florida Native Seminole and settler men in South Florida, but to markedly different ends. By placing contemporary styles, like screen printed T-shirts, in conversation with garments considered "traditional," such as appliqué and patchwork "big shirts," Thompson sheds light on the ways in which dress, and particularly Euro-American dress, has been used to both negotiate settler colonialism and to assert Seminole sovereignty. Countering this is a parallel exploration of the phenomenon of "playing Indian" through dress as a defining component of settler identity—one used as a strategy of dominion over Florida Native Seminole people, and which upholds constructs of white settler masculinity. Through this investigation, Thompson re-frames ordinary garments as powerfully political tools that have been deployed throughout history to, on the one hand, dispossess Native North Americans and uphold settler ideology and dominance, and, on the other, as a powerful tool for re-defining the contours of American citizenship.

In Chapter 7, Einav Rabinovitch-Fox recounts the little-known history of the National Association of Fashion and Accessories Designers (NAFAD)—an organization founded by a group of Black women designers in 1949 to promote their contributions to the canon of American design. In addition to publicizing Black design and helping its members to navigate racial and gender barriers in the American fashion industry, NAFAD emerged as a leader in the Black struggle for equality during the mid-twentieth century. Having carved out a space of power from the margins in its own time, Rabinovitch-Fox rightly argues that NAFAD deserves to be recovered from the margins of American fashion history, too.

In the final chapter of this section, Chapter 8, Victoria Rose Pass employs the framework of "primitivizing accessories" to analyze the short-lived trend for "slave jewelry" in the 1920s. Serving as more than an accessory, she argues that these bracelets, when donned by white American women, served the dual purpose of reinforcing dehumanizing stereotypes about African Americans and upholding constructs of modern, white femininity. Far from being an isolated phenomenon, Pass situates this dark chapter in American fashion history within a longer trajectory primitivizing accessories—from nameplates to doorknocker earrings—that function as tools of white supremacy.

## Notes

1. Nancy Green, *Ready-to-Wear, Ready-to-Work: A Century of Industry and Immigrants in Paris and New York* (Durham, NC: Duke University Press, 1997), 15.
2. Christopher Breward, *Fashion* (Oxford and New York: Oxford University Press, 2003), 194.
3. Claudia B. Kidwell and Susan C. Christman, *Suiting Everyone: The Democratization of Clothing In America* (Washington, DC: The Smithsonian Institution Press, 1974), 15.
4. Rebecca Arnold, *The American Look: Fashion, Sportswear and the Image of Women in the 1930s* (London: I. B. Tauris, 2009).
5. See Nancy Diehl, ed., *The Hidden History of American Fashion: Rediscovering 20th-century Women Designers* (London: Bloomsbury, 2018) and Elizabeth Way, ed., *Black Designers in American Fashion* (London: Bloomsbury 2021).
6. See Christina H. Moon, *Labor and Creativity in New York's Global Fashion Industry* (New York: Routledge, 2020).

5

# *Rags*

## The Birth of Personal Style in Print

Laura McLaws Helms

Existing for only thirteen issues, *Rags* was a counterculture fashion magazine that sought to explicate the changes going on in American society by illustrating real people's dress. Making its debut in June 1970, *Rags* looked to the street, rather than to couture or Seventh Avenue, for its content.

According to curators Amy de la Haye and Cathie Dingwall, "Streetstyle" can refer to both subcultural clothing and "individual, generally youthful, expressions of style that do not emanate from the catwalk" and which are an "entirely personal statement..."[1] The concept that a unique personal style—effortlessly pulled together from several sources—was something to be documented and celebrated can primarily be charted back to *Rags*. Unlike any other contemporary publication, *Rags* cataloged subcultures (including hippies and bikers) alongside the dress of "normal people" (waitresses and meter maids). By choosing to see all dress as integral to daily life and therefore worthy of discussion, *Rags*' engagement with niche arenas of clothing led to a greater understanding of society as a whole.

In her nationally syndicated column "Inside Fashion," the doyenne of American fashion journalism, Eugenia Sheppard, stated that "*Rags* simply had to happen. There had to be a down-to-earth complete antithesis of the beautiful, fantasy fashion magazine."[2] *Rags* set out to be and was in many ways the opposite of traditional fashion publications, yet it was also set apart from the rest of the countercultural press. Working independently, *Rags* elevated everyday dress and revealed it a subject worthy of investigation—leading the way for a new approach to personal style within fashion and underground media.

**Figure 5.1** Cover, *Rags*, June 1970. Photograph by Baron Wolman. From the Rags 50th Anniversary Archive © The Waverly Press. Courtesy Dagon James.

## Background on fashion and underground press

In the 1960s, American fashion media (outside of the fashion pages in daily newspapers) could easily be grouped into three separate, but mutually supportive, categories: trade publications for those in the industry (most prominently, *Women's Wear Daily*); high fashion glossies (*Vogue, Harper's Bazaar*, and *GQ*); and more specialty magazines focused primarily on a specific age group (*Seventeen, Mademoiselle*, and *Glamour*).[3] With clearly defined parameters concerning what types of fashions they showed and how they wrote about them, each category and publication remained constant in terms of overall vision despite wider changes in society. Their major concern was supporting the fashion trends each season as declared by designers, manufacturers, and department stores (i.e., the magazine's main advertisers), leading publications to shun individuality in dress in favor of following trends. Until the mid-1960s, outliers who developed their own styles and identities separate from the fashion world—bohemians, artists, and creatives—only appeared in the fashion press if they were truly exceptional or wealthy.

Separate from the mainstream media was the underground press. Speaking for the counterculture—a culture, in the words of Theodore Roszak, "so radically disaffiliated from the mainstream assumptions of our culture that it scarcely looks to many as a culture at all, but takes on the alarming appearance of a barbaric intrusion"[4]—the underground press was as loose and rambling as the often-ragtag movements it represented. Roszak (who coined the term "counterculture") considered it a mix of two cultures:

> To one side, there is the mind-blown bohemianism of the beats and the hippies; to the other, the hard-headed political activism of the student New Left...I think there exists...a theme that unites the variations and which accounts for the fact that hippy and student activist continue to recognize each other as allies. Certainly there is the common enemy against whom they combine forces, but there is also a positive similarity of sensibility.[5]

As varied as the counterculture was—by politics, race, religion, and social class—they were united by a desire to be different than mainstream America as well as by a wish to overthrow society. To the counterculture, mainstream society had become lulled into docility by consumerism, materialism, capitalism, and industrial society, allowing a technocracy to flourish[6]—so intent on buying the newest television that they did not notice their rights being taken away. The counterculture's hopes and dreams for the future—whether created through drugs or bombs—were vividly spooled out across the newspapers of the underground press. Generally considered to have started in 1964 with the launch of the *Los Angeles Free Press,* the underground press reached its high point in the late 1960s when there were around 6,000 counterculture papers (though many only lasted an issue). Uniting the varied publications were bold, psychedelic art often printed in lurid color; rambling and unstructured articles; and no censorship of language or subject.

The 1974 book *Other Voices: The New Journalism in America* breaks down the underground press into three periods. First was the "hippie period, 1964–1967," which was characterized by "psychedelic art and essays on drug use, sexual freedom, and Eastern religion." From 1967 to 1970 was the "radical period," during which "hippies were politicized and blended with the New Left and other radical political groups." The final "period of internal dissension and new complexity" was from 1970 until the book's publication; internal political schisms occurred within periodical staffs, causing the breakdown of many papers. Those that survived staff dissension and debate, moved "closer to conventional standards" in their style of writing and layout.[7] The underground press—no matter the angle—spoke to a different consumer than the fashion press. Within the counterculture, writing about fashion was frivolous; subjects of interest were instead LSD, meditation, student uprisings, and the Vietnam war.

## Fashion in the underground press

The 1960s were marked by a groundswell of anger and agitation against the status quo, particularly among young people. More holistic than only politics and civil rights, this anger expanded into a renunciation of fashion rules and a rejection of high fashion's high cost in favor of personal style. The tenets of proper dress enforced by women's magazines—requiring girdles, pantyhose, and more sedate outfits—were spurned in favor of clothes that were homemade, secondhand, and utilitarian. Small boutiques began to open around America and in other countries that sold the work of local designers, crafters, and artists. These new counterculture styles and spaces were not covered in their original form by the fashion or mainstream press; instead, they were diluted and reworked by major designers and manufacturers to fit a trend message.

In 1965, *Vogue* launched its "Vogue's Own Boutique" column to tap into the growing youth fashion movement. Experiencing the counterculture from the remove of immense privilege, the column documented high society debutantes visiting "groovy" boutiques around New York City.[8] In the same way that fashion manufacturers attempted to copy and repackage youth counterculture styles for the masses, the magazine industry took the same approach of watering down the zeitgeist to make it palatable for all. For example, Hearst's short-lived *Eye* magazine is generally considered a prime example of consumerism cashing in on the youth boom. It ran for fifteen issues from March 1968 to May 1969; Helen Gurley Brown was a senior editor, and her influence can be seen in the *Cosmopolitan*-ilke headlines.[9] Too capitalist for the counterculture and too offbeat for the general public, *Eye* was a money-losing disaster for the publishing house.

To understand the thoughts of the underground press on fashion, I undertook a study of underground periodicals and their mainstream counterparts. Thorough page-by-page examination of most issues of approximately thirty underground periodicals, both major and minor, showed that this distancing from fashion and dress continued across the underground press. Careful analysis of these periodicals presents a counterculture absorbed in its various obsessions—LSD, meditation, revolution, Vietnam—yet unwilling to speak about the clothing that signaled their beliefs to the wider world. At most, counterculture dress was shared through photographs from love-ins, sit-ins, and protests, or through hand-drawn advertisements for boutiques. *The East Village Other, The Oracle of Southern California, The Organ*, and *The Berkeley Barb* were all influential underground press titles that did not (based on my own visual inspection of most issues) feature any articles on fashion. Even overseas there was no greater prevalence of fashion in the underground press; in *The Directory of British Alternative Periodicals 1965–1974,* John Noyce painstakingly cataloged thousands of UK-based counterculture publications yet there are no mentions of style, fashion, or dress in the directory. There have been no prior scholarly studies on fashion within counterculture publications, and fashion/dress is not brought up in any books or articles on the underground press.

For all the diversity of viewpoints covered within the underground press, what was lacking was any discussion of fashion, dress, or style. Dress was an essential part of countercultural identity, regardless if one was a hippie, a Hells Angel, a Black Panther, or a feminist. In Dick Hebdige's seminal analysis of subcultures, he wrote: "...the challenge to hegemony which subcultures represent is not issued directly by them. Rather it is expressed obliquely, in style. The objections are lodged, the contradictions displayed...at the profoundly superficial level of appearances: that is, at the level of signs."[10] The beads, the afro, and the painted leather jacket were all signs used by the counterculture to signal their dissent and their allegiance against the status quo. The mass media, then and now, reinforced expectations of subcultural dress through the publication of articles and photographs detailing their "delinquency."[11] The ideology and the clothes were seen as one, yet the counterculture media rarely, if ever, spoke of or discussed clothing. The dissemination of countercultural dress occurred through in-person encounters and via the mass media.

One of the few commentaries on fashion within the underground press was a column called "Flame's Hip Fashions" in the Los Angeles weekly *Open City*. Written by the pseudonymous Flame, the column was introduced in June 1967; "And what everyone thinks, from 'HER HIPPINESS' (me) to the 'straights', about that thing you put on your back and why you put it."[12] For five weeks, Flame wrote about countercultural dress using the terminology and grammar of the movement. The final column was a list of sights she had witnessed at a love-in: "…2. a dancing girl in a long green satin Victorian dress…4. a girl in a net body stocking covered with colored chicken feathers (handing them out one by one)…"[13] The types of garments mentioned are more easily discernible in the photographs shared in a separate part of the issue, as documentation of the event rather than as fashion news. Focusing on description versus information and without an engagement with high or mass fashion, "Flame's Hip Fashions" column was a brief experiment.

The earliest interrogation of fashion within countercultural media was the *Village Voice*'s "Outside Fashion" column in 1967. Due to its founding in 1955, the *Village Voice* can be understood as a progenitor of underground press, but whether it qualifies as a member has been up for debate. Robert Glessing, the author of *The Underground Press in America*, considered the *Voice* to have a "pioneering position in the history of the underground press"[14]; contrarily, in *Other Voices,* Everette Dennis and William Rivers wrote, "if the underground is defined as growing out of the psychedelic subculture of the 1960s, oriented to young people, and printed by offset lithography, the *Voice*…hardly qualifies."[15] Developed as a local paper for the bohemian Greenwich Village community, the *Village Voice* would become a highly profitable and provocative weekly, but it never sought the complete revolution of the counterculture press it inspired. While not of the counterculture, by dint of how established it was and its (comparative) professionalism, the *Village Voice* was one of the primary news sources of the growing counterculture movement. As other papers struggled to get distribution, by 1967 the *Voice* was the best-selling weekly newspaper in America, with a single-day circulation higher than 95 percent of big-city dailies.[16]

Ads for hip clothing stores and mail-order counterculture garb filled the pages of the *Voice* throughout the sixties, but it was not until the "Outside Fashion" column debuted in the November 16th issue that fashion was centered. Written by Stephanie Harrington and later Blair Sabol, it sought to expose the marketing fabrications of the Seventh Avenue fashion industry while also publicizing little-known, counterculture creators. According to Sabol, the name was a response to Sheppard's "Inside Fashion." Syndicated in hundreds of American newspapers, Sheppard's column made her the most influential fashion arbiter of the 1950s and 1960s—a true fashion insider, able to make or break careers on a mass scale. Printed on a non-set schedule, Harrington's columns directly responded to the high fashion world. Her first columns were reviews of Oscar de la Renta and

Krizia fashion shows, written from the perspective of a young leftist woman peering into a world she found ridiculous, old-fashioned, and elitist.

When Sabol took over in 1968, her concept for the column was, "semi antifashion but it was taking fashion from the street at the time because I was a hippie with a big Afro and I had flunked out of high school and really wasn't a writer, had no business doing any of this..."[17] For historian Anne Hollander, antifashion was an opposition to participation in elaborate bourgeois fashion and a "means of indicating objections to existing social, economic, and sexual standards"[18]—Sabol considered herself somewhere in-between, an "anti-fashion fashion statement."[19] Calling herself the "Abbie Hoffman of fashion" (after the radical founder of the Yippies), Sabol went to the major fashion shows and reviewed them as one interested in clothing but not swept away by the dictates of fashion—a completely new viewpoint on dress and the industry. Unlike fashion magazines that had a prescriptive approach to dress, "Outside Fashion" instead veered between ridicule (anyone caught in the past, anyone elitist, and anyone trying desperately to be young and hip) and support (of exploited creators and artisans).

The same month that "Outside Fashion" premiered, so did the magazine *Rolling Stone*. Founded as a biweekly in San Francisco by Jann Wenner and Ralph Gleason, it was focused on the counterculture music scene. *Rolling Stone* set itself apart from the underground press by omitting radical politics and by embracing a more traditional journalistic style to the writing and publication form.

## The Birth of *Rags*

Inspired by "Outside Fashion" and *Rolling Stone*, two former assistants at the major glossies, Daphne Davis and Mary Peacock, developed an idea to expand this concept into a full underground fashion magazine. They reached out to Baron Wolman, *Rolling Stone*'s first staff photographer, for advice. In 2020, Wolman recalled:

> They were inquiring about a new magazine that they had in mind to publish. It would be similar to *Rolling Stone*, but fashion would be the subject rather than music—although both subjects often overlapped. They weren't asking me to participate; they just wanted some direction and insight because they know that I knew how to put together a publication. I had learned a lot from being involved in *Rolling Stone*...from how to make a magazine, to the various components, to the staff, to the printing, to distribution.[20]

**Figure 5.2** Mary Peacock and Blair Sabol visit Betsey Johnson at her New York studio for their story on Johnson, which appeared in the first issue of *Rags* in 1970. Photo by Baron Wolman. From the *Rags* 50th Anniversary Archive © The Waverly Press. Courtesy Dagon James.

The trio decided to collaborate. Davis and Peacock felt that, according to Wolman, "the way the fashion world was presenting itself at the time…was soulless. For them real fashion was what they saw on the streets. This desire to show and comment upon real fashion was the driving force of the magazine we were creating…"[21]

Wolman cashed in some *Rolling Stone* stock to pour into start-up costs and moved the nascent team into recently vacated *Rolling Stone* offices. A self-produced prospectus helped to attract several investors, friends of Wolman's who had previously invested profitably in *Rolling Stone*. Taking into consideration their inspiration and the centrality of New York to the American fashion industry, they approached Blair Sabol about setting up an office there for the new project.

She joined as a contributing editor, intent on expanding the irreverent principles of "Outside Fashion" to a broader purview.

The team tested out the names *Scene* and *Faces*, before settling on *Rags*. From the first rough prototype, *Rags*' vision was clear: to discuss beauty, food, and fashion in the counterculture milieu, through unposed candid shots of people on the streets. As the sole counterculture publication devoted to fashion, it was to follow the same format as a traditional fashion magazine; encompassing all aspects of a lifestyle, with dress at its core. According to Wolman, "Mary, Daphne, and Blair had such a clear and brilliant vision; they knew right away what they wanted to see in terms of fashion content. My editorial contribution was the creation of a number of life-style sections including Astrology, Finances (titled 'Common Cents'), Fine Art Photography, as well as various cultural editorial subjects."[22] Breaking away from the solely analytic approach of "Outside Fashion," *Rags* was to be more prescriptive—showing what people were wearing on the street, explaining where to get it, and featuring informative articles about "how to stud your clothes or paint your boots"[23] Their approach was in reaction to the proscriptive technique taken by magazines like *Vogue*, which decreed the new styles readers must buy and regulated the way they were worn; for summer 1970, midis were to be worn with "red cotton boots, bare brown legs" but warned of "the skirt that hits just at mid-calf."[24]

More similar in look to counterculture publications like *Rolling Stone* and *International Times*, *Rags* was printed on newsprint. A higher-quality paper was used for the front and back cover, with an insert of the same paper in the center featuring a portfolio by established or emergent photographers. The newsprint provided an immediacy to the images that was starkly different from the gloss of fantasy of high-end fashion magazines. While production was limited (starting at 50,000 copies per issue and rising to around 100,000 by the end), the thirteen issues of *Rags* had a far-reaching power.

## Revolutionizing fashion media

Arriving on newsstands in mid-May 1970, *Rags* immediately garnered attention from the mainstream media due to its novel form and content. On the cover was an attractive, white couple seemingly stepping out of another, indistinct period—him tall with long hair, handle-bar mustache, cowboy hat, denim shirt and jeans, and gun holster holding a flower; her with hair pulled back in an old-fashioned style, wearing an antique embroidered white dress with a velvet cloak atop. With only the logo in color and the photo bordered with wide whitespace, it is a cover gripping in its simplicity; markedly different than the saturated full-color, borderless photos commonly used by fashion magazines. While the logo and double border frame used on all pages were leftovers from designer Bruce Day's work on the second prototype, the art directors on the first issue were Alfred Marty and Barbara Kruger—the latter later to become famous as a conceptual artist and collagist. A full-page Levi's ad was featured on the inside cover, proving a credibility boost to all possible advertisers.

Though ignored by the counterculture press, over their first few months *Rags'* editors were interviewed in the *Washington Post, Time, Los Angeles Times, San Francisco Chronicle, Philadelphia Inquirer,* and by Sheppard for "Inside Fashion." The reviews were generally flattering, though bemused. Of particular interest to all was "on the street," a section of candid photos taken across the country showing real people's dress. A photo of riot cops pushing a long-haired male up against a wall is opposite two more photos of "longhairs," one in a tie-dye shirt and floppy hat, the other in an American flag-patched jean jacket. There is nothing fancy to the clothes shown in any of the photos; they are lived-in, worn items. Fashion writers found the approach interesting and the fashions unsavory. Rubye Graham wrote in the *Philadelphia Inquirer*, "Everyone seems to be doing his own thing, as far as clothes go, the only fashion trend being a sloppy, dirty look. You can see, I'm not one of the group!"[25] The photos are documentary style—the same as any you would come across today in a library archive, documenting the sociological and sartorial rites of the counterculture—but removed from that context, and re-represented in a fashion format. At that time, magazines like *Vogue* (then under the editorship of Diana Vreeland) were known for their hyperbolic copy, wildly imaginative editorials, and an interest in couture and ready-to-wear that reflected "vitality and excitement."[26] Vastly different in look and effect from contemporary *Vogue*, "on the street" used the historical language of fashion magazines—an illustrative image and descriptive copy —to recontextualize these candid shots into what later became known as "street style photography."[27]

While they morph from reportage to editorial when accompanied by fashion-oriented copy—either quotes from the wearer or short descriptions of them—these images are not selling anything. For Nancy Hall-Duncan, to be considered a fashion photograph there must be a commercial element and a "fashion intent."[28] Unlike fashion editorials featuring models inhabiting city streets—described by Agnès Rocamora as "a celluloid *marchande de mode*...[who] has entered the fashion system to promote its products"[29]—the clothes in *Rags'* street photographs are not for sale. In keeping with the counterculture's anti-consumerist ethos, one woman in a floral-print muumuu shares, "[This dress is] made out of old curtains that I ripped off of this house from which I was evicted..."[30]

From the editors' perspectives, they were simply disseminating what was already happening on the street; as Mary Peacock told *Time*: "Fashion is not fashionable any more. The slick magazines are always telling you how you should look. We do it the other way around. We report what people are wearing without trying to change them."[31] The premiere issue included an interview with a tie-dye artist, a profile of Betsey Johnson, and a cartoon-photomontage of pop art-style T-shirts. The monthly

**Figure 5.3** "on the street," *Rags*, July 1970. From the *Rags* 50th Anniversary Archive © The Waverly Press. Courtesy Dagon James.

"Clothesfreak" column reviewed boutiques around the country, while "Supermarket" featured short descriptions of stores nationwide that sold goods desired within the counterculture—from patched leather tunics to quilted pinafores and incense.

Alongside telling people where to find items, *Rags* also published helpful information on how to make them—thereby providing the tools to achieve countercultural personal style.

Old clothes, workwear, uniforms, military surplus, homemade clothing, "eco fashions"—many of the stylistic elements of personal style that *Rags* celebrated were outside the elite fashion industry, instead falling under what Jennifer Craik termed the "everyday fashion system."[32] By teaching people how to sew their own caftans or telling them where to buy the cheapest fatigues, the editors were subverting fashion, thereby providing readers with the tools to attire themselves fully outside of the fashion industrial complex.

As Wolman stated at the time, "Style, that's important. Fashion, that's unimportant. What's alive is the idea of personal style. That everyone can have an identity—be themselves."[33] *Rags* was engaged with making the individual the focus, not the nameless model or unapproachable socialite—a different perspective from the "beautiful people" celebrated by fashion magazines or the ideal housewife praised by women's periodicals. *Rags* elevated the dress of people hanging out on the street, those hand-making garments to sell in boutiques, and small companies working outside the mass-fashion industry; these were *Rags*' stars. According to Wolman, *Rags*' philosophy was about "expressing what's going on with young people today. Music and clothes are manifestations of what's going on today. Clothes are just a mirror of society."[34] This was achieved by documenting a greater spread of society than that of other fashion periodicals—from meter maids to cowboys to Stephen Burrows' innovative designs.

From issue 5 onwards, *Rags*' editors began to shift certain aspects of the magazine—they put a greater emphasis on strong journalism while also changing "on the street" from strictly candid photography to a gossip column and clothing news section collected from different sources. With less of an emphasis on street style, there came a greater focus on in-depth reporting of niche arenas of clothing that allowed for a more holistic understanding of society. Treating their subjects with a wit and irreverence that would become the *Rags* mode, among their major stories were an investigation of the clothes worn by Catholic priests, rabbis, and Hare Krishnas ("Dressing for God," issue 10), and an exploration of the little-known world of clothing manufactured for the deceased and sold through funeral homes—cleverly titled "What Corpses are Wearing (or, True Underground Fashion)." This article featured interviews with makers of "casket couture" to highlight the absurdity of fashions for the dead: "He reaches a plump hand in and takes out a bridesmaid-type model in baby blue, the latest in funeral fashion. Holding up this bit of fluff, he says, 'Romaine crepe is our best model because it doesn't wrinkle' (for restless sleepers?)."[35] By choosing to see all dress as integral to daily life and therefore worthy of discussion, *Rags* modified the conversation from solely a deification of high fashion clothing.

Unlike the high-end glossy magazines, *Rags* was unconstrained by advertiser pressures (a positive to cheap newsprint)—thus providing them the space to be

**Figure 5.4** "Stud & Patch & Paint & Bleach," *Rags*, July 1970. From the *Rags* 50th Anniversary Archive © The Waverly Press. Courtesy Dagon James.

cheeky, intellectual, and at times combative. A special report on "Fashion Fascism: The Politics of Midi" exposed the efforts the fashion industry and press were undertaking to push the midi on American women. Mary Peacock explained their reasoning in an interview: "We're against the way the midi is being forced on the public. That's part of a plastic environment, what you fall into by not thinking."[36] In addition to an interview with media theorist Marshall McLuhan about the mini vs. midi debate—during which he declared, "The mini will never die. It's a tribal costume. It is Fashion that is dead"[37]—the *Rags* team visited department stores and boutiques around the country, investigating the lengths that were taken by store owners to silence salespeople's personal opinions about this longer-length garment. Positing that the development of the midi was Paris's way of taking back control of the fashion narrative after it had been wrestled away by the street, *Rags* saw the battle between the styles as a political one that mirrored larger societal conflicts. They wrote,

> The mini has always had a political character as a costume. At first the mini was *us against them*, youth against older people whose values they had grown to distrust more and more. Even after it had weathered the vulgarity and commercialism of Big Fashion, and graduated from style to costume, it retained political overtones. Because mini was something women had *chosen*, Big Fashion be damned. It was a statement for its wearers that they would wear what *they* wanted to wear. They would not be dictated to…The mini skirt is a declaration of difference. The Midi skirt is only a fashion stamp of sameness.[38]

By being willing to confront the corruption and manipulation of "Big Fashion," *Rags*' editors set themselves apart from the rest of the fashion media at the time; the closest was contributing editor Sabol's continuing work with "Outside Fashion" at the *Village Voice*. Their revelatory investigative journalism was not limited to high fashion; *Rags* also scrutinized the counterculture it emerged from. A special report "boutiques & hip capitalism" analyzed the abundance of hip boutiques across America and the paradox of trying to be part of the underground while also making money in an inherently capitalist way, retail. Nonetheless, *Rags* never examined the complexity of their own situation—making a for-profit magazine that featured both items for sale and items to make, skirting somewhere between the anti-capitalist nature of the counterculture (and the financially floundering papers of the underground press) and the wildly successful mass-media.

For much of the counterculture, the selling of countercultural style was contrary to their anti-capitalist message. While many stylish young hippies were eager to purchase wares from boutiques (both local artisans and co-opters of the aesthetic), for others their beliefs went much deeper. San Francisco collective The Diggers believed in creating a society free from the dictates of capitalism and money. Digger-member and actor Peter Coyote later wrote, "Much of the counterculture was a re-stylizing of what had gone before…The Diggers understood that recostuming the drama of capitalism was not going to lead anyone to liberation. We established a Free Store where the goods, services, and roles were free for the most imaginative to seize."[39] At their free store (which was publicized in their free news pamphlets), they gave away clothes; they also ran free medical clinics and soup kitchens. While stylistically Diggers could easily have appeared in the "on the street" pages, in terms of a shared belief system they were far removed from *Rags*.

## The end of *Rags* and its impact

*Rags*' emphasis on only taking advertising from like-minded companies resulted in a complete lack of operating capital. While *Rags* was steadily increasing its print runs and sales, it was proceeding at a slower pace than hoped. At the end of 1970 and the beginning of 1971, Wolman was consumed with trying to raise more investment; he raised some from previous investors and put his savings in, but it was not enough to balance the losses. He cut back on essential personnel, dispiriting the remaining employees. The penultimate issue, May 1971, featured a financial statement that indicated a net loss from July through December 1970 of $58,000. In his accompanying statement, Baron Wolman proclaimed that the magazine would soon reach a break-even point of fifteen ad pages and 100,000 circulation. By the following month, *Rags* was closed, with Mary Peacock stating to the press that they were "financially ruined" due to a "lack of professional management and from not enough money."[40]

*Rags* had both an immediate and an enduring impact on fashion media. In 2020, Wolman remembered, "At the end of the day, *Rags* was the perfect magazine at the wrong time, we were at least a decade ahead of the curve. I don't harbor any ill feelings for how it played out. It was an artistic and critical success, but admittedly a financial failure."[41] During the year of its existence, it was among the most-watched publications by others in the fashion industry and press. Before *Rags*' brief publication period, high fashion culture had already begun to co-opt aspects of the counterculture and each issue of *Rags* simply accelerated the commercialization of the movement. By the time *Rags* released its final issue in June 1971, *Women's Wear Daily* had begun to incorporate more candid street photographs and was engaging with street style with less condescension. In 1973, Sabol left the counterculture behind to write for *Vogue*, while Daphne Davis went on to work for *Vanity Fair*. Bringing everything full circle, in the 1980s Mary Peacock was fashion editor of the *Village Voice*, where she hired Amy Arbus to shoot a column called "On the Street."

Many of the ideas that *Rags* propagated slowly made their way into the fashion media and helped reconfigure the industry. In 1978, the *New York Times* premiered Bill Cunningham's seminal column "On the Street." Two years later British style magazine *i-D* became known for its "Straight Up" spreads, where ordinary people—dressed in "apparent disregard of dominant fashion

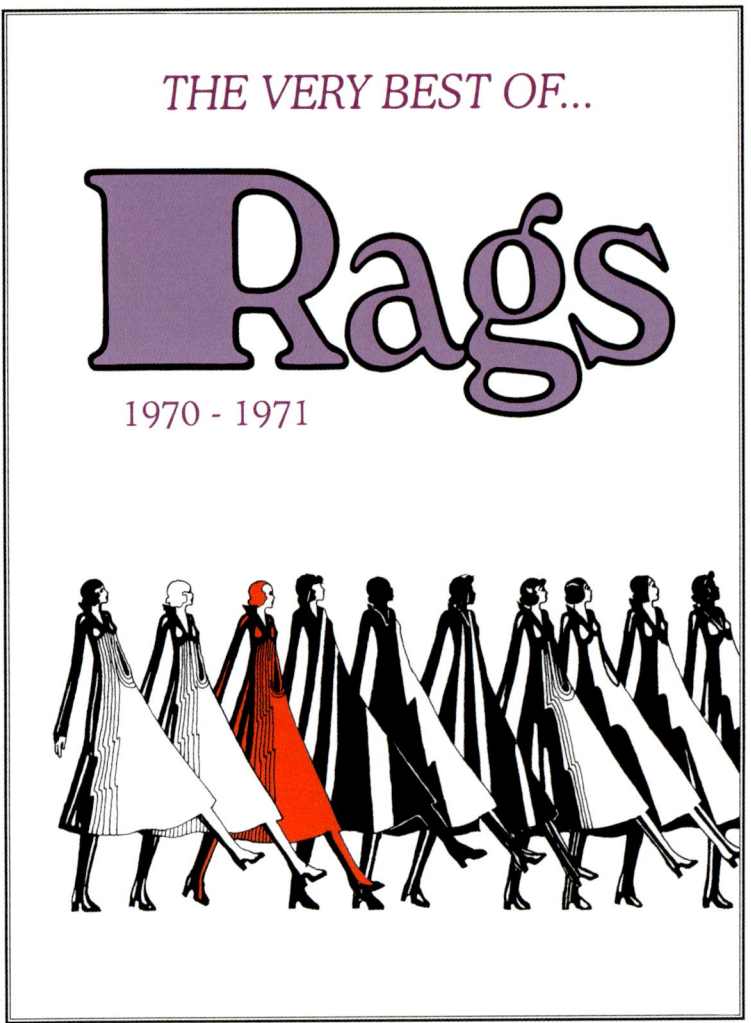

**Figure 5.5** Cover, *The Very Best of Rags 1970–1971* © The Waverly Press. Courtesy Dagon James.

codes"—were photographed on the street against a blank wall.[42] Combined with "snatches of conversation," the "straight up" closely follows the format and concept of the *Rags*' "on the street" section.[43] *Rags,* Arbus, Cunningham and "Straight Up" laid the groundwork for the current proliferation of candid street fashion photography on social media—all presenting "the fashionable street dweller as a representative of the city and its inhabitants, and a kind of shorthand for the vitality and creativity of the street."[44] With the development of the internet, blogs and social media, *Rags*' ideas have become increasingly central to mainstream fashion media today—even Vogue.com publishes street style alongside coverage of vintage, sustainable fashion, personal style, and artisanal clothing. Similarly, the idea of the "individual as star" that *Rags* supported became a cornerstone of fashion blogging and has only grown in importance with the rise of Instagram where "personal style" has become an industry and a way for like-minded outsiders to find each other.

In 1970, *Rags* was the sole voice writing about fashion in witty, investigative, or anti-capitalist ways. While the inner workings of the fashion industry have shifted significantly since then (possibly in part due to the rising influence of the street, along with the development of fast fashion), more broadly read voices now write in a similar manner. Specialized fashion articles like "Casket Couture" were the first of their kind; in recent years digital magazines and websites like YouTube have allowed for a proliferation of stories on the wackier and lesser-known parts of fashion through this more humorous lens. Likewise, their revelatory investigative journalism is reflected in the work of the Instagram account Diet Prada and news website Business of Fashion. *Rags*' critiques of the underground can be understood as an early forerunner of the call-out culture that has bred rampant on the internet.

A true snapshot in time, each of the thirteen issues is a wealth of information on the counterculture in America in 1970—from the lingo to personal style, from politics to food. Wolman passed away in late 2020; before his death he wrote the foreword to *Rags* fiftieth-anniversary limited-edition box-set: "I never expected that anyone would care about or remember *Rags* fifty years down the line, but I am proud that it is a magazine people still enjoy when they come across a copy, and more importantly, delighted that we produced a publication that has influenced changes in the mainstream fashion media, and inspired so many future generations of print and online fashion journalists and contemporary fashion designers."[45]

Though printed on flimsy newsprint, its power to influence went far beyond the contents. *Rags* symbolized a different way of seeing our world and our clothing choices within that—a vision that took in the reality of people's lived experience and shared desire for fantasy, and how these intermingle in a community skirting on the edges of capitalism. In his publisher's letter in the prototype for *Rags*, Wolman explained: "Changes are going down in America...Out in the streets is where it's all happening. You can *see* who is into the changes, because how people dress and adorn themselves is a function of how they think, how willing they are to accept new ideas about themselves and their environment."[46] Only decades later has the fashion media caught up to the changes illustrated so clearly by *Rags*.

## Notes

1. Amy de la Haye and Cathie Dingwall, *Surfers, Soulies, Skinheads & Skaters* (London: Victoria & Albert Museum, 1996), 3.
2. Eugenia Sheppard, "Inside Fashion: 'Rags' to Riches," *New York Post,* May 11, 1970.
3. Joel Lobenthal, *Radical Rags: Fashions of the Sixties* (New York: Abbeville Press, 1990), 158–69.
4. Theodore Roszak, *The Making of the Counter Culture* (Garden City: Anchor Books, 1969), 42.
5. Ibid, 56.
6. Ibid, 1–22.
7. Everette E. Dennis and William L. Rivers, *Other Voices: The New Journalism in America* (San Francisco: Canfield Press, 1974), 139–40.
8. "Vogue's Own Boutique," *Vogue*, February 15, 1966: 61.
9. "It Happened In 1968," *Rolling Stone*, February 1969: 16.
10. Dick Hebdige, *Subculture: The Meaning of Style* (London: Routledge, 1979), 17.
11. "Dropouts with a Mission," *Newsweek*, February 6, 1967: 92–5.
12. "Flame's Hip Fashions," *Open City,* June 9–16, 1967: 4.
13. "Flame Love-In," *Open City,* July 7–13, 1967: 12.
14. Robert Glessing, *The Underground Press in America* (Bloomington, IN: Indiana University Press, 1970), 14.
15. Dennis and Rivers, *Other Voices*, 138.
16. Louis Menaud, "It Took a Village," *The New Yorker,* December 28, 2008, https://www.newyorker.com/magazine/2009/01/05/it-took-a-village?mbid=social_tumblr (accessed May 21, 2022).
17. Blair Sabol, interview with author, April 27, 2019.
18. Anne Hollander, *Seeing Through Clothes* (New York: Viking, 1978), 364.
19. Ibid.
20. Baron Wolman, "Foreword," in *The Very Best of Rags: 1970–1971*, ed. Dagon James (New York: The Waverly Press, 2020), 1.
21. Ibid, 2.
22. Ibid, 4.
23. Sheppard, "Inside Fashion: 'Rags' to Riches".
24. "Summer in America," *Vogue*, May 1970: 169.
25. Rubye Graham, "Rags on Newsstands for Young and Hip," *Philadelphia Inquirer*, May 26, 1970.
26. Polly Devlon, *Vogue Book of Fashion Photography* (New York: Quill, 1979), 140–1.
27. Agnès Rocamora and Alistair O'Neill, "Fashioning the Street: Images of the Street in the Fashion Media," in *Fashion as Photograph: Viewing and Reviewing Images of Fashion*, ed. Eugénie Shinkle (London: I. B. Tauris, 2008), 185–99.

28 Nancy Hall-Duncan, *The History of Fashion Photography* (New York, Alpine Book Co., 1979), 9.
29 Agnès Rocamora, *Fashioning the City: Paris, Fashion and the Media* (London: I. B. Tauris, 2009), 146.
30 "on the street," *Rags,* July 1970: 9.
31 "A New Eye for Fashion," *Time,* August 10, 1970.
32 Jennifer Craik, *The Face of Fashion: Cultural Studies in Fashion* (London: Routledge, 1993), xi.
33 Alan Cartnel, "The Rags Man Speaketh," *Los Angeles Times,* December 1, 1970: F1.
34 Joan Chatfield-Taylor, "An Underground Fashion Rag," *San Francisco Chronicle,* June 1, 1970.
35 Susan Berman, "What Corpses are Wearing (or, True Underground Fashion)," *Rags,* May 1971: 33.
36 Brendan Riley, "New 'Hip' Fashion Magazine Eloquent 'Counterculture,'" *The Austin Statesman,* October 9, 1970: 26.
37 Catherine Court, "An Interview with Marshall McLuhan: Mini Skirt Tribalism," *Rags,* October 1970: 23.
38 "Fashion Fascism: The Politics of Midi," *Rags,* October 1970: 22.
39 Peter Coyote, "Making Visions Real," in *Notes from a Revolution: Com/co, the Diggers & the Haight,* eds. Kristine McKenna and David Hollander (New York: Foggy Notion Books, 2014), 11.
40 "No Riches for Rags," *Washington Post,* July 2, 1971: D3.
41 Wolman, "Foreword," 11.
42 Rocamora and O'Neill, "Fashioning the Street: Images of the Street in the Fashion Media," 186.
43 Ibid, 187.
44 Eugénie Shinkle, "Introduction," in *Fashion as Photograph,* ed. Eugénie Shinkle (London: I. B. Tauris, 2008), 11.
45 Wolman, "Foreword," 11.
46 Baron Wolman, "Letter from the Publisher," *Rags* (second prototype), 3.

# Bibliography

Craik, Jennifer. *The Face of Fashion: Cultural Studies in Fashion*. London: Routledge, 1993.

de la Haye, Amy and Cathie Dingwall. *Surfers, Soulies, Skinheads & Skaters*. London: Victoria & Albert Museum, 1996.

Dennis, Everette E. and William L. Rivers. *Other Voices: The New Journalism in America*. San Francisco: Canfield Press, 1974.

Glessing, Robert. *The Underground Press in America.* Bloomington, IN: Indiana University Press, 1970.

Hall-Duncan, Nancy. *The History of Fashion Photography*. New York, Alpine Book Co., 1979.

Hebdige, Dick. *Subculture: The Meaning of Style.* London: Routledge, 1979.

Hollander, Anne. *Seeing Through Clothes*. New York, Viking, 1978.

James, Dagon, ed. *The Very Best of Rags: 1970–1971.* New York: The Waverly Press, 2020.

Lobenthal, Joel. *Radical Rags: Fashions of the Sixties.* New York: Abbeville Press, 1990.

Noyce, John. *The Directory of British Alternative Periodicals 1965–1974.* Hassocks: The Harvester Press, 1979.

Rocamora, Agnès. *Fashioning the City: Paris, Fashion and the Media*. London: I. B. Tauris, 2009.

Roszak, Theodore. *The Making of the Counter Culture.* Garden City: Anchor Books, 1969.

Shinkle, Eugénie, ed. *Fashion as Photograph: Viewing and Reviewing Images of Fashion.* London: I. B. Tauris, 2008.

# 6

# Playing *Seminole* Indian

## The Cultural Appropriation of Seminole Men's Fashion

Amanda Thompson

In a 2010 photo Mitchell Cypress, Chairman of the Seminole Tribe of Florida, shakes hands with Florida Governor Charlie Crist to solidify a compact between the two governments.

Cypress and Crist each engage in strategic political fashioning through clothing. Crist wears a white button-down shirt and tie — garmenting historically

**Figure 6.1** "HOLLYWOOD, FL – MAY 05: Mitchell Cypress and Governor Charlie Crist attend A Celebration of the Seminole Compact at Seminole Hard Rock Hotel on May 5, 2010 in Hollywood, Florida." May 5, 2010 Photo by Larry Marano/Getty Images.

encoded with Euro-American men's political and economic power. Mitchell wears a short-sleeved, brightly colored shirt with bands of contrasting fabrics including one featuring an otter—the symbol of his tribal clan—which is both modern and attendant to traditions of Seminole design. A silhouette innovated by Jimmy Osceola (Seminole), Cypress' shirt—a style which he might wear everyday—asserts Seminole distinction and self-determination.[1]

Meanwhile, on the University of Miami's campus, students in the school's most prestigious honor society, Iron Arrow, dress in Seminole jackets to indicate their membership, which few Native people have attained.[2] In recent years, Native American students and faculty have advocated against Iron Arrow's appropriations of Native American cultures, which also include wearing war paint, beating drums, and electing "Chiefs" and "Medicine Men." While the society claims it honors Florida's Native people, this stereotyping, like Native mascots, can be harmful to Native peoples. In the words of Shelby Rowe (Chickasaw):

> Cultural appropriation adds to the message we constantly get as Natives that our culture is dead, and that our existence is an inconvenience for society…[It] not only fails to honor and preserve the traditions of American Indians, it could actually be increasing the risk of suicide for our Native youth, especially our boys…By presenting our cultures as that of a dying/extinct society, it leaves no space in the modern world for Native Americans to exist.[3]

This damaging cultural appropriation is not new; rather Iron Arrow participates in a century-old tradition of non-Native people in Florida dressing up in the fashions of Seminoles for parades and reenactments.

In this chapter, I consider fashion as a "political language" strategically deployed or subverted by both Seminole and settler men to contest Indigenous claims to sovereignty in the ongoing colonial context of South Florida.[4] I use the term "Seminole" herein referring to the shared culture of the two Florida Native Nations, the Seminole Tribe of Florida and the Miccosukee Tribe of Indians, as well as independent Seminole people, and to Florida Native people prior to these Tribe's organizations around 1960; I use "settler" referring to white Euro-American immigrants and their descendants who take part in the US's national settler colonial project. I track a history of Seminole men's political fashioning, such as Chairman Cypress's shirt, alongside a history of settler men dressing as Seminoles. Drawing on the work of Indigenous scholars Philip Deloria and Shari Huhndorf, who each explored the phenomena of settlers "playing Indian" or "going Native" as a defining component of American settler identity, I examine three case studies of

Florida settler men "playing Seminole Indian": American Legionnaires parading in Seminole-made garments from the 1920s to the 1940s; Boy Scouts wearing Seminole-made clothing and making Seminole-style garments around the 1960s; and Seminole War reenactors researching and recreating nineteenth century Seminole-style garments in the 1980s.[5] Contextualizing these performances historically, I argue that they are responsive to both the settler state's policies of domination over and dispossession of Florida Native Seminole people and Florida Native Seminole's resurgent contestations of sovereignty. I support this argument through analysis of historical written sources, images, scrapbooks, and oral histories. I also read Seminole-made clothing as an archive that can reveal Seminole cultural, economic, and political agency.

These performances of "playing Seminole Indian" all take place within the United States' settler colonial structure—that is, the type of colonialism enacted and ongoing in the US wherein settlers claim themselves as native to the land and attempt to cause the disappearance of its actual Native people through means including extermination, deterritorialization, assimilation, and limiting political self-determination and sovereignty.[6] I argue that these performances embody what non-Native scholar Mark Rifkin calls "settler common sense." Rifkin theorized the term to describe how settler governance and settler-colonial imperatives—such as capitalist development, white patriarchal power, and dispossession of lands—get "renewed" and "recreated" through the everyday logics and actions of non-Native people.[7] While some of the performances I describe—whether parades, dances, or reenactments—are not everyday events, they culminate from non-Native men's engagement with organizations or communities through which they define and enact their individual, everyday identities.

Each of the settler groups in my case studies are connected by generational history invested in the perpetuation of a nationalist power structure which privileges a hegemonic masculine citizenship.[8] For example, at its 1919 founding, the veteran's organization the American Legion named Theodore Roosevelt Jr. as its chairman, upholding the inherited ideology reified by his father, President Theodore Roosevelt, that linked civilized masculinity, militarism, and US citizenship, and understood Native masculinity to be savage, uncivilized, and destined to disappear.[9] The American Legion went on to sponsor Boy Scout troops, and some Boy Scouts grew up to be Seminole War reenactors. These three communities renew links, through generations, between militarism, hegemonic masculinity, and playing Indian in the US. More particularly, they bolster what I identify as hegemonic settler masculinity: that is, a normative masculinity which enables, more precisely, white settler masculine dominance over Indigenous peoples.

Clothing can be a means of exerting dominance and expressing power. On arrival at residential schools, Native youth immediately had the clothing of their community taken away and replaced with Euro-American style clothing. This forced re-dressing was considered key to the settler colonial goal of Native assimilation.[10] Native peoples taking on settler clothing is not "playing settler" or appropriation as those are acts of dominance and therefore not possible for those oppressed within a settler colonial context. Rather, in this chapter, I highlight Seminole self-fashioning integrating elements of Euro-American dress as a powerful means of resistance to and a negotiation of the settler colonial context, even as individuals wear it for everyday dress without intending such political messaging. While focusing on Seminole men's wear, women are the primary makers of Seminole garments; Seminole men's self-fashioning might then represent Seminole men's and women's creation of political agency through clothing.

In anthropologist Sandra Niessen's essay "Re-Orienting Fashion Theory," she contends that "The fashion process is about the creation of oppositions through time: that which is (conceived as) current and that which is (conceived as) past."[11] Through analysis of garments and visual representations, I demonstrate that Seminole men's fashioning has always been current and has always been political. I argue that settler common sense though seeks to undermine the political potency of Seminole fashion by fixating on a moment of historical Seminole dress or appropriating Seminole dress as costume, disregarding the currency of Seminole fashion in order to subvert contemporary Seminole political agency.

## Florida Seminole and settler history

The people known as Seminole, who now might be citizens of the Seminole Tribe of Florida, the Miccosukee Tribe of Indians, the Seminole Nation of Oklahoma, or independent Seminoles, largely descend from Indigenous ancestors including peoples of pre- and early colonial Florida and peoples of the greater Southeast, broadly identified by settlers as "Creek," who had traveled throughout Florida for hundreds of years before colonialism. As white settlement pressured Indigenous lifeways in the greater Southeast, these peoples converged into communities in Florida, some of which also integrated freed and self-liberated Blacks.[12] While settlers referred to these distinct communities as "Seminole" from the eighteenth century, the semblance of a collective identity among these people only came about in resistance to US military actions during the so-called Seminole Wars of the nineteenth century. Through these extended aggressions, the US sought to rid North Florida of its Native peoples though slaughter or forced removal to what is now Oklahoma.

Seminole men's dress historically incorporated Indigenous and European influences and included European trade goods.[13] From the 1600s and early 1700s, Spanish and British colonists gifted cloth and European-styled clothing to Florida Native peoples and Creeks during negotiations over land use and other relations.[14] Creeks and Seminoles purchased cotton fabrics—which were especially suited to the warm climate of the Southeast—and sewing notions at trading posts to create clothing that integrated elements of European styles. By the nineteenth century, Seminole men wore cotton shirts falling to the mid-thigh and open-fronted coats ("plain shirts" and "long shirts" respectively) derived from Creek garmenting and influenced by European's men's shirts and jackets.[15] Historical Seminole men's dress demonstrates sustained exchange relationships with European settlers, the ethnogenesis of the Seminole, and the enduring creativity of Seminole fashion.

In 1822, having already conducted the First Seminole War, the US acquired Florida as a territory from Spain. In 1826, between the First and Second Seminole Wars, a Seminole delegation traveled to Washington, DC to resolve increasing skirmishes with white settlers in North Florida. A lithograph of a member of that delegation, Seminole leader Tukose Emathla, shows a man dressed to demonstrate his fluency in both Seminole and U.S. cultures. His plumed turban with a silver scalloped band distinguishes him as Seminole. His finger woven sash, bandolier bag, and garters bear snake-like designs perhaps linked to the Mississippian culture, ancestors to many Native cultures of the Southeast. His coat is similar in silhouette to a contemporary Euro-American frock coat but is also distinct in its use of a patterned fabric and two bands of zig-zagging applique at its knee-level hem. He wears a circular presidential medal and a crescent-shaped gorget (a form denoting rank both within European military culture and Southeast Native cultures) around his neck. In the political context of Washington, DC, Tukose Emathla's self-fashioning is coded to exert nation-to-nation influence, expressing both his rights to negotiate on behalf of his Nation and, in his wielding of US and European objects of power, a favored diplomatic status with US leaders.

**Figure 6.2** Charles Bird King, Tuko-See-Mathla. A Seminole chief, from *History of the Indian Tribes of North America*, c. 1843. Hand-colored lithograph on paper, Smithsonian American Art Museum, Museum purchase, 1985.66.153.308.

Despite the Seminole delegation's attempts, the US continued supporting white settlement in North Florida through legislation, welfare programs, and the military actions of the Seminole Wars. By 1858, the costly wars ended with no clear victor. Significant numbers of Seminoles had been forcibly removed to Indian Country or had perished. Those Seminoles remaining took refuge in the Big Cypress Swamp and Everglades of Southern Florida. Seminoles adapted to this unique, watery environment which provided for their survival and protected them from white men who found the area unnavigable.

**Figure 6.3** Seminole Indians in Florida. *c.* 1912, colored postcard. State Archives of Florida, Florida Memory.

In a photograph from around 1910, seven Seminole men pose amid Euro-American style buildings, perhaps near a trading post in Fort Lauderdale, Fort Myers, or Miami. Most wear big shirts—a style of Seminole men's garment they developed following Seminole acquisition of the sewing machine. The technology's speed enabled a transformation of Seminole dress by encouraging greater piecing and seaming. Big shirts of this period are constructed from a white solid or lightly patterned cotton fabric with appliqued and inset bands or patches of contrasting colors. A waistband cinches the big shirt, replicating the silhouette created by belting earlier long shirts. The men wear neckerchiefs and some further accessorize with items indicative of Euro-American men's political citizenship including suit vests, bowler hats, a conductor's or soldier's cap, and watch fobs and chains. Some add feather plumes to their hats like those worn with Seminole men's turbans, and others display Seminole finger-woven belts and bandoliers under their suit vests. This photo exhibits how Seminole men strategically fashioned identities as Seminoles negotiating their settler colonial context of South Florida through clothing.

Seminoles prospered in the years leading up to this photo, as they found lucrative markets for feathers and hides through the settler trading posts from which they likely purchased these hats and suit vests.[16] These accessories mark them as savvy partners in trade: it was Seminole skill, knowledge, and homelands which provided the goods upon which the traders depended for the health of their own businesses. In taking on elements of suiting—an ensemble which distinguished its wearer as "a model male political and economic actor" in the US—the Seminoles in the image strategically mobilize fashionings of masculine settler hegemony as accessories to their Seminole big shirts.[17] These ensembles demonstrate fashion as a political language: Seminoles fluently assume settler men's accessories of power while embodying Seminole culture and distinction through dress.

## The American Legion, 1920s–1940s

By the 1920s, Seminole lifeways and subsistence had been severely impacted by the state's drainage of the Big Cypress Swamp and Everglades. Drainage enabled settlement, urban development, and agribusiness, all of which contributed to Seminole economic marginalization. In response, Seminoles capitalized on the Florida tourism industry at white- or Seminole-owned tourist "Indian Camps."[18] Fort Lauderdale civic leader August Burghard later recalled, "one of the things that [Seminoles] did…was to sell tourists copies of their very colorful Seminole Indian costumes that they made…Our American Legion band here dressed in Seminole costumes, and it went to Legion conventions all over the country. The Seminoles were widely publicized by people who knew very little about them, and cared less."[19] The Broward County Historical Archives holds one such "costume," a typical Seminole-made big shirt that was worn by a member of Fort Lauderdale's William C. Morris American Legion Post #36.[20]

The big shirts Seminole men commonly wore in the 1920s generally were looser and longer than previous shirt styles, with fabric made entirely of horizontal bands of brightly colored solids and patchwork—the Seminole technique of assembling repeating patterns from small pieces of fabric. Seminole seamstresses innovated the patchwork technique in the late 1910s using the efficient capacity of the sewing machine to make historical Seminole decorative motifs more complex in form and color. While in most Seminole big shirts each band features just one patchwork pattern, the bands of the big shirt acquired by the American Legionnaire includes multiple patchwork patterns. Its deviation from typical Seminole design might demonstrate a difference between garments Seminoles made to be worn by Seminoles and those made to be sold to outsiders.

**Figure 6.4** V.F.W. marching in Seminole Indian dress for Governor's inaugural parade. The Veterans of Foreign Wars, or V.F.W., was another settler veterans' organization who dressed as Seminoles. 1949. State Archives of Florida, Florida Memory.

While patchwork has cultural and community meaning to Seminoles, the Legionnaires, in Burghard's words, did not care. Seminole makers, knowing this, might have pieced together patchwork scraps to complete the big shirts to be sold to the Legionnaires, while big shirts made to be worn by Seminoles highlight the form through consistent bands of patchwork designs.

An undated photograph shows perhaps forty members of American Legion Post #36's Drum-Bugle Corps wearing Seminole big shirts and garrison caps as uniforms parading through a city street under US and Legion Post flags.[21] A veteran in US military uniform looks on, saluting. In 1919, the American Legion passed a resolution devoted to "Protection of the Uniform," which "is as much a symbol as the flag itself" to be "worn with honor."[22] But, despite Legionnaire's respect for the US military uniforms and their valorous associations, Post #36's Corps took on Seminole big shirts as their uniform.

Why would American Legionnaires living in Florida don the clothing of Florida's native Seminole people as uniform? I propose multiple and complex motivations.

**Figure 6.5** Patchwork big shirt, early twentieth century. Ah-Tah-Thi-Ki Museum, Seminole Tribe of Florida, Catalog Number 2005.79.1.

The American Legion was founded in 1919 for First World War veterans. It had an expansive mission including to uphold and defend the US Constitution, foster Americanism, and encourage its members to serve community, state, and nation. The American Legion sought to shore up American masculinity and white patriarchal citizenship from its start, as the First World War's modern warfare had created a crisis of masculine heroism.[23] By dressing up as Seminoles, these veterans appropriated the remembered martial prowess of Seminole warriors like Osceola in the Seminole Wars.[24] Indigenous tactics were not mediated by modern technologies and modes of warfare, therefore neither was Indigenous heroism.

Additionally, Philip Deloria argues in *Playing Indian* that by appropriating Native identities through "playing Indian," settlers feel they become more American.[25] Thus, wearing a Seminole costume might have been considered as a demonstration of patriotism—a way of fostering a collective sense of Americanism, given that American identity rests on an assumed indigeneity. Further, photos of the Corps carousing and "taking" Jacksonville while wearing Seminole big shirts exemplify the "Indianization of misrule," where playing Indian enabled settler men to be more free, wilder, more rebellious.[26]

While wearing Seminole clothing might have made Legionnaires feel more heroic, manly, and American, dressing as a people actively living under colonization and negatively affected by the very policies supported by their organization is an act of domination. The American Legion was complicit in the most impactful disruption of Seminole relationships to the land and lifeways since the Seminole Wars: the draining of the Big Cypress Swamp and Everglades. At its 1919 National Convention, the American Legion passed a resolution in support of the reclamation of swampy lands, such as the Florida wetlands, in order to "present…to discharged soldiers and sailors an opportunity to establish homes and create for themselves a place in the field of constructive effort."[27] This resolution enacts what Goenpul scholar Aileen Moreton-Robinson calls "the white possessive," wherein private property ownership enhances the power and naturalization of white patriarchal sovereignty.[28] To the Legionnaires, US veterans' entitlement to homes rationalized the dispossession of Seminole land and the transformation of the land itself, an ultimate demonstration of ownership.

A 1939 newspaper account of the American Legion's annual national convention parade describes how each state's Posts expressed its state's uniqueness:

> In one block there were Iowans receiving tall cornstalks; in the next were lumberjacks from Wisconsin wiping rain drops from glistening axes…over there were Floridians in gaily striped Seminole costumes; over here Californians leading a live brown bear…[29]

The garments of the Florida Seminole became a metonym—their culturally distinct designs appropriated to demonstrate the uniqueness of the state. Nearly all those state symbols telepath mastery over nature: in reaping corn, felling lumber, or taming a bear. Wearing Seminole garments signifies this as well within a settler colonial system. In the American imagination, Native peoples are connected to the land. I posit that taking on the clothes of Native people signals taking over their relationships to the lands, which government and business interests had already begun through their drainage and development. The Legionnaires' settler common sense furthers government imperatives through this everyday performance.

## The Boy Scouts of America, 1950s–1960s

A newspaper clipping from the *Hollywood* (Florida) *Sun-Tattler* from about 1955 shows a white Boy Scouts of America scoutmaster teaching two Seminole boys wearing Scout shirts and neckerchiefs how to shoot guns. A young Seminole boy wearing patchwork clothing looks on. The caption claims that, "not yet in scouting, [he] is hopeful of exchanging his native dress for a scout uniform someday."[30] Boy Scouts sought to inculcate boys into a model of masculine American citizenship. For Seminole boys, this meant assimilating and leaving behind "native dress"; but for settler Boy Scouts, dressing up as Native people was essential to their training.

The roots of the Boy Scouts date to 1902, when author Ernest Thompson Seton began instructing boys in his conceptions of Native American values and traditions, founding the organization Woodcraft Tribe and writing a manual called the *Birch Bark Roll*. Around the same time, Lord Robert Baden-Powell, dismayed by the state of masculinity in Britain, sought to teach its boys martial and survival skills and military ethics. His 1908 manual, "Scouting for Boys" which drew heavily on nationalist and imperialist language to inspire its readers, sold widely in the US. In 1910, the Boy Scouts of America began, combining Baden-Powell's military pedagogy with Seton's emphasis on connecting to nature and veneration for supposedly Native American culture.[31]

Uniforms were core to the Boy Scouts' practice. Uniforms encouraged discipline, created a united identity, and delineated rank and prestige, as rights to certain uniforms were granted as Boy Scouts rose through scout levels and badges marked achievements.[32] But taking on the clothing of Native Americans, acting as Native people, performing Native dances, and learning Indian lore, crafts, and technologies (or rather settler constructions of these things) was also an integral part of Boy Scout induction.

As Shari Huhndorf explored in her 2001 book *Going Native,* the scouts had a curiously ambiguous relationship to Native Americans in the early twentieth century.[33] Huhndorf argues that in revering Native American ways through

**Figure 6.6** Patchwork jacket, mid twentieth century. Ah-Tah-Thi-Ki Museum, Seminole Tribe of Florida, Catalog Number 2022.11.2.

learning skills imagined to be meaningful to Native Americans, dressing in Native American clothing, and modeling behavior after imagined Native characteristics, scouts sought to reinscribe white racial dominance while tapping into a cultural unease with modernity. This modeling was only possible, though, because of Native peoples' lack of political and military power at the time. To quote Huhndorf, "Because Natives no longer posed a significant military threat, they could now serve as a military ideal for the dominant culture."[34]

In 1963, members of a Miami Boy Scout Order of the Arrow (OA) Lodge wore Seminole-made jackets representative of Seminole men's fashion of the era. The jacket's design is like the top half of a big shirt with bands of horizontal patchwork and solid-colored fabric and the same tailoring through the shoulders, underarms, and wrists. However, the jacket ends at the waist (to be worn with pants) and has a pointed collar, when older garments had band collars. Seminoles created this men's jacket style with their increasing engagement with settler society, attentive to dominant American men's fashion trends, such as the so-called "Eisenhower jacket" named for the US President, and to the power and opportunity which came with wearing them. But these jackets still distinctly

Seminole. Like when earlier Seminole men took on Euro-American fashion accessories, these jackets materialize Seminole men's negotiation between settler and Seminole culture through fashion.

Claiming to be the first Florida scouts to ever wear Seminole clothing, this lodge intentionally arrived late at the 1963 OA National Meeting and rolled a red carpet from their bus to ensure other lodges from throughout the country noted the Florida Scouts' entrance in bright patchwork jackets they commissioned from Seminole seamstresses.[35] They made themselves distinctive by wearing the distinctive garments of the Seminole. The lodge also performed what they claimed to be a Seminole Green Corn Dance, an annual spiritual event deeply enmeshed in the perpetuation of Seminole clan relations and social order.[36] But the Scouts did not wear the short, pointed-collar jackets they commissioned in their Green Corn Dance. Rather, they fabricated garments that they believed to be more representative of nineteenth century Seminole clothing. By performing a Seminole dance in "historical" clothing of their own creation, these scouts undermined the authenticity of contemporary Seminole dress and ongoing rituals of social and spiritual renewal, and therefore the legitimacy of contemporary Seminole political claims based on their rights as an Indigenous Nation.

This same mid-century period was pivotal in Seminole political organizing.[37] In the 1950s, Florida Seminoles successfully fought the US government's proposed termination policy that would have severed trusteeship and cut federal services. Building on this success, in 1957 some Seminoles drafted and approved a Tribal Charter and Constitution and achieved federal recognition as the Seminole Tribe of Florida, affirming a nation-to-nation relationship with the US government. Another group, some of whom went on to organize the Miccosukee Tribe of Indians in 1962, made headlines for refusing recognition, which they viewed as a capitulation to the US federal government. They advocated for the necessity of maintaining their culture, language, and education systems. In their most arresting statements, widely publicized in South Florida newspapers, they insisted that all Southern Florida belonged to its Native people and demanded its return by the settler state.

In articulating Florida as a settler state, the Miccosukee forced increased settler awareness of their own positionality as settlers. I contend that this awareness instigated a renewal of a settler colonial drive to replace the Native enacted in Boy Scouts by wearing Seminole garments and crafting their own historical Seminole-style garments to perform as Seminoles. The very modernity of the Miccosukee and Seminole—in making jackets for sale, in claiming Florida lands, in demanding rights to self-determination, and in organizing Tribal governments—opened a space of possibility for the Boy Scouts to step into what they believe to be more authentic Indian selves based on Seminole *history* rather than Seminole *present*. While they framed this performance as appreciative of Florida Native culture and history, I propose that by claiming a past era as more authentic than the present, these scouts suggested the illegitimacy of modern Miccosukee and Seminole political agency, again acting with settler common sense.

## Seminole War reenactors, 1980s–1990s

Since the 1980s, settler living historians or reenactors have painstakingly crafted their own nineteenth-century Seminole-style garments to play Seminole Indian in reenactments of Seminole War battles. The archive of the American Museum of Natural History holds years of correspondence on Boy Scouts of America Central Florida Council letterhead from reenactor and former OA Scout Rick Obermeyer diligently inquiring about garments in the museum's collection: he sent a bead sample card so collection staff could identify the beads used on Seminole bandoliers and drew elaborate diagrams of small tailoring details for collection staff to confirm.[38] He published his research as step-by-step instructions for making Seminole garments in 1991's *19th Century Seminole Men's Clothing*.[39] The Seminole War reenactment scene, and its attention to recreating historic Seminole fashions, grew out of and carries on the culture of OA Scouts playing Indian. Reenactors also have built respectful personal and professional relationships of reciprocity with Seminole individuals often founded around the sharing of knowledge about historical Seminole techniques.

That Seminole War reenactments developed within a decade of the end of the Vietnam War invites more specific interpretations of early settler participants' motivations. The two wars have much in common. The Vietnam War and the Seminole Wars both were fought in tropical ecosystems unfamiliar to US soldiers. US soldiers were largely unprepared for the guerilla tactics used against them by those Indigenous to the places that became battlegrounds. Both wars dragged on for decades and ended without a US victory, marring the perception of US exceptionalism. Susan Jeffords has argued that post-war representations of the Vietnam War worked toward the "remasculinization" of US culture, or the strengthening of patriarchal systems of power and dominance over women and non-white subjects.[40] She contends they do this through focusing on the performance of action rather than the end results, among other means.

Reenactments embody this tactic: the weekend-long performances are about the preparation, the spectacle, and the community of reenactors rather than the pre-ordained end of the battle.

Reenacting a historical war might have mollified unease over American masculinity in the post-war moment while reinforcing the specific masculine settler hegemony of Florida. In taking on the "Unconquered" Seminole role, reenactors perhaps reconcile their own conflicted relations to hegemonic masculinity, power, and the US state and its colonial and imperial practices following the Vietnam War. In *Playing Indian*, Philip Deloria writes of "counterculture Indians," that is non-Native people who took up symbols and language of Indian-ness to mark their independence and protest the US government and the Vietnam War in the 1960s. Deloria saw that "countercultural rebels became Indian to move their identities away from Americanness altogether...To play Indian was to become vicariously a victim of US imperialism."[41] By playing Seminole Indian, reenactors could both become fearsome and unconquered warriors and assert their own independence from the settler state's actions.

It is also conspicuous that Seminole War reenactments became popular soon after the Seminole Tribe of Florida's successful litigation of its rights to run high-stakes gambling on reservation lands. The 1981 US Federal Court decision in the Seminole Tribe's favor changed the economic future of the Seminole Tribe, and of Tribal Nations throughout the US. Through this assertion of sovereignty, the Seminole Tribe again shifted power dynamics within the settler state of Florida.[42] Meanwhile, the coincident Seminole War reenactments presented Seminoles as peoples of the past, whose Native-ness could be taken on through study and martial performance, and specifically through reconstructing and wearing nineteenth-century Seminole's men's garments. These reenactments give power to historical Seminole fashion and thereby symbolically diminish the legitimacy of the impactful Seminole political, legislative, economic agency in the present.

# Conclusion

Through these three cases studies, I've explored how settler men have used Seminole dress to play Seminole Indian and, in doing so, negotiate their own hegemonic settler masculinity in performances that embody settler common sense through the twentieth century. Although imagined to be a reenactment of the past, playing Seminole Indian is actually a phenomenon primarily responsive to the concurrent settler colonial negotiations of sovereignty in South Florida. These boys and men take on Seminole men's fashions to mobilize claims to Native-ness which justify the settler development of Florida and undermine Seminole political agency. At the same time, Playing Seminole provides a means to resolve their own conflicted relationships to hegemonic settler masculinity or, for Boy Scouts, to grow into it. Taking on the brightly colored and patterned clothing of the Seminole—and taking off the pants and neutral clothing of Euro-American masculinity—can, ironically, affirm hegemonic settler masculinity by highlighting Indigenous difference and enacting the dominance of appropriation.

While many of these men sincerely feel they honor Seminole peoples, their acts of self-fashioning cannot be separated from the settler colonial context in which they occur and its ongoing harm to Native peoples. Playing Indian, in the multiple variations I've documented in this chapter, expresses settler power and domination.[43] It creates stereotypes of Native people and signals Native-ness through simplified markers which diminish the living breadth of Native identities and cultures. For instance, in Florida, those who play Seminole Indian don't reflect on, say, how living in a matrilineal culture, like Seminole, might impact their masculine identities; rather, they take on Seminole clothing to perform an imagined Indigenous masculinity, acting out gender expressions significant to and supportive of the perpetuation of hegemonic settler masculinity.

I have also documented nearly two centuries of Seminole men using Seminole fashions to assert their political agency and citizenship, negotiate settler colonialism, and pursue Seminole sovereignty. Settler attempts to deny the power of contemporaneous Seminole fashion by using it as costume or researching and recreating historic dress in fact prove its potency as a political language. Seminole fashion must be appropriated, or its currency denied as it indicates the ultimate failure of settler colonialism by evidencing the vibrance, rather than the disappearance, of Seminole people and the futility of damaging assimilative programs of the settler state. When Seminole Tribal Chairman Mitchell Cypress wore a Seminole shirt to codify an agreement with the state of Florida, he embodied Seminole resistance to the hegemony of the settler state through fashion.

## Acknowledgments

This chapter relates to my in-progress dissertation on settler colonialism and Florida Miccosukee and Seminole arts with research funded by the American Philosophical Society, Bard Graduate Center, Decorative Arts Trust, Hagley

Museum and Library, and the Smithsonian American Art Museum. Thanks to the individuals who shared their knowledge, experiences, and feedback with me and the museum and archive staff who facilitated this research.

## Notes

1. William C. Sturtevant, "Seminole Men's Clothing," in *A Seminole Sourcebook*, ed. William C. Sturtevant, *The North American Indian* (New York: Garland, 1987), 192.
2. Among *The Miami Hurricane*'s reporting on Iron Arrow, see Jesse Lieberman, "Iron Arrow Eliminates Decades-Old Native American Traditions after Two-Year Review," *The Miami Hurricane*, August 27, 2020, https://www.themiamihurricane.com/2020/08/27/iron-arrow-eliminates-decades-old-native-american-traditions-after-two-year-review/
3. Quoted, Vincent Schilling, "Boy Scouts 'Have Been One of the Worst Culprits' of Cultural Appropriation," *Indian Country Today*, https://indiancountrytoday.com/news/boy-scouts-have-been-one-of-the-worst-culprits-of-cultural-appropriation
4. Jean Marie Allman, ed., *Fashioning Africa: Power and the Politics of Dress*, African Expressive Cultures (Bloomington, IN: Indiana University Press, 2004), 1.
5. Philip Joseph Deloria, *Playing Indian*, Yale Historical Publications (New Haven: Yale University Press, 1998); Shari M. Huhndorf, *Going Native: Indians in the American Cultural Imagination* (Ithaca: Cornell University Press, 2001).
6. Patrick Wolfe, "Settler Colonialism and the Elimination of the Native," *Journal of Genocide Research* 8, no. 4 (December 2006): 387–409.
7. Mark Rifkin, *Settler Common Sense: Queerness and Everyday Colonialism in the American Renaissance* (Minneapolis, MN: University of Minnesota Press, 2014), 10.
8. R. W. Connell and James W. Messerschmidt, "Hegemonic Masculinity: Rethinking the Concept," *Gender and Society* 19, no. 6 (2005): 832.
9. Gail Bederman, *Manliness and Civilization: A Cultural History of Gender and Race in the United States, 1880–1917*, Women in Culture and Society (Chicago: University of Chicago Press, 1995), 170–215.
10. Shawkay Ottmann, "Indigenous Dress Theory," *Fashion Studies* 3, no. 1 (2020), https://www.fashionstudies.ca/indigenous-dress-theory
11. Sandra Niessen, "Re-Orienting Fashion Theory," in *The Fashion Reader*, eds. Linda Welters and Abby Lillethun (Oxford; New York: Berg, 2007), 106.
12. "The Seminole Ancestors," Semtribe, https://www.semtribe.com/stof/history/the-seminole-ancestors (accessed February 1, 2023); Andrew K. Frank, "Red, Black, and Seminole: Community Convergence on the Florida Borderlands, 1780–1840," in *Borderland Narratives: Negotiation and Accommodation in North America's Contested Spaces, 1500–1850*, eds. Andrew K. Frank and A. Glenn Crothers (Gainesville, FL: University Press of Florida, 2017).

13 Dorothy Downs, *Art of the Florida Seminole and Miccosukee Indians* (Gainesville, FL: University Press of Florida, 1995), 10–82; Sturtevant, "Seminole Men's Clothing."

14 Laura E. Johnson, "Cloth and the Rituals of Encounter in La Florida: Weaving and Unraveling the Code," in *The Oxford Handbook of History and Material Culture*, eds. Ivan Gaskell and Sarah Anne Carter, Oxford Handbooks Online (New York: Oxford University Press, 2020), 397–413; Caroline Wigginton, "In a Red Petticoat: Coosaponakeesa's Performance of Creek Sovereignty in Colonial Georgia," in *Native Acts: Indian Performance, 1603-1832*, eds. Joshua David Bellin and Laura L. Mielke (Lincoln, NE: University of Nebraska Press, 2011).

15 I follow the English-language garment nomenclature codified in Sturtevant, "Seminole Men's Clothing."

16 Harry A. Kersey, *Pelts, Plumes, and Hides: White Traders Among the Seminole Indians, 1870–1930* (Gainesville, FL: University Press of Florida, 1975).

17 Stephen Kantrowitz, "'Citizen's Clothing': Reconstruction, Ho-Chunk Persistence, and the Politics of Dress," in *Civil War Wests: Testing the Limits of the United States*, eds. Adam Arenson and Andrew R. Graybill (Oakland, CA: University of California Press, 2015), 244.

18 Patsy West, *The Enduring Seminoles: From Alligator Wrestling to Casino Gambling*, rev. and expanded edn., Florida History and Culture Series (Gainesville, FL: University Press of Florida, 2008).

19 Transcript, August Burghard Oral History Interview, December 19, 1973, Samuel Proctor Oral History Program Collection, P. K. Yonge Library of Florida History, University of Florida.

20 Broward County Historical Archives, 1978.4.1.

21 Ibid.

22 Quoted, George Seay Wheat, *The Story of the American Legion* (New York: G. P. Putnam's Sons, 1919), 200.

23 George Lewis, "The End of Military Heroism? The American Legion and 'Service' Between the Wars," in *Warring Over Valor: How Race and Gender Shaped American Military Heroism in the Twentieth and Twenty-first Centuries*, ed. Simon Wendt (New Brunswick, NJ: Rutgers University Press, 2018), 21–36.

24 Mikaëla M. Adams, "Savage Foes, Noble Warriors, and Frail Remnants: Florida Seminoles in the White Imagination, 1865–1934," *The Florida Historical Quarterly* 87, no. 3 (2009): 417–20.

25 Deloria, *Playing Indian*, 7.

26 Broward County Historical Archives, 1978.4.4; Deloria, *Playing Indian*, 25.

27 Quoted, Wheat, *The Story of the American Legion*, 200–1.

28 Aileen Moreton-Robinson, *The White Possessive: Property, Power, and Indigenous Sovereignty*, Indigenous Americas (Minneapolis, MN: University of Minnesota Press, 2015).

29 "The Great Parade Swings Down Michigan Avenue," *The National Legionnaire* 5:10 (October 1939): 6.
30 Mrs. Frances Sheldon Scrapbook, Broward County Historical Archives, 1976.14.1.
31 Schilling, "Boy Scouts."
32 Tammie Proctor, "Scouts, Guides, and the Fashioning of Empire, 1919–39," in *Fashioning the Body Politic: Dress, Gender, Citizenship*, ed. Wendy Parkins (Oxford and New York: Berg, 2002), 125–44; Jennifer Craik, *Uniforms Exposed: From Conformity to Transgression*, Dress, Body, Culture (Oxford: Berg, 2005).
33 Huhndorf, *Going Native*, 69–78.
34 Ibid., 75.
35 Collection file, Florida Museum of Natural History, 2010.4.1.
36 Order of the Arrow lodges throughout the country still "play Indian," perform protected dances, and create replicas of ceremonial regalia. See Vincent Schilling, "Order of the Arrow Is a 'Secret' Scout Society 'in the Spirit of the Lenni Lenape'—a Lenape Leader Disagrees," Indian Country Today, https://indiancountrytoday.com/news/order-of-the-arrow-is-a-secret-scout-society-in-the-spirit-of-the-lenni-lenape-a-lenape-leader-disagrees (accessed June 25, 2022).
37 Harry A. Kersey, *An Assumption of Sovereignty: Social and Political Transformation among the Florida Seminoles, 1953–1979*, Indians of the Southeast (Lincoln, NE: University of Nebraska Press, 1996).
38 "Alanson Skinner Museum Exped. 1910.54," American Museum of Natural History Department of Anthropology Archives.
39 Rich Obermeyer, "19th Century Seminole Men's Clothing," http://www.nativetech.org/seminole/index.php (accessed June 19, 2022).
40 Susan Jeffords, *The Remasculinization of America: Gender and the Vietnam War*, Theories of Contemporary Culture, v. 10 (Bloomington, IN: Indiana University Press, 1989).
41 Deloria, *Playing Indian*, 161.
42 Jessica R. Cattelino, *High Stakes: Florida Seminole Gaming and Sovereignty* (Durham, NC: Duke University Press, 2008).
43 Deloria, *Playing Indian*, 186.

# Bibliography

Adams, Mikaëla M. "Savage Foes, Noble Warriors, and Frail Remnants: Florida Seminoles in the White Imagination, 1865–1934." *The Florida Historical Quarterly* 87, no. 3 (2009): 404–35.

Allman, Jean Marie, ed. *Fashioning Africa: Power and the Politics of Dress*. African Expressive Cultures. Bloomington, IN: Indiana University Press, 2004.

Bederman, Gail. *Manliness & Civilization: A Cultural History of Gender and Race in the United States, 1880-1917*. Women in Culture and Society. Chicago: University of Chicago Press, 1995.

Cattelino, Jessica R. *High Stakes: Florida Seminole Gaming and Sovereignty*. Durham, NC: Duke University Press, 2008.

Connell, R. W. and James W. Messerschmidt. "Hegemonic Masculinity: Rethinking the Concept." *Gender and Society* 19, no. 6 (2005): 829–59.

Craik, Jennifer. *Uniforms Exposed: From Conformity to Transgression*. Dress, Body, Culture. Oxford: Berg, 2005.

Deloria, Philip Joseph. *Playing Indian*. Yale Historical Publications. New Haven: Yale University Press, 1998.

Downs, Dorothy. *Art of the Florida Seminole and Miccosukee Indians*. Gainesville, FL: University Press of Florida, 1995.

Frank, Andrew K. "Red, Black, and Seminole: Community Convergence on the Florida Borderlands, 1780–1840." In *Borderland Narratives: Negotiation and Accommodation in North America's Contested Spaces, 1500–1850*, edited by Andrew K. Frank and A. Glenn Crothers. Gainsville, FL: University Press of Florida, 2017.

Huhndorf, Shari M. *Going Native: Indians in the American Cultural Imagination*. Ithaca: Cornell University Press, 2001.

Jeffords, Susan. *The Remasculinization of America: Gender and the Vietnam War*. Theories of Contemporary Culture, v. 10. Bloomington, IN: Indiana University Press, 1989.

Johnson, Laura E. "Cloth and the Rituals of Encounter in La Florida: Weaving and Unraveling the Code." In *The Oxford Handbook of History and Material Culture*, edited by Ivan Gaskell and Sarah Anne Carter, 397–413. Oxford Handbooks Online. New York: Oxford University Press, 2020.

Kantrowitz, Stephen. "'Citizen's Clothing': Reconstruction, Ho-Chunk Persistence, and the Politics of Dress." In *Civil War Wests: Testing the Limits of the United States*, edited by Adam Arenson and Andrew R. Graybill, 242–64. Oakland, CA: University of California Press, 2015.

Kersey, Harry A. *Pelts, Plumes, and Hides: White Traders Among the Seminole Indians, 1870-1930*. Gainesville, FL: University Press of Florida, 1975.

Kersey, Harry A. *An Assumption of Sovereignty: Social and Political Transformation Among the Florida Seminoles, 1953–1979*. Indians of the Southeast. Lincoln, NE: University of Nebraska Press, 1996.

Lewis, George. "The End of Military Heroism? The American Legion and 'Service' Between the Wars." In *Warring Over Valor : How Race and Gender Shaped American Military Heroism in the Twentieth and Twenty-First Centuries*, edited by Simon Wendt, 21–36. New Brunswick, NJ: Rutgers University Press, 2018.

Lieberman, Jesse. "Iron Arrow Eliminates Decades-Old Native American Traditions after Two-Year Review." *The Miami Hurricane*, August 27, 2020, https://www.

themiamihurricane.com/2020/08/27/iron-arrow-eliminates-decades-old-native-american-traditions-after-two-year-review/

Moreton-Robinson, Aileen. *The White Possessive: Property, Power, and Indigenous Sovereignty*. Indigenous Americas. Minneapolis, MN: University of Minnesota Press, 2015.

Niessen, Sandra. "Re-Orienting Fashion Theory." In *The Fashion Reader*, edited by Linda Welters and Abby Lillethun, 105–10. Oxford and New York: Berg, 2007.

Obermeyer, Rich. "19th Century Seminole Men's Clothing," http://www.nativetech.org/seminole/index.php (accessed June 19, 2022).

Ottmann, Shawkay. "Indigenous Dress Theory." *Fashion Studies* 3, no. 1 (2020), https://www.fashionstudies.ca/indigenous-dress-theory

Proctor, Tammie. "Scouts, Guides, and the Fashioning of Empire, 1919–39." In *Fashioning the Body Politic: Dress, Gender, Citizenship*, edited by Wendy Parkins, 125–44. Oxford, New York: Berg, 2002.

Rifkin, Mark. *Settler Common Sense: Queerness and Everyday Colonialism in the American Renaissance*. Minneapolis, MN: University of Minnesota Press, 2014.

Schilling, Vincent. "Boy Scouts 'Have Been One of the Worst Culprits' of Cultural Appropriation." Indian Country Today, https://indiancountrytoday.com/news/boy-scouts-have-been-one-of-the-worst-culprits-of-cultural-appropriation (accessed June 28, 2022).

Schilling, Vincent. "Order of the Arrow Is a 'Secret' Scout Society 'in the Spirit of the Lenni Lenape'—a Lenape Leader Disagrees." *Indian Country Today*, https://indiancountrytoday.com/news/order-of-the-arrow-is-a-secret-scout-society-in-the-spirit-of-the-lenni-lenape-a-lenape-leader-disagrees (accessed June 25, 2022).

Semtribe. "The Seminole Ancestors," https://www.semtribe.com/stof/history/the-seminole-ancestors (accessed February 1, 2023).

Sturtevant, William C. "Seminole Men's Clothing." In *A Seminole Sourcebook*, edited by William C. Sturtevant, 160–74. *The North American Indian*. New York: Garland, 1987.

West, Patsy. *The Enduring Seminoles: From Alligator Wrestling to Casino Gambling*. Revised and expanded edition. Florida History and Culture Series. Gainesville, FL: University Press of Florida, 2008.

Wheat, George Seay. *The Story of the American Legion*. New York: G. P. Putnam's Sons, 1919.

Wigginton, Caroline. "In a Red Petticoat: Coosaponakeesa's Performance of Creek Sovereignty in Colonial Georgia." In *Native Acts: Indian Performance, 1603–1832*, edited by Joshua David Bellin and Laura L. Mielke. Lincoln, NE: University of Nebraska Press, 2011.

Wolfe, Patrick. "Settler Colonialism and the Elimination of the Native." *Journal of Genocide Research* 8, no. 4 (December 2006): 387–409.

7

# Working from the Periphery

## The National Association of Fashion and Accessories Designers (NAFAD) and the Promotion of Black Fashion

Einav Rabinovitch-Fox

Black designers were always part and parcel of the fashion industry, as producers of cloth and of clothing, and they continue to shape and be shaped by it. For African American women in particular, fashion served, both during and after slavery, as a means of shaping ideas regarding Black women's bodies and appearance and a route to claim freedom and inclusion in American culture.[1] However, despite this continued involvement, pattens of discrimination caused much of Black designers' work and influence to remain outside the mainstream industry well into the twentieth century. Aware of this marginal position and acknowledging the need to create an organization and a support network to change it, a group of Black women designers decided in 1949 to found the National Association of Fashion and Accessories Designers (NAFAD). NAFAD would become one of the most prominent organizations to champion opportunities for Black professionals in the fashion industry, seeking to integrate the business rather than maintain a separatist approach. As NAFAD's president Jeanetta Welch Brown argued in 1951: "Too long have we operated in a vacuum—sometimes through force and at other times through choice...If in our efforts we are able to establish a wider knowledge of the work and worthiness of Negro designers, this Association will have acquitted itself in fair measure."[2] For Brown and the other NAFAD officers, the goal was not only to increase the visibility of Black designers in mainstream society, but they also wanted to turn fashion into a valuable route of empowerment and racial uplift in their own communities.

NAFAD's mission was to carve a place for African Americans in the fashion industry so they could insert their influence. It sought to "foster complete integration of its membership in all phases of the fashion industry through the extension of educational and economic opportunities, ... the dissemination of pertinent information, the offering of local and national scholarships, and the display of fashion in good taste."[3] As part of this mission, NAFAD organized conferences and meetings, published a monthly newsletter, and worked to foster connections between members and people and institutions in the business.[4] These activities were geared towards gaining a foothold and claiming a professional status within the industry. Indeed, NAFAD founders saw themselves first and foremost as professional fashion designers and they fought to get the recognition they deserved as such. They did not admit everyone who claimed to be a designer or who agreed to pay the dues for the organization but demanded that they will adhere to strict professional standards, and that their designs will be original and of high quality.

Yet, NAFAD was more than just a professional organization. Affiliated with and supported by Mary McLeod Bethune and the National Council of Negro Women (NCNW), it became part of the organized Black struggle for racial equality in the mid-twentieth century, using fashion as a means for promoting civil rights. Like the NCNW's mission, NAFAD sought to increase the recognition of the worth of Black design both among African Americans and whites, espousing an integrationist view that aimed to join the mainstream and to provide Americans with everyday clothing. As they navigated both racial and gender barriers in an industry which favored whites and males, these women used fashion into a realm of empowerment and a way to claim their status as equal.

Although NAFAD has long been at the forefront of promoting Black design and Black designers, and the organization is still active today, it has stayed very much on the margins of scholarly attention as well as the general public. The names of many of the women who led NAFAD remain obscure and its activities and presence in the fashion world have been almost forgotten. By exploring how NAFAD carved a space of power from the margins, this chapter points to the intricate ways through which Black women used fashion to challenge their place in society as women and as Blacks, demanding to have a voice in an industry that often marginalized or ignore them. These women sought to provide everyday solutions for their clients, making not only the industry accessible to Black designers, but to make "good design" for everyday wear accessible to African Americans. By using archival records and coverage in Black newspapers and magazines such as the *Chicago Defender* and *New York Amsterdam News*, this chapter sheds light onto this organization and its role in making Black fashion and designers an integral part of the industry. Shifting the focus to the periphery and the everyday instead of the glamourous, this chapter expands the conversation to the ways in which we tell the history of fashion in the United States and who do we include in it.

## Crafting female networks

NAFAD was officially founded in 1949, yet its story begins in the 1930s and 1940s, which were remarkably good years for American fashion, despite the hardships of the Great Depression and the Second World War. The economic crisis and more forcefully the Nazi occupation of France after 1940, caused the domestic fashion industry to look inward toward American designers rather than to Paris as sources of inspiration.[5] The fashion industry was also especially welcoming to women, offering them professional opportunities not available to them in any other field. By 1940, nearly 84 percent of female executives in the United States (218 out of 260) held positions in a fashion-related field, using the industry to advance and legitimize their career aspirations.[6] Although the fashion industry was very much segregated, Black designers managed to carve themselves a professional space within it, and they too benefited from the rise of the domestic industry in the 1930s and 1940s. New York, the nation's fashion capital, became a center for Black professional designers who found Harlem's middle class as well as its growing entertainment scene in the interwar period a great potential source of profits.[7] Yet, Black designers also found a thriving pool of customers among many of the urban centers in the North and Midwest that welcomed African Americans during the first Great Migration.[8]

Much like the beauty industry, fashion design and dressmaking offered a sense of autonomy and a venue to express one's creativity, and it soon became a lucrative business route for many African American women who sought to escape domestic work.[9] Dressmaking, which demanded neither substantial capital investment nor a specific working space, proved an especially attractive occupation for many new migrants, who could launch their businesses at home with the rental or purchase of a sewing machine.[10] This was the case for future NAFAD members, designers Zelda Wynn Valdes, Ruby Bailey, and Amanda Wicker. Wynn opened her first business in 1935 in White Plains, New York, and in 1948 opened a store on Broadway in New York City, which became an important fashion resource for the local community.[11] Bailey, whose designs ranged from sportwear to eveningwear to millinery, also served the Harlem community as well as the Broadway theater scene.[12] Wicker began her career as an apprentice to Mrs. Addie Clarke in Washington DC, and after migrating to Cleveland in 1924, she opened her own business and a dressmaking school.[13] Whereas the bulk of Black designers' clientele usually came from the Black community, designers such as Ann Lowe, who designed the dress Jacqueline Bouvier wore to her wedding to John F. Kennedy in 1953, achieved national fame and acquired a long list of white customers.[14] Selling both custom-made and ready-to-wear dresses, Black women designers like Wicker, Wynn, Bailey, and Lowe served as important financial pillars of their communities and played a pivotal role in bringing fashion within Black women's reach.

Unlike white American designers, who by the mid-twentieth century enjoyed a celebrity status and name recognition with the American public—even while catering to ready-made fashions—Black designers remained completely anonymous. Thus, Black designers saw the importance of creating their own professional and support networks, which they perceived as useful in promoting Black design. Often shunned from the mainstream industry, Black designers participated in their own separate system, holding fashion shows that were covered primarily by the Black press.[15] However, even if keeping offices and showrooms on Seventh Avenue—where the Garment District in New York City was located—was not a possibility or a wanted choice for many of these designers, they still understood the importance of cultivating relationships with buyers and sought to break ground within the mainstream fashion business that was controlled by whites.

The decision to form NAFAD came in 1948 after Wynn integrated a fashion show celebrating New York City's golden jubilee of the consolidation of the five boroughs. Despite the initial exclusion of Black designers, show organizers agreed that Wynn's design, together with leather goods accessories by Helen Cornele Cuyjet, would represent Harlem in the event, showcasing Black design to white audiences.[16] Acknowledging the need to create a more permanent organization to represent Black designers' interests, Wynn—who was one of NAFAD's founding members—pushed for action. In 1949, with the support of Bethune and the NCNW, NAFAD was founded as an independent organization with Jeanetta Welch Brown as its first president.

The connection with the NCNW influenced much of the organization's character in its first years. NAFAD fit the NCNW's mission to augment the political and professional power of Black women as well as the more elitist image that put an emphasis on respectability and racial uplift.[17] It was a combination of a professional club and a civil rights movement, and while never officially closed to men, membership in the first years of the organization was almost entirely composed of Black women who gained a reputation for themselves in the fashion trade.[18] Like many of the affiliated organizations of the NCNW, NAFAD was also imagined as a "sisterhood" and was known at first as "Rho Delta Phi—a national sorority for designers and models."[19] The affiliation with the NCNW also determined NAFAD's headquarters location, which was in Washington DC and not in New York City, where most of the fashion industry was located. Yet, the organization was always national in scope. By 1954, the organization had branches across the country, ranging from New York, Washington, DC, Philadelphia, Detroit, Chicago, Newark, Cleveland, St. Louis, Kansas City, Boston, Brooklyn, NY, Atlanta, Houston, and Los Angeles. Each branch had its own officers and activities that were relatively independent from the national organization, although all reported to the national leadership.

The affiliation with NCNW also impacted the religious character of the organization. Like in many other civil rights organizations, the church functioned as a community space where women activists engaged in networking. Many of NAFAD's members were pillars of their communities not only because of their professional work, but also because of their standing in the church. When these women began to organize around fashion, they brought with them the customs they were used to from their work in the church and other women's clubs.[20] The organization designed an emblem and a hymn, similar to sororities, and board meetings often opened with a prayer. The emblem itself, in the shape of a shield, contained five elements: The hands signify praise and thanks to God for creative hands. The scales represent balance in life and balance in design. The torch represents leadership, guidance light and education in the fashion fields and in our local communities. The key signifies the open doors of opportunity, integration, study, travel, and employment. And the clasped hands represent unity of purpose and strength in union. The colors of the organization: blue and gold stood for truth and depth of understanding of the aims and purposes of the organization; and for purity of design, excellence in performance, and refinement of talent, respectively.[21]

Although the organization was professional in character, its mission was wrapped up in a civil rights discourse that viewed the issue of professional status and economic independence as crucial to ideas of citizenship and racial equality. In 1950, Vice President Sara Turner framed NAFAD's purpose as the accomplishment of four rights: The right of equal opportunity, the right to equal chance to use skill and knowledge, the right to be a first-class citizen, and the right to bring about the highest standard of fashion and good will. Turner's

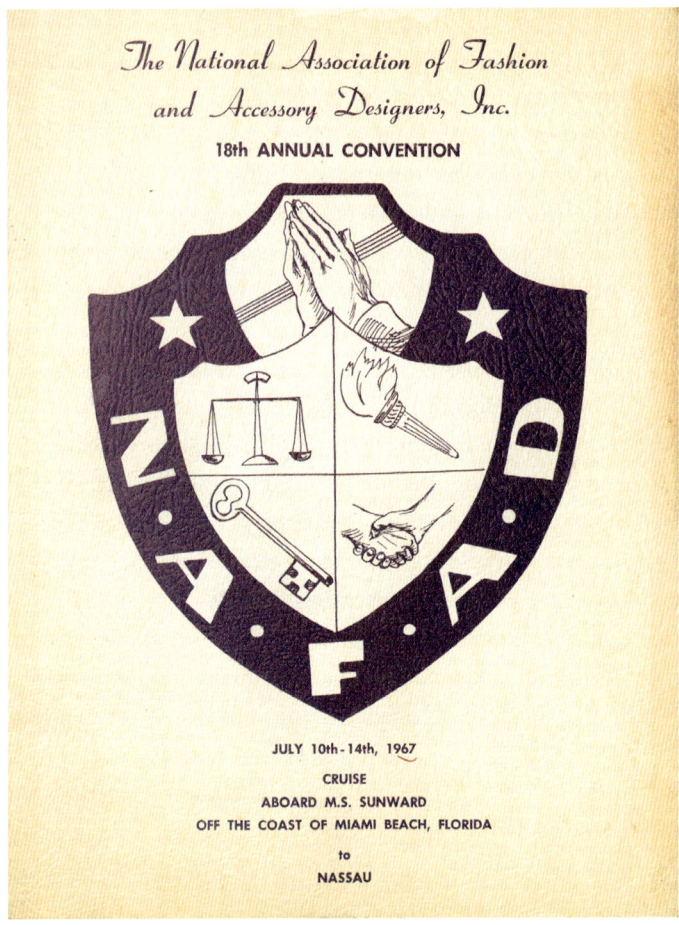

**Figure 7.1** NAFAD Emblem. Courtesy of National Association of Fashion and Accessory Designers (NAFAD) Inc. Records, National Archives for Black Women's History, National Park Service Museum Resource Center.

emphasis was on the fashion industry, and she addressed these rights in the context of breaking down discrimination in the fashion world. Yet, she also made the effort to connect NAFAD into a broader coalition and struggle for racial equality and civil rights, seeing fashion not as a disconnected realm but as another avenue for racial uplift and advancement.[22]

## Promoting Black design

NAFAD members took pride in the organization and its uplifting mission, but mostly in its insistence to adhere to the highest standards of design. Organizational correspondence shows that there was a continuous discussion about how to define a "fashion designer" and who was eligible to join the organization. In the recruitment stage, personal letters from Brown and Bethune were sent to those who "create and sell fashions, have a most challenging and interesting career," and with their "ingenuity and resourcefulness inspired by…knowledge…contribute largely to America and the world."[23] While board members decided that modeling, together with millinery, clothing, and accessories design would be under the purview of NAFAD, hairdressers and wig makers were left out of the organization. However, despite the will to maintain a high bar for joining, the constant need of members, and especially of their annual membership fees, caused the organization to have quite inclusive membership criteria. Members in NAFAD could be people trained in the fields of clothing and design, people who may have no formal training but have served as apprenticeship or have market experience, or people practicing types of art directly related to the fashion field. The latter group was often models, fashion photographers and journalists, and managers of PR and modeling casting companies. Regardless of their background, however, all members were expected to be able to create original designs and make adaptations from historic and contemporary costumes to qualify for a membership, thus assuming a level of sewing and crafting skills that were deemed sufficient for working in the industry.[24]

Moreover, while the organization centered its efforts in promoting Black designers as part of an inward-facing ideology of racial uplift, they also invested in outward-facing efforts, seeking to foster connections with influential people and institutions in the white fashion world, again being in line with the NCNW. "We…believe that we can contribute an untapped reservoir of creative talents, heretofore, overlooked by the industry," argued Vice President Sara Turner in 1950.[25] From its inception, NAFAD worked to obtain affiliation with the Costume Institute of the Metropolitan Museum of Art so members could use its collections for inspiration for their designs.[26] NAFAD also invited white speakers to its annual conventions, working with prominent figures in the fashion industry such as Eleanor Lambert, Claire McCardell, Jo Copeland, and Diana Vreeland. Many of those women were part of the Fashion Group, a mirror organization to NAFAD that was founded in 1931 and sought to promote women in the fashion business.[27] Both organizations sought to fulfill the need for professional networks, especially for women, that could serve as a space to advocate for social change. And although the racist structures of the industry prevented NAFAD's members from gaining the public attention that the Fashion Group attracted, the two organizations collaborated with each other and helped to make Black designers' presence more visible.[28]

As NAFAD wanted to position itself as a professional power in the industry, there was a constant negotiation between the will to create a community of designers and the need to be recognized by the mainstream society. Unlike the Fashion Group, which only accepted members who had already made a name for themselves in the industry, NAFAD was more invested in cultivating a younger generation of designers who would help to sustain the organization in the long run. Indeed, like other affiliates of the NCNW, much of NAFAD's activities revolved around education and professional development. It looked not only to promote existing designers, but to also encourage young people to enter the field. To this end, NAFAD organized conferences and meetings that offered informational sessions and workshops beyond the regular networking opportunities. Lectures included topics such as "Successful Designing, Promotion and Marketing of Fashion Merchandise," "New Trends and Techniques in Fashion Apparel," and "Getting the Know-How from the Experts," which provided members with valuable information on the inside of the industry and offered a more holistic view on how African Americans can get their equal place in the business. If lectures and panels were geared towards raising the profile and influence of African Americans in the fashion industry, conventions also included "Do-it Yourself" and "How to" workshops that focused on the technical and professional aspects of design and sought to attract more younger crowds. Yet, true to their civil rights mission, and especially during the 1960s when the national movement took off, convention workshops also offered legal information such as "Equal Employment" that meant to help members to navigate their place in the field.[29]

NAFAD invested a lot of effort in attracting young talent into its ranks, trying to convince them that the fashion field was a viable career option. It encouraged the presence of the Rho Delta Phi sorority in universities, and awarded scholarships and financial aid for "young men and women with interest and creative ability...that they may develop their potential to the fullest degree and to place them in contact with unlimited opportunities in the fashion field."[30] Local chapters created junior chapters, where young members were supposed to be initiated into the profession through mentoring by senior members and active participation in NAFAD's activities. Each junior chapter was required to offer its members professional workshops about topics ranging from patterns, knowledge of materials and color coordination, to fashion show coordination and tools used in the trade.[31] In places like Cleveland, Ohio for example, NAFAD member Amanda Wicker's Clarke School of Dressmaking and Fashion Design specifically focused on preparing young people for work in

*Working from the Periphery* 149

the garment industry, providing them with scholarships and teaching them how to operate industrial machinery and other skills such as pattern-making related to mass production.[32]

Another medium for increasing networking, professional development, and member outreach was the organization's monthly newsletter, *Fashion Cue*. The newsletter included a column by the president, updates from the local chapters, and occasionally also professional reports on the latest trends in the industry. What started as an amateur machine-typed four-page brochure developed into a professional-looking publication typeset with photographs from the different activities. *Fashion Cue* served not only as a forum for members to share news and publicize their work, but to also build a sense of community and pride in the organization with reports on members' inroads into the industry.[33]

Expanding job opportunities for African Americans in the fashion industry and increasing the visibility of Black design was a top priority for NAFAD. Annual conventions were not just a time for networking and professional development, but first and foremost a chance to showcase members' designs to manufacturers and retailers. Both the National NAFAD and the local chapters routinely organized fashion shows to celebrate members and to increase their visibility within their communities. NAFAD members used their connections

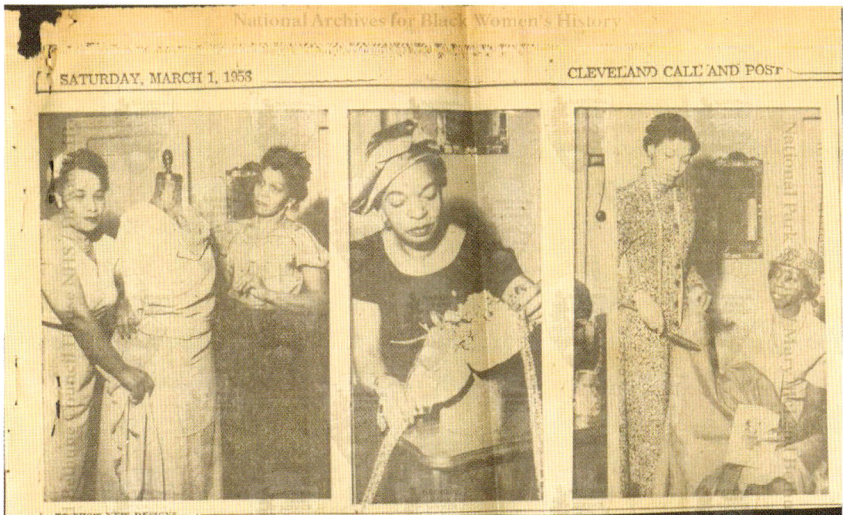

**Figure 7.2** "Cleveland NAFADs to Show Spring, Summer Collection," *Cleveland Call & Post*, March 1, 1958. Image published with permission of ProQuest LLC. Further reproduction is prohibited without permission.

with Black publishers to publicize the organization's fashion shows and members' designs, giving attention not only to the clothes but also to the women who made them.

Articles about NAFAD and its activities often included photographs of models wearing African American designs, with credit to the designers. Some articles also included photographs of "designers at work" which raised their celebrity status.[34] In 1954, NAFAD began to collaborate with *Ebony* magazine on its "Best Dressed Women of the Year" poll, raising their profile in the Black press. NAFAD also worked to publicize its shows in the white press, and, mainly with the help of Eleanor Lambert, often succeeded to grab reporters' attention to its annual conventions' shows.[35] The fashion shows demonstrated the constant need to navigate between these two worlds. While NAFAD took a great pride in making a name for itself within the Black community, leadership always sought white approval and recognition, seeing their mission to integrate the fashion industry as the most important. Yet, despite collaborations with white designers and the Fashion Group, NAFAD never managed to completely break racial barriers within the industry and most of its influence remained confined within the Black community.

## The style of Black empowerment

As part of this negotiation, NAFAD leadership also sought to cater to white taste in terms of styles. Fashion shows were carefully crafted, as designers were encouraged to produce original and innovative designs, while also adhering to quality. "All original design is not necessarily good design," reminded NAFAD President Freddye Henderson. "We must make sure that ours adhere closely to the principles of balance, proportion, harmony, rhythm and emphasis as possible, for they and only they be adjudged good."[36] Fashion shows presented custom-made pieces, often made specifically for the show, but the designs were always constructed with the intention of being mass-produced, often serving a sample to convince buyers to manufacture on a large scale.

As an organization, NAFAD promoted more conservative taste when it came to styles. In a letter addressed to Jeanetta Welch Brown, the writer suggested that designers who want to appeal to white buyers should stick to more conservative style: "The type which can be worn by a majority of women...The 'spectacular' type of clothing is out...special thought should be given the detail of the clothing, with the idea in mind that such small points determine new trends in garments, materials should be chosen with care and conservatism while bearing in mind the fact that new combinations make for interest and originality."[37] As NAFAD's purpose was to carve themselves a foothold in the mainstream industry, their attitude toward fashion was more vocational than artistic. Despite emphasizing the importance of "good design" and "good sewing," the idea was always to create clothes that ordinary people could wear. For them, "good design" always meant popular design, one that could appeal to the masses, and that was meant for everyday use.

Indeed, although many NAFAD designers preferred to focus on custom dressmaking and eveningwear—as it demanded more skill and commanded a higher price than sportswear—NAFAD became a big proponent of everyday wear. Recognizing that the retail and ready-made field can be a better avenue for African American integration in the business, NAFAD put most of its efforts in promoting designers in that field. It believed that the wholesale business, always in search of new ideas and talent, would be much more open to integrate Black designers. Moreover, since many of the wholesale designers remained anonymous to the buying public, NAFAD hoped it would enable Black designers to overcome discrimination and reluctance of white employers in hiring, who did not want to showcase the fact that Black designers are responsible for their merchandise.[38] Although Black designers who concentrated on couture and custom wear also suffered from anonymity, NAFAD believed this would be less of a disadvantage in the retail business. Alongside evening gowns and wedding dresses, fashion shows sponsored by NAFAD also featured sportswear and play clothes that appealed to a broader market audience and prices, and demonstrated the versatility of designers.[39]

The national fashion shows that were part of the annual convention were the one of the most important activities of the organization, but local branches also organized their own shows to support their members.[40] Often these local events served as a stepping-stone for designers to achieve national recognition when outfits from the local shows were featured in NAFAD's annual conventions. Moreover, as the hosting of the annual convention rotated yearly between chapters, each had the opportunity to showcase its local talents to national buyers and manufacturers. One of such examples is a brown sportswear suit designed by Wicker that demonstrates how members used their skills in creating a functional outfit suitable for everyday wear that would appeal to a broad consumer base. Outfits like these not only positioned Wicker on the national level but also boosted her reputation among her personal clients.[41]

**Figure 7.3** Amanda Wicker, Suit Ensemble, *c.* 1950s. Chisholm Halle Costume Wing, Western Reserve Historical Society, Cleveland, Ohio.

## The politics of Black design

NAFAD sought to maintain its standing as a professional organization, focusing mainly on opening opportunities for Black designers. Yet, as the 1950s progressed, and the Civil Rights Movement started to get more public attention, NAFAD itself became more radicalized, demanding not just racial equality but racial visibility. Staying true to its uplift mission and the legacy of Mary McLeod Bethune, NAFAD fought for civil rights goals through its mission to promote African American design. In 1963, NAFAD's President Lois Alexander declared: "We are in the midst of a great revolution as we as designers must keep pace with the youngsters of the country giving them our support in the fight for freedom."[42] For members, fashion, and especially what they perceived as good design, became a form of activism, just like marches, sit-ins, and voter registration efforts. By showcasing their talent and by investing in the next generation's education, NAFAD members believed they could convince white society to acknowledge their worth. Thus, design became an everyday practice of resistance, both for the women who made the clothes, and those who designed them. Dressing well became a political statement, and NAFAD members sought to provide their communities with the means to do so.

However, in much of the same way that generational disagreements unsettled the Civil Rights Movement, rifts between generations regarding the best path forward caused NAFAD to lose some of its prominence. Some voices within the organization called for more direct action to protest Black designers' exclusion from the industry, suggesting staging demonstrations and protests that would receive media attention and draw publicity to NAFAD's demands. The purpose of such demonstrations was less about bringing change (which NAFAD board was skeptical about), but more to expose the industry's racism and to force prominent figures in the industry to own their positions and try to defend them. However, the majority preferred a more diplomatic approach, trying to deal with manufacturers and retailers behind the scenes in order to get Black designers a foot in the door. Instead on insisting to use an official NAFAD label, or to showcase fashions under the NAFAD brand, the organization put an emphasis on selling designs and patterns for everyday wear, not on name recognition, believing that might be a better way to integrate the industry.[43]

Moreover, the relative conservatism of NAFAD's leadership, especially with regard to style and appearance, limited their influence among a younger generation of designers who were more invested in exploring their African heritage and in celebrating Black Power. As a photograph of the San Francisco

**Figure 7.4** San Francisco Junior Chapter NAFAD. Courtesy of National Association of Fashion and Accessory Designers (NAFAD) Inc. Records, National Archives for Black Women's History, National Park Service Museum Resource Center.

Junior Chapter shows, many of the young members adopted the afro and soul styles of the 1970s, sporting overalls and jumpsuits.

Yet, it was only in 1973 that a model with an afro appeared on the runway in a NAFAD show.[44] Despite the recognition that NAFAD would need "to meet the challenges in present society" in order to maintain relevance, leadership kept insisting on the need to maintain professional standards that not always kept with young members' views and tastes.[45] NAFAD leadership were determined to change the profession *as* professionals, but as the 1970s progressed it was more difficult to convince young designers in the necessity of the organization.

Although NAFAD lost much of its power by the mid 1970s, and today the organization is almost forgotten, this is certainly not due for the lack of their efforts. For at least two decades, NAFAD provided a model of Black resilience, and an example of how Black women can find creative ways to work around white discrimination and marginalization without relying on separatism and exclusion. In many ways, NAFAD never managed to break the color barriers of the industry, and its power remained largely at the periphery within the local communities where it was active. Yet, the organization's actions and initiatives did pave a way for a generation of Black designers who found jobs and a voice within the fashion world. In an industry that often ignored Black people, both as producers and as consumers of fashion, NAFAD designers managed to carve themselves a niche from which they could make a difference.

# Notes

1 Jonathan Michael Square, "Slavery's Wrap, Liberty's Weft: A Look at the Work of Eighteenth- and Nineteenth-Century Enslaved Fashion Makers and Their Legacies," in *Black Designers in American Fashion*, ed. Elizabeth Way (London: Bloomsbury, 2018), 29–46.
2 "Speech," 1951, folder 37, box 7, series 5, National Association of Fashion and Accessory Designers Inc. Records, National Archives for Black Women's History, National Park Service Museum Resource Center (NAFAD hereafter).
3 "Constitution of National Association of Fashion and Accessory Designers, Inc.," folder 15, box 7, series 5, NAFAD.
4 "Do You Design Clothes? Here's a New Outlet," *Baltimore Afro-American*, April 2, 1949: B11.
5 Rebecca Arnold, *The American Look: Fashion, Sportswear, and the Image of Women in 1930s and 1940s New York* (New York: I. B. Tauris, 2008), 75–6; Sandra Stansbery Buckland, "Promoting American Designers, 1940–1944: Building Our Own House," in *Twentieth-Century American Fashion*, eds. Linda Welters and Patricia A. Cunningham (Oxford: Berg, 2005), 112–13.
6 Sheryl Leipzig, Jean Parsons, and Jane Farrell-Beck, "It is a Profession that is New Unlimited and Rich: Promotion of the American Designer in the 1930s," *Dress* 35, no. 1 (2008): 38–9; Marie Clifford, "Working with Fashion: The Role of Art, Taste, and Consumerism in Women's Professional Culture 1920–1940," *American Studies* 44, no. 1/2 (Spring/Summer 2003): 80.
7 Joy Davis, "Ruby Bailey: Making for Oneself, A Regional Fashion Designer Case Study," in *Black Designers in American Fashion*, ed. Elizabeth Way (London: Bloomsbury, 2021), 97.
8 The first Great Migration refers to the period between 1916 and 1930 when over one million African Americans, many of them young women, left the rural South to settle in urban centers, mainly in the Northeast and the Midwest. These migrants sought better lives and to improve their economic status, as well as to escape the violence of Jim Crow. With the mobilization to the Second World War, another wave of migration occurred, this time mostly to Western States where much of the military jobs were concentrated. On Black experience during the first Great Migration, see Davarian L. Baldwin, *Chicago's New Negroes: Modernity, the Great Migration and Black Urban Life* (Chapel Hill, NC: University of North Carolina Press, 2007); Carol Marks, *Farewell—We're Good and Gone: The Great Black*

*Migration* (Bloomington, IN: Indiana University Press, 1989); Daniel Johnson, *Black Migration in America: A Social Demographic History* (Durham, NC: Duke University Press, 1981); Ann Douglas, *Terrible Honesty: Mongrel Manhattan in the 1920s* (New York: Noonday Press, 1995).
9 For further discussion about the economic possibilities cosmetics that enabled African American women see: Tiffany Melissa Gill, *Beauty Shop Politics: African American Women's Activism in the Beauty Industry* (Urbana, IL: University of Illinois Press, 2010).
10 Tera W. Hunter, *To 'Joy My Freedom: Southern Black Women's Lives and Labors after the Civil War* (Cambridge, MA: Harvard University Press, 1997), 111–12; Victoria Wolcott, *Remaking Respectability: African American Women in Interwar Detroit* (Chapel Hill, NC: University of North Carolina Press, 2000), 28; Patricia Edmonson, "Lifting as We Sew: Amanda Wicker and The Clarke School of Dressmaking," unpublished paper in the author's possession.
11 Nancy Deihl, "Zelda Wynn Valdes: Uptown Modiste," in *The Hidden History of American Fashion: Rediscovering Twentieth-Century Women Designer*, ed. Nancy Deihl (London: Bloomsbury, 2018), 224–5.
12 Davis, 'Ruby Bailey,' 94–7.
13 "Clarke School of Dressmaking and Fashion Design First Fall Fashion Carnival," October 21, 1951, box 1, folder 1, Clarke School of Dressmaking and Fashion Design Records, 1941–83, MS 4490, Western Reserve Historical Society, Cleveland OH.
14 Rosemary E. Reed Miller, *Threads of Time, the Fabric of History: Profiles of African American Dressmakers and Designers, 1850 to the Present* (Washington, DC: Toast and Strawberries Press, 2002), 34–7.
15 Davis, "Ruby Bailey," 97.
16 "Jubilee Fashion Show Accepts Negro Girl," *New York Amsterdam News*, August 21, 1948: 1, 23.
17 Rebecca Tuuri, *Strategic Sisterhood: The Council of Negro Women in the Black Freedom Struggle* (Chapel Hill, NC: University of North Carolina Press, 2018), 2–3, 20.
18 Membership Lists 1951–58, folder 45, box 7, series 5, NAFAD.
19 Letter from Jeanetta Welch Brown, March 17, 1949, Series 2, Box 2, Folder 1, NAFAD.
20 Tuuri, *Strategic Sisterhood*, 25.
21 Board of Directors Meeting, July 10–15, 1962, folder 11, box 6, series 4, NAFAD.
22 Sara Turner, "Statement of Purpose," 1950, folder 4, box 1, series 1, NAFAD.
23 Letter from Jeanetta Welch Brown, March 17, 1949, Series 2, Box 2, Folder 1, NAFAD papers; Letter to Mary Lou, Margaret, Barbara and Willi, March 5, 1957, folder 14, box 1, series 1, NAFAD.
24 "NAFAD Handbook" folder 11, box 8, series 6, NAFAD; Mary McLeod Bethune to Miss Mattie Bailey, February 21, 1949, folder 2, box 1, series 1.
25 Turner, "Statement of Purpose."

26 "Designers Set to Study Plans for New York Office," *Baltimore Afro-American,* April 28, 1951: 11.
27 Although the Fashion Group did not have a formal policy to exclude Blacks, the nature of its membership, which was based on personal endorsements, and the segregated nature of the fashion industry and media, led to their de-facto absence. Only in 1955, twenty-five years after the founding of the Fashion Group, the first African American member, Mrs. Artie Bell from Washington, DC, was admitted to the organization. Annual Report 1955–6, folder 2, box 6, series 5, NAFAD.
28 Mary McLeod Bethune to Mrs. Kay Linden, December 15, 1948, folder 1, box 1, series 1, NAFAD; Jeannetta W. Brown to Mrs. Ethel Kreemer, May 20, 1950, folder 4, box 1, series 1, NAFAD.
29 Letter from Freddye Henderson to Lois Alexander, May 25, 1953, folder 11, box 1, series 1, NAFAD; "8th Annual Convention Plan," June 20–3, 1957, folder 9, box 2, series 2, NAFAD; Minutes of the Convention, July 15, 1964, folder 17, box 3, series 2.
30 "NAFAD's First Ten Years," Convention Program, folder 11, box 2, series 2, NAFAD.
31 "Junior NAFAD Handbook," n.d. NAFAD Scrapbook 1948–75, Box 10, NAFAD.
32 "Congressional Record, March 18, 1974," folder 2, box 1, Clarke School of Dressmaking and Fashion Design Records, 1927–79, MS 4605, Western Reserve Historical Society, Cleveland, OH.
33 "NAFAD Make Inroads in Fashion Industry," *Fashion Cue*, June 1953, 4, folder 8, box 8, series 6, NAFAD.
34 "600 View '57 Clothes of Cleveland Designers," *Cleveland Call & Post*, March 23, 1957; "Cleveland's NAFADs to Show Spring Summer Collections," *Cleveland Call & Post*, March 1, 1958, 3B; "Designers Talk Shop," *Colored Magazine*, July 1951, all in NAFAD Scrapbook, box 10, NAFAD.
35 "Unusual Color Combinations," *Women's Wear Daily,* April 16, 1951, 3; "Negro Designers Display Fashions," *New York Times*, April 16, 1951: 34.
36 Freddye Henderson, "Bulletin #2," folder 20, box 2, series 1, NAFAD.
37 Letter to Jeanetta Welch Brown, n.d., folder 3, box 1, series 1 NAFAD.
38 "Meeting the Challenge," n.d., folder 8, box 1, series 1 NAFAD.
39 Marion B. Campfield, "Designers Bid for Nod from Fashion Industry," *Chicago Defender*, April 28, 1951, 12; "NAFAD Stage First Designers Show Friday," *Cleveland Call & Post*, February 16, 1952, 1C.
40 "NAFAD 'The Queen Reigns Program' 1953," in NAFAD Scrapbook, box 10, NAFAD; "NAFAD Stage First Designers Show Friday."
41 Edmonson, "Lifting as We Sew."
42 Board Meeting National Convention 1963 Minutes, folder 15, box 3, series 2, NAFAD.
43 NAFAD Planning Meeting Minutes, October 10, 1969, folder 23, box 6, series 4, NAFAD.
44 "'To Build a Better You,' 24th Annual Convention book," 1973, folder 26, box 3, series 2, NAFAD.

45 "A Search for Relevance," NAFAD Newsletter, May 1968, folder 15, box 8, series 6, NAFAD.

# Bibliography

Arnold, Rebecca. *The American Look: Fashion, Sportswear, and the Image of Women in 1930s and 1940s New York*. New York: I. B. Tauris, 2008.

Clarke School of Dressmaking and Fashion Design Records, Series I & II, Western Reserve Historical Society, Cleveland, OH.

Clifford, Marie. "Working with Fashion: The Role of Art, Taste, and Consumerism in Women's Professional Culture 1920–1940." *American Studies* 44, no. 1/2 (Spring/Summer 2003): 59–84.

Davis, Joy. "Ruby Bailey: Making for Oneself, A Regional Fashion Designer Case Study." In *Black Designers in American Fashion*, edited by Elizabeth Way, 91–107. London: Bloomsbury, 2021.

Deihl, Nancy. "Zelda Wynn Valdes: Uptown Modiste." In *The Hidden History of American Fashion: Rediscovering Twentieth-Century Women Designers*, edited by Nancy Deihl, 223–36. London: Bloomsbury, 2018.

Gill, Tiffany Melissa. *Beauty Shop Politics: African American Women's Activism in the Beauty Industry*. Urbana, IL: University of Illinois Press, 2010.

Hunter, Tera W. *To 'Joy My Freedom: Southern Black Women's Lives and Labors After the Civil War*. Cambridge, MA: Harvard University Press, 1997.

Leipzig, Sheryl et al. "It is a Profession that is New Unlimited and Rich: Promotion of the American Designer in the 1930s." *Dress* 35, no. 1 (2008): 29–47.

National Association of Fashion and Accessory Designers (NAFAD) Inc. Records, National Archives for Black Women's History, National Park Service Museum Resource Center.

Reed Miller, Rosemary E. *Threads of Time, the Fabric of History: Profiles of African American Dressmakers and Designers. 1850 to the Present*. Washington, DC: Toast and Strawberries Press, 2002.

Square, Jonathan Michael. "Slavery's Wrap, Liberty's Weft: A Look at the Work of Eighteenth- and Nineteenth-Century Enslaved Fashion Makers and Their Legacies." In *Black Designers in American Fashion*, edited by Elizabeth Way, 29–46. London: Bloomsbury, 2018.

Stansbery Buckland, Sandra. "Promoting American Designers, 1940–1944: Building Our Own House." In *Twentieth-Century American Fashion*, edited by Linda Welters and Patricia A. Cunningham, 99–12. Oxford: Berg, 2005.

Tuuri, Rebecca. *Strategic Sisterhood: The Council of Negro Women in the Black Freedom Struggle*. Chapel Hill, NC: University of North Carolina Press, 2018.

Wolcott, Victoria. *Remaking Respectability: African American Women in Interwar Detroit*. Chapel Hill, NC: University of North Carolina Press, 2000.

8

# Primitivizing Accessories

## "Slave Jewelry" and the Construction of White Femininity in 1920s America

### Victoria Rose Pass

In March 1926 legendary fashion columnist Lois Long declared, "the slave bracelet mode...simply refuses to die the death." In her characteristically arch style, Long describes the explosion of the slave collar trend: "Woolworth's has gotten out its own version of the plain gold or silver necklet (thereby making it unnecessary for many young women to morn that the tin rings around Heinz pickle jars are not bigger)."[1] *Vogue* described the staying power of this fashion somewhat differently:

> When the slave bracelet came to being sold for ten cents, along with Christmas tree ornaments, several seasons ago, its fate seemed to be sealed. And yet, it still shines among the precious jewelry at such shops as Cartier and Dreicer and in the semiprecious versions on novelty jewelry counters.[2]

The term "slave jewelry" referred to a range of accessories: simple metal bands worn around the neck as chokers, bangle bracelets often worn in multiples, chain linked bracelets or necklaces, and hoop or chain linked earrings. It reached its peak of popularity in 1926.

Gertrude Lawrence in *Charlot's Review* and Ina Claire in *The Last of Mrs. Cheyney* both wore slave jewelry styles to great acclaim on Broadway stages.[3] *Women's Wear Daily* reported on the success of these styles all across America and the *New York Times* attributed an increased demand for jewelry to the "adoption of the slave bracelet."[4] Slave jewelry was frequently worn by Hollywood celebrities too, such as Colleen Moore in *Motion Pictures Classics*, or Joan Crawford in *Our Dancing Daughters* (1928).

**Figure 8.1** Joel Gutman & Co. advertisement for "Slave Jewelry," *The Evening Sun*, Baltimore, March 4, 1926.

By September, Long was fed up, writing in her *New Yorker* column:

> bracelets are so much in evidence that they are positively junk. There are millions of them in every window—the same old slave bracelet idea, but gone completely mad with cabochon stones of every color. To me they are so much trash, but everybody is buying them.[5]

Long found this style tacky precisely because it was no longer exclusive and dismissed the trend of wearing multiple pieces as generally in bad taste.[6] That certainly didn't deter many women of all classes from participating in the trend.

These chain links and simple band styles of jewelry were not new in the 1920s. Indeed, these styles of jewelry are ancient and present in many different cultures. What *was* new in the 1920s was using the term "slave" to describe this jewelry. The term gave this style of jewelry a meaning in the 1920s that was particularly resonant with the cultural moment—enmeshing it within in the popular rhetorics of Orientalism and Primitivism, lending it sex appeal and connecting

**Figure 8.2** At center, "Colleen Moore all bound round with the 'slave bracelets,' dear to the heart of flappers," in *Motion Picture Classic*, January 1925. Courtesy of the Media History Digital Library.

it to jazz culture. White femininity in the United States was being reconstructed by a generation of women who were newly enfranchised with the vote and were moving into the public sphere in increasingly visible ways. At the same time, Black culture, particularly jazz, was becoming an international phenomenon just as white supremacist violence was surging in the US. White women, while afforded increasing freedom, were still required to adhere to white feminine qualities in order to maintain the status their race accorded.[7] Slave jewelry offered a space of racial and sexual exploration while also maintaining patriarchal and white supremacist values.

By examining the representation of this jewelry in popular fashion magazines, newspapers (including African American newspapers), advertisements, fashion

**Figure 8.3** Joan Crawford in *Our Dancing Daughters*, 1928. © Michael Ochs Archives / Stringer

industry periodicals, and works of fiction we can see how these styles were racialized through the language of slavery, Primitivism, and Orientalism. As Cheryl Buckley and Hazel Clark observe, "an item of clothing may have once been extraordinary or part of an ensemble that was extraordinary, but over time, regular use, or a changed context, it has become ordinary, or routine."[8] Over time, slave jewelry moved from the extraordinary to the everyday for many women. This is significant because it offers an example of how racism can be reinforced through everyday practices of self-fashioning. Slave jewelry was but one small material manifestation of racism in American everyday life. White women's self-expression through this fashion came at the expense of Black people, and particularly Black women. As this chapter argues, looking back to the 1920s and the fashion for "slave jewelry," can offer insight into the ways that racialized language continues to be used in fashion to deploy Blackness as a kind of accessory to whiteness across history, and the damage it does.

## Jazz, primitivism, and exoticism in the 1920s

"Slave bangles" began appearing in the American media in the early twentieth century. At first the term described various styles of metal bands that were worn tight on the upper arm, also called Cleopatra bracelets.[9] Slave jewelry was available at a wide variety of price points, and was made from a huge array of materials, both precious and costume. In the 1920s, chain-linked styles and simple bands were made from precious metals, ivory, tortoise shell, as well as plastics such as celluloid and galalith.[10] The popularity of slave jewelry styles cut across lines of both class and race. In 1926 at high-end department store Bonwit Teller a "slave-link bracelet with semiprecious carnelian, chalcedony, chrysoprase or onyx rings and cushion cabochons," cost $85 and a simpler "slave-link bracelet of French brilliants combined with links set in semi-precious onyx of chrysoprase, or synthetic emeralds of sapphires," was $45.[11] For $2.50 in 1924, a *Women's Home Companion* reader could order a "slave link bracelet of green and white gold plate."[12] The Namm Store in Brooklyn offered gold plated slave-link bracelets for 47¢ while Wanamaker's offered them for $2 with matching necklets for $3.50.[13] They were $12.50 at Saks Fifth Avenue and 29¢ at Kann's in Washington, DC.[14]

"Slave jewelry" appears in an ad for gifts under $5 in the African American paper the *New York Amsterdam News*.[15] In 1927, Elsievans, a fashion columnist for the African American newspaper the *Chicago Defender,* cautioned readers against wearing inappropriate accessories, including slave bracelets with broken links. She suggested it was better to go without than ruin an ensemble with a damaged piece of jewelry.[16] A year later, a society story in the paper reported that slave bracelets were presented as keepsakes to members of Entre Nous, a club of African American high school sub-debs from Flushing, New York.[17]

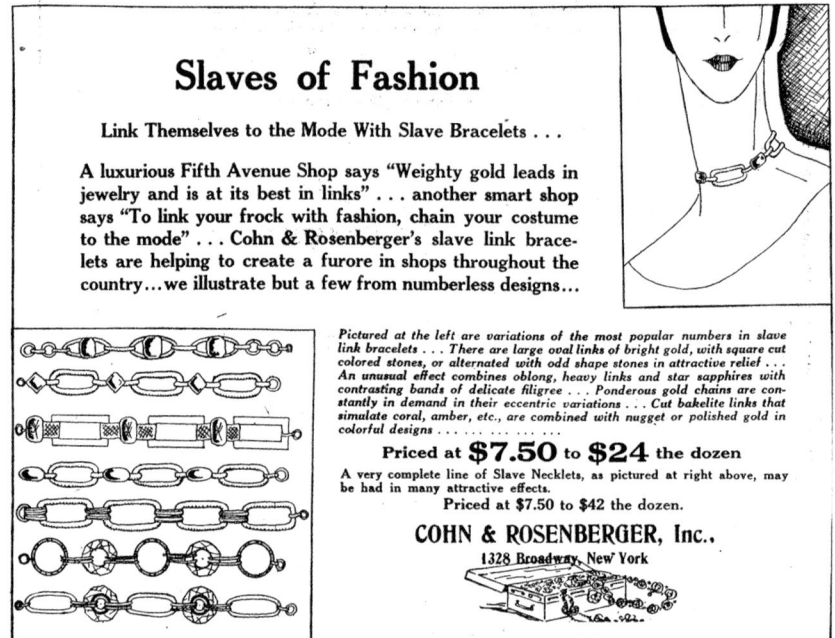

**Figure 8.4** Cohn & Rosenberger, Inc. Advertisement for "Slave Bracelets," *Women's Wear Daily*, April 1, 1926.

As ubiquitous as they were, however, the origin of this style remains unclear. Some early accounts note slave bracelets being worn by society women in London, and others mention Paris.[18] Some papers connected the trend to the broader interest in Egyptian styles in the period sparked by the 1922 discovery of King Tutankhamun's' tomb. In December 1927 an associated press article ran comparing the modern flapper who "decorated her wrist with a slave bracelet, pencils her eyebrows and rouges her cheeks" to the "well-dressed woman of ancient Egypt 5,000 years ago."[19]

While there was certainly a connection to Egyptomania, in order to untangle the significance of term "slave" as it was applied to this style of jewelry, it is essential to understand the increasing prominence of Black culture, particularly jazz, among white audiences in the 1920s. In her book *Negrophilia: Avant-Garde Paris and Black Culture in the 1920s*, Petrine Archer-Straw documents the fascination with Black culture that defined the Parisian avant-garde. She shows how the racist theories of the nineteenth century that defined ideas about "primitive" and "civilized" or "modern" were precisely what made Black culture appealing. Of the very loaded term "primitive," she explains, "the Parisian avant-garde exploited the word's more negative readings—its links with Blackness, savagery and deviance—because it suited their need to outrage."[20] Archer-Straw's intervention is to insist that we look not at "Primitivism" in the culture of the years between the wars—and indeed the ways that it persists in our own time—but rather at the ways that whites "primitivized" other cultures.[21] To primitivize a culture—and in this case the styles, garments, dances, and music that have been associated with it by the dominant culture—means positioning it as innocent, naive, and pure in contrast to modern Western culture.[22] Negrophiles, according to Archer-Straw, were searching for an alternative to a society that they viewed as hollow. Western civilization's obsession with rationalism and science had led to the horrifying mechanization of killing in the First World War.[23] The way avant-garde artists like Picasso and Matisse engaged with African aesthetics and Primitivism filtered down to high end design and fashion, and ultimately to the mass market in a style that has been called Black deco or Jazz Moderne.[24] This second name highlights the important connections being made by creatives in the period between jazz and Africa.

Two other terms, exoticism and Orientalism, also frequently come into play in the fashion and popular culture of the early twentieth century. Exoticism is a more generic means of othering a culture through a fascination and curiosity about it. Exotic was a term used to suggest, "an exciting, sensual and decorative vision that carried the dynamics of nineteenth century colonialism into a global future."[25] At its root, this is a term that is used to position non-Western and non-white cultures as other, and relies on racist stereotypes that view those cultures as more sexual, earthy, and primitive. Orientalism is also deeply rooted in fashion culture and, as Susan Hannel has pointed out, is often linked to Jazz culture.[26] In his 1979 book, *Orientalism*, Edward Said dissects the importance of the Orient to the way that the Occident (the West) defines itself. Going back to antiquity, Europe has imagined the Orient as "a place of romance, exotic beings, haunting memories and landscapes, remarkable experiences."[27] Said considers Orientalism a discourse, explaining that "Orientalism can be discussed and analyzed as the corporate institution for dealing with the Orient…in short, Orientalism [is] a Western style for dominating, restructuring, and having authority over the Orient."[28] In visual culture, Westerners have represented the Orient as a barbarous, decadent, sensual, and decaying, supporting the argument for the benevolence of imperial rule.[29] Orientalism is an important framework for understanding slave jewelry since Orientalist fantasies so frequently involve slave markets and harems, which were often depicted as a kind of sexual slavery.[30] This was precisely the kind of imagery famously evoked by

**Figure 8.5** Georges Lepape, Denise Poiret at 'The Thousand and Second Night' party, 1911. Gouache on paper. ©Universal Images Group via Getty Images.

French fashion designer Paul Poiret in his theatrical "Thousand and Second Night Party" in 1911 used to promote his new collection which included harem trousers. In George Lepape's iconic portrait of Denise Poiret she wears three bracelets and three anklets in what would later be called the slave jewelry style.[31]

Minh Ha T. Pham has shown how Poiret used the rhetoric of Orientalism to mitigate men's anxiety about white women's growing political and social power in the early twentieth century, which was represented by trousers, an exceptionally controversial garment for women. Instead of appropriating the trousers of white men, and thus emasculating them, Poiret's customers stole their trousers from Oriental men thus leaving the power of white men intact.[32]

## Sexuality and embodied primitivism

While the colonial context of Europe and the apartheid policies of the United States in the era of Jim Crow were certainly different, Primitivism, Exoticism, and Orientalism were as much a part of American popular culture, and especially fashion, as in Europe. Jim Crow laws and the racist violence that enforced them were designed to maintain white supremacy and also to guard against miscegenation, or the mixing of races through sex and marriage. In spite of this context, and in fact because of it, many white Americans were deeply engaged in the vogue for primitivizing Black people and Black culture. Indeed, for white audiences, engaging with taboo Black culture was part of its appeal.[33]

African American musician and doctor Rudolf Fisher observed this new white obsession with Blackness in 1919 when he returned to Harlem from Washington, DC, describing how he found himself the only Black patron in clubs now catering to white audiences: "some think it's just a fad. White people have always more or less sought Negro entertainment as diversion," but he argued the cabaret was a different kind of space than a theater since it was participatory, "when they bodily throw themselves into Negro entertainment."[34] This was a significant insight. As the Charleston took the country by storm a moral panic about this and other popular jazz dances followed closely behind.[35] Part of the panic was certainly the open displays of sexuality that were part of these dances but also the prospect of Black men and white women dancing together—though that was generally impossible in the segregated night clubs of the period.

In 1930, Mary Roberts Rinehart looked back on the heyday of jazz dancing with disdain. Writing for *Ladies' Home Journal*, she described, "the vogue of eccentric dancing, mainly borrowed from the Negros on the Southern levees, to music borrowed from the savages of the African jungles," and expresses horror that this takes place in the public space of the night club. Rinehart described "short and angular garments," which demanded different jewelry, "heavy, ungraceful, so-called slave bracelets; exaggerated earrings; cigarette holders a foot long. And with them the vogue for strong primitive colors, often in hideous barbaric conjunction."[36] Rinehart explicitly connected slave jewelry to other "African" styles and used language which primitivizes them. While she never makes the threat of miscegenation explicit in her text, it is the subtext as she laments fashions that invite sex: "a girl who is partially unclothed, who is innocently or knowingly forcing her attractions on him becomes a question to be answered. He makes advances he would otherwise not dream of."[37] The bodily engagement with jazz culture was threatening because it was sexualized. That sexuality is rooted in racist ideas about the hyper-sexuality of Black people, fears of miscegenation, and ultimately the fear of diluting or losing all together white cultural supremacy.

## Jazz, the plantation, and Africa

Rinehart also freely conflated Africa and African Americans revealing how whites understood and consumed Black culture in a way that was rooted in the legacies of slavery. The term slavery was often used in a broad way in relation to this slave jewelry, as in a 1926 Brock and Company ad describing necklaces "worn about the throat like a slave collar of long ago."[38] Looking at images surrounding jazz makes it clear that on some level the slavery referenced was the European and American chattel slavery system. Romanticized images of the Antebellum South were often used as décor for jazz clubs in Harlem catering to white patrons in the 1920s.[39] Slave bracelets were a way for whites outside of New York to engage this Harlem jazz culture, combining references to Africa and to the enslavement of Africans in the United States.

Descriptions of slave jewelry also used primitivizing language to connect these accessories with Africa. In 1920, Dorothy Dignam declared:

> shades of the slave market, brown bodies and leopard skin! Here's a barbaric mandate that decrees bangle bracelets and hoops around the neck for every slave of fashion. Anklets that jangle to the floor and earrings that dangle to the shoulders will further mark our servitude to style…The "slave bangle" comes from Livingston's Africa but stopped over in Paris long enough to receive the blessing of her sanction.[40]

In 1928 the *Washington Post* made similar connections to Africa: "slave bracelets and ring necklaces, both inspired by primitive African costumes—or lack of costumes," and "a bangle that is a copy of a jungle native's bracelet of teeth."[41] Writing for the *Post* in 1931, Elizabeth Harvey declared: "Seven is the lucky number of bracelets to wear when your accessories go native."[42] The article also describes a trend for "Algerian" and "bright barbaric" jewelry.[43] The primitivizing language and the use of stereotypical images of the imagined African jungle used across these articles, as well as the citation of specific places in Africa as the origin for this jewelry, ultimately gave it value for the consumer. Many explicitly compared flappers and their jewelry to African women. A 1925 *New York Times* article, "Flappers of Africa are much like Our Own," included an illustration of "African flappers," wearing stacks of bangle bracelets and hoop earrings.[44] The following year, *The New York Amsterdam News*, an African American paper, reported "in the matter of beads, necklaces and bangles, too, our women seem to have taken a leaf out of the Matabele book."[45]

This jewelry was not only connected to African styles, but it was also framed through allusions to Orientalism. For instance, *The Allen Monthly*, a trade journal published by Benjamin Allen & Co. in Chicago, heavily promoted slave jewelry for Easter 1924 touting, "the new Slave bracelets, made of links, for links have always bound slaves; and local sheiks could find themselves irresistibly drawn to a bracelet that binds a fair one's wrist in slavery."[46] The writer uses sheiks to refer to the "jazz sheik," a white man who played or danced to jazz, the companion to the flapper. The term came from the 1921 film *The Sheik* whose plot hinged on this fantasy of sexual slavery. Slave jewelry is one example of the many ways that Orientalism informed jazz fashion and culture: "the style for slave collars was [easily] transferred between Oriental and African-inspired fashion."[47] The rhetorics of Orientalism and of Primitivism freely overlap in the description of these accessories. Rudolf Valentino, the original Sheik, infamously wore a slave bracelet. His second wife Natacha Rambova designed and gave him the platinum chain link bracelet in 1924. A copy of it was available to fans through the "Hollywood Shopping Service" in 1928.[48]

## The contingent meanings of slave jewelry

Slave jewelry offered a space of racial and sexual fantasy for white women—as did Rudolph Valentino's Sheik, a European man who was passes as Arab—while allowing them to uphold standards of respectable white femininity. Such fantasies are an integral part of white supremacy as bell hooks explains in her essay "Eating the Other,"

> certainly from the standpoint of white supremacist capitalist patriarchy, the hope is that desires for the "primitive" or fantasies about the Other can be continually exploited, and that such exploitation will occur in a manner that reinscribes and maintains the status quo.[49]

By making the other into an item that can be put on and taken off, like a slave bracelet, a white woman can play with that sexuality and otherness temporarily, without threatening her supposed white racial purity. Slave jewelry allowed white women to incorporate references to Africa into their fashion, connecting themselves to the excitement and modernity of jazz culture. The jewelry was also part of creating sexuality, relying on Orientalist fantasies and a racist hypersexualization of Africans and African Americans. It also depended upon an abstracted and romanticized vision of almost four centuries of chattel slavery which had only ended about sixty years earlier in the US in 1863. Couching this slavery as that of an "oriental" harem was a "displacement tactic" to avoid the more radical threat of miscegenation between Black and white people that some believed jazz was causing. Here, I'm borrowing the term displacement from psychology where it describes the ways that an individual might "displace" a negative emotion such as anger onto a safer target, rather than the actual person who caused the anger, as a defense mechanism. In this instance, the threat miscegenation is tempered by displacing slavery from the realities of the American plantation to the fantasy of the Orientalist harem. As Susan B. Kaiser and Sarah Rebolloso McCullough have argued, meaning and signification in fashion, particularly around race, is a knot rather than a straight line.[50] The origin stories that are devised for certain styles and garments are a kind of mythology that functions to fix identity and often to confirm certain pre-existing biases.[51] In the case of slave jewelry these vague and contingent references to slavery, which were sometimes about a romanticized Antebellum South and at other times about an imagined Orient, worked to make slavery into a fantasy about sexual availability rather than a horrific historical reality.

Much of the appeal of this jewelry for white women was in marking the distance between themselves and an imagined primitive and enslaved Black person. An opinion column in the *New York Times* commented on the difficulty of squaring modern fashions and "the picture of the women emancipated." The author notes that in terms of the symbolism of women's dress

> the short skirt and bobbed hair are common sense, freedom, equality. But the powder puff and the lipstick smack of the seraglio. Women confront life more frankly and more courageously than their grandmothers and mothers did, but they do it in silk stockings and high heels...A regular feature of evolution is the 'throw-back.' But perhaps the slave bracelet has its symbolic meaning today. The wearer can throw it off whenever she feels like it.[52]

Here, the author uses an Orientalist reference to the seraglio (women's quarters in an Ottoman or Turkish palace) to underline the symbolic weight of white American women's ability to remove the slave bracelet themselves. Within this context, the bracelet demonstrates white women's mobility as well as their agency. This idea is affirmed in a 1927 essay in which beauty editor Hazel Rawson Cades wrote, "no matter how you look at them [slave bracelets] seem to bring us to the conclusion that woman has reached a position in society where she can dare to effect shackles because she knows they really don't mean a thing."[53] White women had reached this position, but at the expense of Black men and especially women. Indeed, white women were donning accessories that, on the one hand, displayed their embrace of jazz culture, but whose rhetorical framing functioned to bolster the racist ideologies that upheld Jim Crow segregation and racial violence.

## Black women and slave jewelry

While mentions of this jewelry in African American newspapers show that for some Black women these slave bracelets were a way of participating in modern fashion trends and jazz culture, for others their racialization was troubling. In her 1928 semi-autobiographical novel *Quicksand*, Nella Larsen's protagonist Helga Crane talks about wearing such jewelry with discomfort. The novel follows American-born Helga, the daughter of a white Danish mother and African American father, as she struggles to find her place in the world. She flees a repressive teaching job at a school called Naxos in the rural south where respectability is paramount for the promise of cosmopolitan urban life in Harlem, only to feel stifled by the community's obsession with the "race problem." She escapes from Harlem to the home of her relatives in Copenhagen. There she becomes the kind of ethnic commodity that bell hooks writes about in her essay "Eating the Other: Desire and Resistance."[54]

In America, Helga expressed her love of color only in her night clothes (such as a Chinese red dressing gown), or in the objects she used to furnish her rooms (bright nasturtiums, oriental silk, and Chinese-looking pillows), because she had been taught not to stand out.[55] At Naxos the dean of women explained, "'bright colors are vulgar,'" she said "'Black, gray, brown, and navy blue are the most becoming colors for colored people'—'Dark-complected people shouldn't wear yellow, or green or red.'"[56] When Helga arrives in Copenhagen on the other hand, her aunt teases her for her somber wardrobe:

> "Haven't you something lively, something bright?" And, noting Helga's puzzled glance at her own subdued costume, she explained laughingly: "Oh, I'm an old married lady, and a Dane. But you, you're young. And you're a foreigner, and

different. You must have bright things to set off the color of your lovely brown skin. Striking things, exotic things. You must make an impression."[57]

Fru Dahl insists Helga wear more revealing dresses and brighter colors than she would have back in Harlem.[58] Helga understands that she is being shown off by the Dahls and her image is being carefully managed:

> Helga began to wonder. She was dubious, too, and not a little resentful. Certainly she loved color with a passion that perhaps only Negros and Gypsies know. But she had a deep faith in the perfection of her own taste, and no mind to be bedecked in flaunting flashy things.[59]

She describes feeling, "like a veritable savage" on the way to tea, as pedestrians stared at her and whispered.[60] When she dresses for dinner in a reworked gown, now incredibly revealing, she "was thankful for the barbaric bracelets, for the dangling ear-rings, for the beads about her neck," bought for her by her aunt and uncle.[61] Helga is uneasy with the way that her Danish family primitivizes and sexualizes her to show off to their friends, though she also relishes the attention from the men she meets "she was attractive, unusual, in an exotic, almost savage way, but she wasn't one of them. She didn't at all count."[62] Helga is fashioned as an ethnic spectacle by her aunt and uncle. Her new wardrobe of "barbaric bracelets," and bright and revealing dresses confirmed the expectations of her Danish hosts about her exoticism and sexuality. At first Helga enjoys freedom from the violence of American racism, but eventually it becomes clear that in Copenhagen she is obligated to enact a different kind of Blackness through dress, no more liberated than the dull respectable fashions she begrudgingly wears at Naxos. She eventually returns to New York.

Nella Larsen's writing can help us to begin to understand the ways that the commodification of Blackness in fashion had a real effect of Black women. This is a story that remains undocumented in most of the archives we traditionally rely on in fashion, magazines, newspapers, films, and photographs. Helga's struggle to live as fully herself, is made impossible by the intersection of racism and sexism. For white women slave jewelry offered the freedom of temporarily adding an element of sound, spectacle, sexiness, exoticism, and modernity to an ensemble. Helga would always be seen by others through a racist lens. Helga did not have a choice of whether to explore her sexuality through fashion, because it would always be projected onto her. She couldn't freely explore the bright colors and rich textures of fabrics she loved because of the ways that they had been primitivized in fashion culture. When she wore them in Copenhagen they served to confirm ideas that the white people around her already had about her exoticism. Helga would be seen through the lens of racism no matter what she wore, whether that was as an exotic but othered spectacle in Copenhagen, or as a second-class citizen in New York.

## Conclusion

Helga's experience in Copenhagen shows how slave jewelry was never quite totally ordinary. While it might have become an everyday presence in the fashion landscape, its racialized meaning was a part of a broader culture which both celebrated and denigrated Blackness. It made Blackness into a consumable spectacle. We can see a striking parallel to slave jewelry in the ways that white performers repackaged hip-hop culture for white audiences at the turn of the last century. Scholar and cultural critic Lauren Michele Jackson argues that some white female pop stars "declar[ed] bodily autonomy by way of hip-hop" in the early 2000s.[63] Jackson focuses on Christina Aguilera's 2002 album *Stripped* and uses the video for "Can't Hold Us Down" as a prime example of the ways Aguilera uses hip-hop styles to move away from the highly controlled image that Disney produced of her as a teen. Jewelry is a key part of how Aguilera constructs this

**Figure 8.6** Christina Aguilera, featuring Lil' Kim, "Can't Hold Us Down," directed by David LaChappelle. © RCA Records 2003. All rights reserved.

new sexier more grown up image; she wears two bangle bracelets , two pairs of large hoop earrings, multiple necklaces, including a nameplate, a charm bracelet and multiple rings all in gold.[64]

At the time, this jewelry was often referred to as "ghetto gold," and is worn by the other women in the video, who are mostly Black and Latina, including her collaborator Lil' Kim.[65] Tanisha Ford explains how as hip-hop became more visible across America through television and music videos, the stylistic innovations of Black and Latinx women and girls in the 1980s and 1990s became visible to a broader and whiter audience.[66] This connected nameplates, door knocker earrings and gold chains with hip-hop culture and particularly the hyper-visible aesthetic of "ghetto fabulousness."[67]

Much like slave jewelry, it was the popularity of African American music which circulated these styles. Also, as with slave jewelry, sexuality was at the heart of the appeal of these styles for white women. Jackson explains "Christina's entry into hip-hop music, collabs with rap artists, and approximated hood style coincides with her transition from sexually suggestive to sexually explicit."[68] The signification of this jewelry for a white woman relied on the same primitivizing stereotypes of hypersexual Black women that slave jewelry did eighty years earlier. As with white women wearing slave jewelry, pop stars like Aguilera as well as her white fans, "can experiment, get dirty, shock the public, seize their womanhood and then, after the fun is over, walk away like it never happened." Both slave jewelry and "ghetto gold" are accessories that allowed white women to experiment with expressing their sexuality and bodily autonomy, but ultimately at the expense of Black women.

By understanding the history of slave jewelry, we can also understand the persistence of primitivizing fashions and the ways that fashion can act to maintain white supremacy and patriarchal values even as it seems to offer something modern and novel. In the 1920s, when the international influence of African American culture was in the ascendant, as was the social and political power of women, slave jewelry offered a space of play with sexuality for white women that didn't have a permanent effect. White wearers could remove their stacks of jangling bracelets and swinging necklaces and reclaim the social power of white femininity. They could decouple themselves from the edgy world of jazz music and dancing by simply changing their clothes, in the same way that Aguilera could simply change her style and thus create a new image for herself on her next album. For Black women like Helga Crane however, the jewelry simply made visible the ways that whites primitivized and sexualized her. Tanisha Ford expressed a similar frustration with the more recent appropriations of hip-hop fashion:

I hated this dynamic that the institutional culture seemed to support: black culture was better on white women. And I hated even more the feeling it conjured in me, that sense of self-doubt, the feeling that white girls were better than me, the belief that black was inferior. Those feelings had taken root in my mind so early in life, and I had worked so hard over the years to shake them.[69]

Fashion is not only a powerful tool in the construction of self-identity, but also in transmitting the ideology of white supremacy in the everyday

# Notes

1 Lois Long, "On and Off the Avenue," *The New Yorker*, March 6, 1926: 41.
2 "Seen in the Shops," *Vogue*, March 1, 1926:, 86.
3 Ibid., 86. Lois Long, "On and Off the Avenue," *The New Yorker*, January 30, 1929: 34.
4 "The Buisness World," *New York Times*, September 22, 1926. "New Versions of Charlot Necklet Emphasized in Manufacturer's Group," *Women's Wear Daily*, February 4, 1926: 51. "'Charlot' Bag Matches Necklet in Treatment of Gilt Metal Handle," *Women's Wear Daily*, March 20, 1929: 22. "Charlot Necklet Meets Instant Success on Coast," *Women's Wear Daily*, March 18, 1926: 25. "Gold Jewelry and Types to Match New Costumes Sell in Portland Ore," *Women's Wear Daily*, April 1, 1926: 38. "Chicago Firm Reports Activity in Choker and Slave Bracelet," *Women's Wear Daily*, August 26, 1926: 41.
5 Lois Long, "On and Off the Avenue," *The New Yorker*, September 4, 1926: 32–3.
6 Lois Long, "On and Off the Avenue," *The New Yorker*, January 30, 1926: 34.
7 One example of this is the maintenance of slimness in this period, see Sabrina Strings, *Fearing the Black Body: The Racial Origins of Fat Phobia* (New York: New York University, 2019), 189–99.
8 Cheryl Buckley and Hazel Clark, *Fashion and Everyday Life: London and New York* (New York: Bloomsbury, 2017), 7.
9 "Women Admire 'Slave Bangle'," *Buffalo Courier*, December 30, 1906: 39.
10 "Fashion Fancies for Film Fans," *Photoplay*, March 1926: 52. Buffalo Jewelry Manufacturing Company ad, *The Jewelers' Circular*, May 7, 1924: 142. "The Slave Bracelet—The Big Seller," *The Allen Monthly*, April 1924: 1. "A Word About the Jewelry Exhibit at the Leipzig Fair," *The Jewelers' Circular*, May 7, 1924: 65.
11 Bonwit Teller & Co. ad., *Vanity Fair*, November 1926: 7.
12 "For Tree and Stocking," *Women's Home Companion*, December 1924: 102.
13 The Namm Store ad., *The Brooklyn Daily Times*, September 30, 1926: 8. Wanamaker's ad., *The Philadelphia Inquirer*, March 16, 1926: 13.
14 Saks-Fifth Avenue ad., *New York Times*, November 19, 1925. Kann's ad., *Washington Post*, April 9, 1926.

15 American Watch & Diamond Co. ad., *The New York Amsterdam News*, December 21, 1927.

16 Elsievans, "The Trend of Fashion," *Chicago Defender*, October 29, 1927.

17 Bessye J. Bearden, "Tid-Bits of New York Society," *Chicago Defender*, September 8, 1928.

18 "The Slave Bracelet," *Women's Wear Daily*, September 11, 1920: 5. "'Slave' Bangles the Latest; They Come from Paris—5 Sizes," *The Brooklyn Daily Eagle*, November 2, 1920: 20.

19 "Flapper Inherits Beauty Aids from Nile Maids of 3000 B.C.," *Atlanta Constitution*, December 11, 1927.

20 Petrine Archer-Straw, *Negrophilia: Avant-Garde Paris and Black Culture in the 1920s* (New York: Thames & Hudson, 2000), 11.

21 Ibid., 12.

22 Camara Dia Holloway, "Afrochic: Africa in the Modernist Imagination," in *African Diaspora in the Cultures of Latin America, the Caribbean, and the United States*, ed. Persephone Braham (Newark: University of Delaware Press, 2015), 94.

23 Archer-Straw, *Negrophilia*, 18.

24 Archer-Straw extends the meaning of Black deco, a term coined by Rosalind Krauss, *Negrophilia*, 71. Ghislaine Wood refers to Jazz Moderne in "The Exotic," in *Art Deco 1910-1939*, eds. Charlotte Benton, Tim Benton, and Ghislaine Wood (London: V&A Publications, 2003),135.

25 Wood, "The Exotic," 125.

26 Susan L. Hannel, "The Influence of American Jazz on Fashion," in *Twentieth-Century American Fashion*, eds. Linda Welters and Patricia A. Cunningham (New York: Berg, 2005), 70–3.

27 Edward W. Said, *Orientalism* (New York: Vintage Books, 1979), 1.

28 Ibid., 3.

29 Linda Nochlin, "The Imaginary Orient," in *Race-ing Art History: Critical Readings in Race and Art History*, ed. Kymberly M. Pinder (New York Routledge, 2002), 69–85.

30 One American example is the 1921 film *The Sheik*, directed by George Melford and starring Rudolf Valentino and Agnes Ayres.

31 Leon Bakst's costumes for the Ballet Russe's *Scheherazade* (1910), Poiret's inspiration for the collection common also included stacks of bracelets as well as necklaces and swags of pearls worn by both male and female dancers.

32 Minh-Ha T. Pham, "Paul Poiret's Magical Techno-Oriental Fashions (1911): Race, Clothing, and Virtuality in the Machine Age," *Configurations* 21 (2013): 1–26.

33 Eric Lott has written extensively about this idea in *Love and Theft: Blackface Minstrelsy and the American Working Class* (New York: Oxford University Press, 1993).

34 Rudolf Fisher, "The Caucasian Storms Harlem," in *Keeping Time: Readings in Jazz History*, ed. Robert Walser (New York: Oxford University Press, 1999), 64.

35 Wendy Buonaventura, *Something in the Way She Moves: Dancing Women from Salome to Madonna* (Cambridge, MA: Da Capo Press, 2004), 184–6.
36 Mary Roberts Rinehart, "The Effect of Fashion on Manners," *Ladies Home Journal* (October 1930): 7.
37 Ibid., 80. This threat is also made clear in the illustration of the woman from 1926 who dances in front of a Black musician, the only man illustrated with the article, on page 6.
38 Brock and Company ad., *Los Angeles Times*, February 28, 1926: C3.
39 See for instance Cab Calloway's description of the Cotton Club quoted in Robert Kronenburg, *This Must Be the Place: An Architectural History of Popular Music Performance Venues* (London: Bloomsbury, 2019), 83, or the description of New York restaurant/cabaret "The Plantation" in "The New York Season Speeds Gaily to its Close," *Vogue*, May 1, 1922: 35.
40 Dorothy Dignam, "In Fashion's Jewel Box," *The Washington Post*, November 14, 1920: 84.
41 "Art of Congo Jungle is Fashtion in Paris [sic]," *The Washington Post*, January 12, 1928: 3.
42 Elisabeth Harvey, "Algerian Motifs Inspire Jewelry and Accessories," *The Washington Post,* March 1, 1931: A1.
43 Ibid.
44 Erick Berry, "Flappers of Africa Are Much Like Our Own," *New York Times*, May 17, 1925: 14.
45 Matabele refers to Nedeble women in Zimbabwe "African Natives Set Style in Bobs," *The New York Amsterdam News*, October 13, 1926: 5.
46 "Never a Better Time for Business," *The Allen Monthly*, April 1924: 7, 9.
47 Hannel, "The Influence of American Jazz on Fashion," 72–3.
48 Hollywood Shopping Service ad. in *The Alumni Register of Duke University*, January 1928, 163.
49 bell hooks, "Eating the Other: Desire and Resistance," in *The Consumer Society Reader*, eds. Juliet Schor and Douglas B. Holt (New York: New Press, 2000), 344.
50 Susan B. Kaiser and Sarah Rebolloso McCullough, "Entangling the Fashion Subject Through the African Diaspora: From *Not* to *(K)not* in Fashion Theory," *Fashion Theory* 14:3 (2010): 380–1.
51 Ibid., 371.
52 "Topics of the Times," *The New York Times*, December 8, 1926: 26.
53 Hazel Rawson Cades, "Fashions as Follows," in *Mirrors of the Year: A National Review of the Outstanding Figures, Trends and Events of 1926–7*, ed. Grant Overton (New York: Frederick A. Stokes Company, 1927), 121.
54 hooks, "Eating the Other: Desire and Resistance," in *Black Looks: Race and Representation* (Boston: South End Press, 1992), 21–40.

55 Nella Larsen, *Quicksand* (New York: Alfred A. Knopf, 1928), 1, 14, 33, 151, https://www.google.com/books/edition/Quicksand/dPdaAAAAMAAJ?hl=en&gbpv=0
56 Ibid., 38.
57 Ibid., 149.
58 Ibid., 150.
59 Ibid., 151.
60 Ibid., 152.
61 Ibid., 154–5.
62 Ibid., 155.
63 Lauren Michele Jackson, *White Negros: When Cornrows Were in Vogue. . .and Other Thoughts on Cultural Appropriation* (Boston: Beacon Press, 2019), 17.
64 Ibid., 10. For more on the significance of nameplate jewelry to women of color see: Isabel Flower and Marcel Rosa-Salas, "Say My Name: Nameplate Jewelry and the Politics of Taste," *QED* 4, no. 3 (2017): 109–26.
65 Ibid, 116–7. See also Tanisha C. Ford, *Dressed in Dreams: A Black Girl's Love Letter to the Power of Fashion* (New York: St. Martin's Press, 2019), 176.
66 Ford, "Bamboo Earrings," in *Dressed in Dreams*, 164.
67 Flower and Rosa-Salas, "Say My Name," 117–8.
68 Jackson, *White Negroes*, 22.
69 Ford, *Dressed in Dreams,* 175.

# Bibliography

Archer-Straw, Petrine. *Negrophilia: Avant-Garde Paris and Black Culture in the 1920s*. New York: Thames & Hudson, 2000.

Buckley, Cheryl and Hazel Clark. *Fashion and Everyday Life: London and New York*. New York: Bloomsbury, 2017.

Buonaventura, Wendy. *Something in the Way She Moves: Dancing Women from Salome to Madonna*. Cambridge, MA: Da Capo Press, 2004.

Flower, Isabel and Marcel Rosa-Salas. "Say My Name: Nameplate Jewelry and the Politics of Taste." *QED* 4, no. 3 (2017): 109–26.

Ford, Tanisha C. *Dressed in Dreams: A Black Girl's Love Letter to the Power of Fashion*. New York: St. Martin's Press, 2019.

Hannel, Susan L. "The Influence of American Jazz on Fashion." In *Twentieth-Century American Fashion*, edited by Linda Welters and Patricia A. Cunningham, 57–77. New York: Berg, 2005.

Holloway, Camara Dia. "Afrochic: Africa in the Modernist Imagination." In *African Diaspora in the Cultures of Latin America, the Caribbean, and the United States*, edited by Persephone Braham, 93–101. Newark: University of Delaware Press, 2015.

hooks, bell. "Eating the Other: Desire and Resistance." In *The Consumer Society Reader*, edited by Juliet Schor and Douglas B. Holt, 343–59. New York: New Press, 2000.

Jackson, Lauren Michele, *White Negroes: When Cornrows Were in Vogue. . .and Other Thoughts on Cultural Appropriation*. Boston: Beacon Press, 2019.

Kaiser, Susan B. and Sarah Rebolloso McCullough. "Entangling the Fashion Subject Through the African Diaspora: From Not to (K)not in Fashion Theory." *Fashion Theory* 14, no. 3 (2010) 361–86.

Lott, Eric. *Love and Theft: Blackface Minstrelsy and the American Working Class*. New York: Oxford University Press, 1993.

Nochlin, Linda. "The Imaginary Orient." In *Race-ing Art History: Critical Readings in Race and Art History*, edited by Kymberly M. Pinder, 69–85. New York: Routledge, 2002.

Pham, Minh-Ha T. "Paul Poiret's Magical Techno-Oriental Fashions (1911): Race, Clothing, and Virtuality in the Machine Age," *Configurations* 21 (2013): 1–26.

Said, Edward W. *Orientalism*. New York: Vintage Books, 1979.

Strings, Sabrina, *Fearing the Black Body: The Racial Origins of Fat Phobia.* New York: New York University, 2019.

Wood, Ghislaine. "The Exotic." In *Art Deco 1910–1939*, edited by Charlotte Benton, Tim Benton and Ghislaine Wood, 125–37. London: V&A Publications, 2003.

# Section Three

# Recovering the Everyday

Hazel Clark and Lauren Downing Peters

How are histories of American everyday fashion reconstructed, where are they recovered, and what actions may be undertaken to ensure that they don't go overlooked or forgotten? These are all questions that are central to the chapters in the last section of this book, and which, in a departure from preceding chapters, are more self-reflexive in their discussion of methods and sources.

As Heike Jenss writes in the introduction to *Fashion Studies: Research Methods, Sites and Practices* (2016), "figuring out one's method/s in the conducting of fashion research is anything but a straightforward process."[1] This is due in large part to the breadth and diversity of fashion as industry, object, idea, and embodied practice, and what Francesca Granata has notably described as the "in-between-ness" of fashion studies. With this term, Granata is describing the "liminal" place the field of fashion studies occupies between the disciplines of visual culture, dress history, art and design history, cultural studies, and performance studies, and the challenges that have come with developing a clearly-defined set of methods and approaches for the study of fashion.[2] Yet, even as a "methodological canon" remains largely undefined in fashion studies, both Jenss and Granata have noted how fashion studies scholars have become adept at adopting multimodal, multimethodological, and increasingly fluid (and, one could argue, *innovative*) approaches to the study of fashion and dress. Appropriately, these methods are "tailored" or "fashioned" in response to the researcher's "exchange with the agents (human and nonhuman) and site/s of exploration...along with the shaping of research interests and contexts."[3]

While every research project will have its own methodological challenges, in the study of everyday fashion, a common obstacle that researchers are likely to run up against is a lack of formalized archives of ordinary dress. Indeed, "museums can play significant roles in institutionalizing specific forms of knowledge," and up until very recently, "museums have...underrepresented the importance of fashion in everyday lives."[4] It is because of this institutional deficit that so few of the authors in this volume draw upon archival materials and, when they do (as, for instance, in Rebecca Jumper Matheson's chapter in Section One) they supplement them with oral histories, snapshots, and other ephemeral accounts and materials that help to better illuminate how people experienced and practiced fashion in everyday life, and which help to destabilize the "single, superior point of view" of historical narrative in favor of more localized and intimate "microhistories."[5] Although, as Alexis Romano points out in Chapter 10, oral history remains an underutilized method in the field of fashion studies, it holds a central place in the scholarship in this section. While the potential pitfalls of oral history are legion—from romanticizing events in hindsight to jumbling dates—its upsides are even greater. Indeed, as Lou Taylor observes, "the value of oral history lies in its ability to clarify the individuality of each human life and yet to reveal the contribution of each person within their wider community."[6] Circling back to Greenblatt's definition of self-fashioning as a "formation of self" in response and relation to wider social forces,[7] oral history, as a tool, helps us to understand these complex entanglements between fashion, the self, and society.

In Chapter 9, authors Alison Bazylinski, Lynn Heidelbaugh, and Rachel Lifter discuss their collaborative research project, the Postal Workwear Oral History Project, which explores the dress practices of America's postal workers. Sitting at the intersection of fashion and public history, the authors employ material culture methodologies, oral history, and a Foucauldian approach to media analysis to understand "what postal people think—about the clothes they wear, the jobs they do, and the roles they play within American society." In addition to expanding accepted definitions of "workwear," their project importantly documents ordinary dress and "uniforming" practices not traditionally accounted for in formal fashion archives or in museum storytelling.

Adopting a similar methodology, in Chapter 10 Alexis Romano explores women's experiences of shopping and getting dressed in 1970s America through a cross-analysis of garments, images, and oral histories. While the image of 1970s fashion—from garish color palettes to body-skimming silhouettes rendered in Lycra, Ultrasuede, and lurex—is familiar to many, the experiences of "anonymous everyday practitioners" of fashion, and specifically those of female consumers, have gone largely overlooked in the fashion literature. Romano seeks to rectify this omission by collecting oral testimonies from women who lived through this iconic fashion era, and in doing so, reframing them "as agents and fashion authors." By further layering the wearer's experience with archival materials and established narratives (i.e., published histories of 1970s fashion, advertisements, and editorials), Romano aims to test the "potentialities and pitfalls" of such an integrative approach for the study of everyday fashion and dress.

Like traditional oral history, crowd-sourced digital archives and public-facing humanities projects are increasingly being used to capture the everyday and fleeting experiences of self-fashioning in American life. In Chapter 11, Michelle McVicker discusses several recent projects that are seeking to document Latinx sartorial expression. The jumping off point for McVicker's timely chapter are recent discussions surrounding the overwhelming "whiteness" of museum fashion archives, and the subsequent marginalization of the dress histories of people of color. Until museums create inclusive and forward-thinking collecting missions that center the voices and experience of Latinx people, McVicker argues that social media photo archives are themselves a valid (and important) repository of Latinx style and material culture—especially given the extent to which they offer contributors "ownership and agency" over their visual representation.

In the final chapter in the volume, Chapter 12, Diana Baird N'Diaye offers a case study in crowd-sourced, collaborative history making in her discussion of her work on the years-long "Will to Adorn" project at the Smithsonian's Center for Folklife and Cultural Heritage. With a focus on African American sartorial and creative expression, the "Will to Adorn" project brought together various communities and organizations from across the country to try to document the diversity of African American fashion, dress, and bodily adornment through oral histories and site visits. While there are myriad challenges to organizing and orchestrating such a large and long-term research project, N'Diaye writes that there was no better (or other) approach for capturing the breadth and beauty of African American sartorial expression and for "revealing the intersections between everyday fashion, craft, and cultural identity."

# Notes

1  Heike Jenss, "Introduction" in *Fashion Studies: Research Methods, Sites and Practices*, ed. Heike Jenss (London: Bloomsbury, 2016), 2.
2  Francesca Granata, "Fashion Studies In-Between: A Methodological Case-Study and Inquiry into the State of Fashion Studies," *Fashion Theory* 16, no. 1 (2012): 67–82.
3  Jenss, "Introduction," 12.

4 Cheryl Buckley and Hazel Clark, "In Search of the Everyday: Museums, Collections, and Representations of Fashion in London and New York," in *Fashion Studies: Research Methods, Sites and Practices*, ed. Heike Jenss (London: Bloomsbury, 2016), 26.
5 John Brewer, "Microhistory and the Histories of Everyday Life," *Cultural and Social History* 7, no. 1 (2010): 89, quoted in Cheryl Buckley and Hazel Clark, *Fashion and Everyday Life: London and New York* (London: Bloomsbury, 2017), 16.
6 Lou Taylor, *The Study of Dress History* (Manchester: Manchester University Press, 2002), 259–60.
7 Stephen Greenblatt, *Renaissance Self-Fashioning: From More to Shakespeare* (Chicago: University of Chicago Press, 1980).

9

# Extra-ordinary Americans

## Oral History, Workwear, and the US Postal Service

Alison Bazylinski, Lynn Heidelbaugh, and Rachel Lifter

We use this chapter to introduce postal workwear into the study of everyday dress and to identify oral history as a key method through which to collect, record, and examine it. In doing so, we also establish everyday fashion as a unique access point for the museological study of the history of the United States Postal Service (USPS). We write this chapter collaboratively and also from our independent perspectives. Alison and Lynn are curators at the Smithsonian's National Postal Museum (NPM), and Rachel is Clinical Assistant Professor and Director of the master's program in Costume Studies at New York University (NYU).

Our collaboration started in the classroom. In Spring 2021, with her colleague Nancy Deihl, Rachel created and taught a special projects class on the US postal uniform. The course offered students an opportunity to forge original accounts of the uniform—as a diverse set of objects, as represented in texts and images, and as worn as a form of everyday dress—and thus contribute new stories to the evolving historiography of American fashion. Rachel pitched the class to Lynn as an opportunity for institutional cooperation, and the coronavirus pandemic shaped how we worked together. Because all teaching was held over Zoom, Lynn, Alison, and their colleague Susan Smith were able to regularly join class sessions, sharing their own research as well as information about the museum's workwear holdings and its future collecting goals. This virtual, cross-institutional environment sparked lively conversations about, among other themes, the uniform's evolution to keep up with contemporaneous fashions, the expansive industry that emerged to produce and supply regulation textiles and finished uniforms, and the many (and often humorous) depictions of postal workers in popular culture. On this last theme, readers might be glad to know, the NPM holds within its collection Cliff Clavin's uniform from the long-running television series *Cheers*.

One class discussion focused on methodologies for examining postal people. Uniforms do not simply exist as inanimate objects. Like all forms of dress, they are worn, on the body, animated by living people: in this case, postal workers. The session was divided into three methodological approaches. First, Lynn shared her ongoing research on a dispatch bag within the NPM's collection, its unique label hinting at the identity of its carrier, a Sioux woman working for the Indian Agency at Standing Rock around 1880. Next, Rachel used contemporary media coverage of the USPS, which she also discusses below, to illustrate a Foucauldian approach to analyzing representations: that is, seeing identities as produced *within*, not before, the texts and images that cover them.[1] And, finally, we invited Shannon O'Neill, curator for Tamiment-Wagner Collections at NYU Special Collections, to introduce best practices for oral history research.[2] Our rationale for this last was simple: the best way to learn what postal people think—about the clothes they wear, the jobs they do, and the roles they play within American society—is by asking them. This conversation planted the seeds of the Postal Workwear Oral History Project, the anchor of the present chapter.

The project examines postal services and workplace clothing, two aspects of Americans' daily life that are so ingrained that they often go overlooked in histories. We look beyond the quotidian USPS uniform, instead applying the term "workwear" to encompass the lived experiences of postal workers whose dress, though not mandated, nevertheless meets the demands, environment, and culture of their workplace. Many non-uniformed positions tend to have fewer interactions with customers—in processing, transportation, and office jobs—and thus, have less need to be publicly conspicuous. Expanding the project's definition to workwear has enabled us to consider this entire labor force, which USPS reported in 2021 was "composed of more than 653,000 people in more than 2,000 functions, including letter carriers, mail processing clerks, tractor-trailer operators, engineers, mail handlers, nurses, postmasters, mechanics and more—all the way up—to the postmaster general."[3]

As outlined on the NPM's website, "The Postal Workwear Oral History Project seeks to document the experiences of current and past postal workers in order to learn about what they wear on the job and how they feel about it; how workwear is selected, designed, and produced for postal jobs; and how workers choose and adapt clothing to fit their daily needs."[4] Three students in the NYU class helped establish its foundations—Elisa Diaz, Victoria Sperotto, and Talia Spielholz—and, at the time of this chapter's writing, collecting has only just begun. The goals of the project are to document the personal experiences not traditionally or readily apparent in the records of the institution of the USPS or the museum's collection of objects (Lynn) *and* to place the dialogue between these experiences and the material culture of the postal workwear at the center of the museum's public-facing storytelling (Alison). To be documented within the project's own historical record is that it was developed at a time when ordinary postal workers were recast as extraordinary Americans (Rachel).

## From ordinary to extraordinary (Rachel, NYU)

Postal workwear offers an excellent case study for research on "fashion and everyday life," to borrow the title of Cheryl Buckley and Hazel Clark's 2017 book.[5] With this term, Buckley and Clark's focus is on "aspects of fashion that typically have been hidden or obscured," in part "overlooked as being too mundane or ordinary."[6] Like everyday dress, uniforms have largely been overlooked. Jane Tynan and Lisa Godson identify uniform as a type of "everyday clothing [that] has been less likely to attract the interest of historians and sociologists of fashion."[7] But postal workwear offers fashion historians a treasure trove of fascinating sartorial and material stories. Take, for example, that of George Nadolleck, Civil War veteran and Detroit letter carrier. Some say it was he who came up with the first uniform, officially mandated for city letter carriers in 1868 by Postmaster General Alexander W. Randall.[8] As reported in an 1895 issue of *The Postal Record*, since 1893 the official representative publication of the National Association of Letter Carriers, Nadolleck "wanted to get some new clothing to show that he had a Government job." The article continues, that when he

> ... drifted into the office first in those new clothes [the postmaster and the chief clerk] said it was the greatest thing on earth, and they immediately hustled him off to a photograph gallery to have some pictures taken, that the same might be sent to the Department at Washington, and the question asked if it would not be a good thing to uniform all the carriers.[9]

*The Postal Record*'s interest in Nadolleck was perhaps piqued by the preceding year's competition for an official Post Office Department uniform contract. As reported in its pages, the department "seeks bids for supplying the entire force—a new departure—a large contract."[10] At the time, the city carrier force numbered "about twelve thousand," and the proposal asked bidders to design summer and winter uniforms. Specifications were given to garment styles and weight and quality of cloth. Fechheimer Bros. & Co. of Cincinnati and Oehm & Co. of

**Figure 9.1** City letter carrier's uniform manufactured by Maher Brothers of Utica, New York, *c.* 1900. Courtesy National Postal Museum, Smithsonian Institution.

Baltimore were the successful bidders, although a wide range of companies continued to supply local markets and advertise in *The Postal Record*, thus expanding consumer options for city letter carriers. The NPM holds within its collection, for example, a jacket from Maher Brothers of Utica, New York, *c.* 1900. Jenise Sileo closely examined it for her final presentation within NYU's collaborative class with the NPM. About the matching trousers, she noted in her final paper, "if you look closely, there's evidence of personal touches added to the standard uniform…The owner of the pants tailored the back seam by adding a gusset of dark gray wool fabric in order to extend the waistline." Through this very brief introduction to the nineteenth-century city letter carrier uniform, I also introduce (albeit faintly) the intersecting processes of regulation, representation, production, and consumption that shape postal workwear as a cultural object and postal identities as they are performed by ordinary Americans. I draw these terms/processes from Paul du Gay et al.'s "circuit of culture," which has proven to be a useful model for sociologists of fashion.[11] Postal workwear thus presents itself as a fascinating and interdisciplinary object of research, hidden in plain sight.

As the NPM-NYU collaboration took off in 2020, however, the USPS was thrust to the center of American politics and popular culture, and strange new identity positions were imprinted upon its uniformed employees. Within the context of a global pandemic, US postal workers—and their counterparts in private service at UPS, FedEx, and Amazon Prime—became first responders, connecting housebound Americans with the outside world. Within the context of a contested American election, USPS workers became "couriers of democracy," to cite an article I discuss below, transporting the will of the American people, from the mailbox to the ballot box. And linked to the explosion of activism under the banner of "Black Lives Matter," postal workers became representatives of American diversity and difference—living, breathing balms against the scourge of white nationalism. The ordinary figure of the postal worker was recast as an extraordinary American icon.

Political discourse did this transformative work. Take, for example, "The Couriers of Democracy"—a photo essay by Philip Montgomery, with context and captions written by Vauhini Vara, that ran in the November 2, 2020 issue of *The New York Times Magazine*.[12] Montgomery documents postal workers at a South Florida post office and the work that they do. The cover photograph is a black-and-white portrait of a white, male postal worker. Shown in extreme close-up, visible are his gator-style face mask, hanging loosely around his neck, and his southern Florida tan, made prominent in the image's grayscale by the pronounced outline of pale skin in the shape of temple-hugging, athletic-style sunglasses. He is bald, sweat glistening on his head, and he squints as he gazes off to the left of the image—a human counterpart to the eagle on his chest, which faces to the right and appears to be captured mid-flight. The portrait is that of a hero, one who has been baked in the Florida sun. The language follows suit, as the title alone—"couriers of democracy"—makes clear: what is being carried is not only the mail, but the future of the country.[13]

Fashion discourse did this work, too. An example is "Look Book," a repeating street style piece on *The Cut*, which is *New York* magazine's digital fashion platform. On July 10, 2020 "Look Book" featured the post office in Jamaica, Queens, New York City.[14] The cover image features a young, Black woman with long blond braids, asymmetrical pink sunglasses, and a leopard-print facemask wrapped around her chin. She is curvy, filling out her regulation short-sleeved button-down shirt and blue-gray wool shorts. Her image could easily be placed in other street style features that celebrate youth, diversity (of body size and racial and ethnic background), and sense of style.[15] The remaining photos expand the visual discourse of street style, focusing on workers young and old,

**Figure 9.2** Letter carrier in New York City, 2020. Photographer Kyle Dorosz.

who appear Black, Asian, Latino, and white. Instead of ages, the featured postal workers are identified by their number of years in service. One older, white, male postal worker has been in service the longest, at forty-one years. Like the woman from the cover photo, he is also dressed in a regulation short-sleeved button-down shirt, blue-gray shorts, and black sneakers, with socks pulled up over his calves. Both postal workers are letter carriers, sharing uniform options and responding to the same environmental concerns. Almost identically dressed, their visible differences in age and race highlight the diversity of this working body, the unintentional (style) heroes of America's urban and suburban streets in 2020.[16]

By turning our critical attention to the USPS, its employees, and the clothes they wear, our class and collaboration with NPM contributed to this explosion of discourse.[17] Reciprocally, this historic re-presentation of postal workers shaped our approach to analysis. We developed the oral history project to highlight the voices of these newly recognized American icons. Clear within our conversations, Lynn had already been considering postal workers' voices as a necessary focus of the NPM collection.

## The material culture of postal workwear (Lynn, NPM)

For several years I had curatorial oversight of the museum's collection of clothing items used by postal workers. The accessioned objects range from issued items like numbered, metal badges used for employee identification in the late nineteenth through the twentieth century to the full-body, leather flight suit that belonged to Eddie Gardner, one of the first pilots to join the Airmail Service in 1918. The variety and number of such items have necessitated a vision not only for ways we choose to refine and grow this collection of workwear—postal workers and their relatives frequently make donation offers to the museum—but also how to activate the objects and their histories through museum programming and access for researchers.

A case study of one accession illustrates an evolving policy and approach to collecting. In 2012, retired postal employee Ann L. Salisbury (1947–2021) contacted the museum with an offer to donate pieces of her former uniform. Her name in the offer's scant information first caught my attention because the museum's collection had comparatively few female workers' uniforms. Thus, the offer held potential to meet intentions in the museum's collecting plan to diversify and increase representation, including gender. On top of that, many of the museum's cataloged uniform items simply lacked the wearers' names. When I telephoned Ann Salisbury to learn more about her and the assorted pins and jackets, she described the objects and shared that they dated to the beginning and middle of a thirty-four-year career, which included various job types, at the Seekonk Post Office in Massachusetts. She explained that her two uniform jackets were in almost-new condition because she wore each for only a couple of years.

**Figure 9.3** Ann Salisbury's Post Office Department uniform (left) and her USPS letter carrier's jacket (right). Courtesy National Postal Museum, Smithsonian Institution.

Salisbury's first job with the Post Office Department began in 1968 and her fitted jacket had to have a patch on the shoulder with her job designation—letter carrier—placed above the department's insignia of a horse and rider embroidered in white on a blue field bordered in maroon. She wore this until new uniform regulations came into effect in 1971 following the Postal Reorganization Act of 1970, which transformed the government agency into the USPS. The new corporate management approach of USPS came with a modern look, and every letter carrier had to purchase a whole new uniform with a logo featuring an eagle designed by Raymond Loewy. Soon thereafter, she switched from neighborhood delivery rounds to the indoor job of a postal clerk. Her nearly pristine USPS letter carrier's jacket went into storage, and she took to collecting the pins that USPS gave clerks to wear during promotions of new Express Mail and Priority Mail service postage rates of the late 1980s to mid-1990s and the USPS sponsorship of the 1992 US Olympic team.

These details are about the extent of what I was able to jot down during our brief conversation. Ann Salisbury's succinct answers formed the basis of the report I submitted to the museum's collections committee, which officially accepted the donation offer. Salisbury shipped the jackets and pins to the museum along with a photocopy of her 1973 interview in the *Seekonk Sentinel* newspaper that gave insights our phone call had not. The local news piece opens with Salisbury offering to give safety instruction in motorcycle riding, one of her hobbies, and continues with a description of some of her job duties, about which she remarked, "driving comes easily to me; I just had to get used to having the wheel on the right side of the truck." Her interests in motorcycles, along with the statement that, "she is the only woman working [at the Seekonk Post Office]," function to position her as a woman in a man's world at the time. Nevertheless, Salisbury's photograph—captioned, "Lady Mailman"—shows her looking directly at the camera wearing a knit cap, her USPS jacket, and matching USPS striped trousers while seated at the wheel of a mail truck, much like any male counterpart in the post office would appear while on the job.[18] The article is kept in the accession file, and together with the thirteen objects and their catalog records that contain my distillation of one phone call and brief correspondence with the donor, they represent the museum's collection of one woman's postal career in the late twentieth century.[19]

Although I did not make note of the emotions and tone of our conversation, I can recall how Salisbury spoke humbly of her career in public service for which she demonstrated recognition of the historic value of her experience and uniforms that might find a place in the NPM's collection. I also remember her brief laugh that struck me as a hint of humor mixed with resignation when she mentioned the expense of and the effort to buy a new uniform so soon after the first. Future researchers reading the accession file for these objects and visitors reading exhibition labels at the museum will have to take my word for this. Ideally, I would rather it have been her words captured in an audio recording with her inflections, her precise descriptions, and her personal impressions about wearing—and keeping—this clothing.[20] For me, the process of accessioning these items raised questions whether the actual clothing itself needs to be in the museum's collection, or can the information in oral history interviews be enough to further our understanding about the wearers, their experiences with USPS, their interactions with postal customers, and perceptions of the role and value of postal service in American life?

My reflections upon accessioning and writing of Ann Salisbury's uniforms raise many possibilities for collecting and interpreting museum objects. As Lou Taylor proposed, "Since clothing is such a fundamental factor within everyday life and human experience, memories of dress should be able to make significant contributions to the field of oral history especially when respondents include both the poorest in society as well as political, social and cultural elites."[21] I believe that our project can likewise make contributions to the study of postal history by including multiple voices and perspectives in the documentation of the personal experiences not readily apparent or typically found within the traditional records of authority, the publications and archives of the institution of the USPS, or the museum's objects themselves. Recording memories of postal workers from all varieties of job types can address some of the silences of the lived experiences missing from the management manuals and memos about workwear. Engaging narrators to tell their own stories and share their insights in understanding material culture also has potential to address diversity and inclusivity within the museum's collection and increase the knowledge base while broadening the meaning-making between postal workers, the museum, and the museum's audiences.

NPM's imperative to prioritize the participation of postal workers as stakeholders in their own history became part of the museum's ten-year interpretive plan developed in 2021 during the Covid-19 pandemic and Black Lives Matters movement that brought about a reexamination of professional practices at NPM and many other museums.[22] Public history and museum professionals have increasingly embraced methods that incorporate community collecting, including oral history, as ways to address the power structures of the institutions and remain relevant in the civic lives of audiences.[23] In this context, the Postal Workwear Oral History Project presented an opportunity for NPM to go directly to the sources and, with the narrators, confront the gap in the written records of postal history with the memories of firsthand experiences.

Through the project, I have sought to consider my role and practices as a curator. For the museum, the project has raised lines of inquiry, such as: How might the project advance the mission of the NPM "[to educate, challenge, and inspire audiences] on the breadth of American experiences?"[24] Why and how could the museum incorporate shared authority in collecting and interpreting postal workwear? In what ways might oral history help increase knowledge and understanding of the roles and perceptions of postal workers in the American experience? The project will address these through the interdisciplinary application of oral history methods and costume studies, thus repositioning the museum and postal institutions in conversation with oral history narrators, their lived experiences, and contemporary material culture of their workwear. Alison is taking this approach to reframe the curation of museum's current and future collections.

## Theorizing material culture and oral history in dialogue (Alison, NPM)

When I began working at the NPM in 2020, I took over as the main curator of the workwear holdings (formally the uniform collection). Much of my historical research utilizes traditional written sources, but I also turn to extant garments, photographs, advertisements, and personal recollections. Thus, my interpretive approach to the museum's collection is one which considers the entire life cycle of the object: processes of design and production, the materials and styles used, who wore clothing and when, as well as affective experiences of wear. I envision a collection of workwear that encourages a multiplicity of meanings and interpretations, one that can tackle technical aspects of design and production *and* one that encourages reflection on how the materiality of workwear influences and affects postal employees. The Postal Workwear Oral History Project dovetails with these goals, in addition to providing an entry point for museum visitors and future researchers to connect with the collection on a personal and experiential level.

Fashion scholars have argued for the importance of materiality to everyday experience. As Leora Auslander writes, fabric and clothing are "psychologically loaded" based on their "intimate relation to the body,"[25] while touch, movement, sound, and texture all influence human interactions with fabric and clothing.[26] These affective experiences of wear, as well as how people select clothing and feelings elicited through wearing, frequently overlap and intertwine.[27] Examining postal workwear provides a case study for understanding the significance of materials and materiality to social relationships when people are forced to choose from specified garments. Conventional workwear that conforms to both official and unofficial expectations embodies specific structural systems that shape "frameworks of interpersonal relations," but are also part of complex social play that can be deliberately appropriated, subverted, or rejected through subtle changes. Therefore, dress codes are far from straightforward in the social and cultural messages they convey. Oral history offers a method of getting at how postal workers feel about workwear, and in conversation with material and historical contexts, illustrates the complexities of how humans wear, view, and interact with fabric and clothing individually and as a society.

However, "the body is not simply a passive vehicle being acted on by the fashion industry"—or in this case, by the federal government.[28] Written sources reveal postal workers often expressed opinions about what they wore, at times questioning necessity, styles, or practicality. There are articles in newspapers and periodicals from the nineteenth century that detailed changes in postal uniforms, and also conflicts within post offices regarding who had to wear uniforms. Internal postal employee sources such as *Postal Life* (1967–92) and union publications including *The Postal Record* (1888–ongoing) demonstrate that at least some postal employees felt compelled to write in with complaints, praise, or in response to queries regarding opinions on uniforms.[29] These types of details provide clues into the everyday lives of these employees who, as a body, ran and maintained one of the great communication systems of the modern age.

For instance, clerks in New York and Chicago openly rebelled against uniforms in the late nineteenth century, to the annoyance of local postmasters. According to one 1877 article, Postmaster James of the New York Post Office was "greatly annoyed" that his request for clerks to wear uniforms was received with "so much adverse criticism."[30] Unfortunately, clerks were not interviewed and their specific critiques have been lost. The case of rebelling Chicago post office clerks, however, received more press coverage in 1899. The postmaster's attempt to put clerks in uniform "raised about his head a storm which he will find some difficulty in quelling."[31] Clerks organized meetings to debate and protest the order, arguing that very few of them came into contact with the public and that the service would "in no way be benefited by their wearing uniforms." Many of them wore shirt sleeves (a collared shirt with no coat) to "facilitate their labor." Comfort and practicality, not visible signs of professional service, seemed to be the main priority.

There are also tantalizing mentions of employees such as Helen Kramer of Shively, Kentucky, who, after serving as postmistress for five years, was appointed letter carrier for Rural Route No. 6. Although rural delivery drivers were not required to wear a uniform, Miss Kramer chose to create her own pattern anyway because the Post Office Department did not provide details on uniforms for women.[32] In an interview with a local newspaper, Kramer detailed her struggles in finding fabric: "I went to a number of stores and asked for the letter carrier gray cloth. Goodness, how they stared at me. Maybe they thought it was something in the way of a new style of dress goods...not being able to find exactly what I wanted, I was at last forced to buy a blue-gray chambray cloth."[33] Kramer designed a "Gibson [shirt] waist" and a "plain skirt," plus the regulation cap, which she had difficulty fitting to her head.[34] Unfortunately, she did not say *why* she felt the need to provide herself with a uniform that cost her time, effort, and money. Helen Kramer's story, fortunately captured in her personal testimony in the news article, demonstrates the intersection of women's labor in and out of the home, sewing, and the federal government, overlaps explored within studies of home economics but rarely in postal history.

More recent issues of workwear include the design of uniforms specifically for women, which did not occur until the 1960s, and the push for (male) letter carriers to wear shorts, forbidden until 1973. Publications written for postal employees provided a forum for expressing opinions and finding like-minded individuals in the pre-internet age, including on the topic of workwear. Volume 1, issue 6 of *Postal Life* contains two such letters. A Pennsylvania carrier agreed with a letter from the previous issue which called for Bermuda shorts to be part of the regulation uniform, noting "my first experience as a letter carrier in summer was the brutal beating from the sun and the containment of the heat in the present uniform. It is an unnecessary cruel burden...the shorts are not for fashion but for health."[35] At the same time, a "female window clerk" from Illinois expressed her desire to see skirts made part of the regulation uniform so she could use her uniform allotment to purchase one and requested to know the thoughts of other clerks on the subject.[36] These two letters, although brief, show how personal experiences and interactions with clothing can highlight changing social norms, gendered differences in decisions on workwear regulations, and uniform allotments and labor negotiations.

Combining material culture approaches, oral histories, and historical contexts, curators at the NPM can consider the full life cycles of workwear from union contract and design to production, marketing, consumption, and uses.[37] Indeed, certain questions are better approached through the medium of oral history, such as who produced uniforms and how did this change with the growth of ready-to-wear and mass production? How did employees choose which pieces to acquire or discard? How have fabrics and designs changed and who has made those decisions? Where do obsolete workwear pieces end up when style changes are instituted? Have definitions of workwear shifted as the number of acceptable options has proliferated, particularly in the late twentieth and early twenty-first centuries? Not all pieces of workwear end up in museums, and not all of them should. NPM's collection does not need to consist of an encyclopedic record of every type of workwear, which would overwhelm storage space without making significant contributions to knowledge. Rather, the oral history program in combination with select objects, chosen based on personal, historical, and vernacular significance, will document the fuller life-cycle and record multivocal perspectives about the material culture.[38]

## Conclusion

Clothing and uniforms, while seemingly a minor aspect of postal history, provide an intimate look at the everyday lives of postal workers and a significant nexus of material culture and identity for workers, management, and the public. The Postal Workwear Oral History Project envisions reaching out to all aspects of the workwear design process, including manufacturers and consultants on quality control and stylistic decisions. Workwear shapes, influences, and remains essential for an individual's capacity to carry out job duties; has repeatedly served as a flash point for postal workers and unions negotiating uniform regulations; and functions as a symbol of and by the postal service and in American culture. Moreover, the relatable, universal experience of clothing amplifies the relevancy between the historic evolution of postal workwear and contemporary life. Oral histories of postal workwear and the practice of meaning making through such records can expand various historiographical areas, including uniforms, textiles, labor, business, and design. While the NPM has included specific anecdotes and personal experiences in the accession records of objects, what might we learn from a collection of oral histories surrounding all aspects of workwear? What might become apparent to future historians looking at this often-unsettled period in postal history? For their own sake, as well as part of the larger stories of postal history and communications, indeed labor and identity, in the United States, these histories must be collected.[39] And our goal in this present chapter is to begin the historical record of this project.

## Notes

1  See, for example, Rachel Lifter "Creating Fashionable Identities," in *Communicating Fashion Brands: Theoretical and Practical Perspectives*, eds. Emily Huggard and Jon Cope (London: Routledge, 2020), 79–94.

2   Shannon also shared materials related to the postal strikes of 1970, which are within the Tamiment-Wagner collections.
3   "Postal Facts," United States Postal Service, https://facts.usps.com/print-all-facts (accessed May 17, 2022).
4   "Postal Workwear," National Postal Museum, https://postalmuseum.si.edu/postal-workwear (accessed May 17, 2022).
5   Cheryl Buckley and Hazel Clark, *Fashion and Everyday Life: London and New York* (London: Bloomsbury, 2017).
6   Ibid., 1.
7   Jane Tynan and Lisa Godson, "Understanding Uniform: An Introduction," in *Uniform: Clothing and Discipline in the Modern World*, eds. J. Tynan and L. Godson (London: Bloomsbury, 2019), 8.
8   Historian, United States Postal Service, "Letter Carriers' Uniform: Overview," May 2002, https://usps.com (accessed June 6, 2022).
9   Photocopy, "The First Letter Carrier's Uniform," *The Postal Record*, 1895, month unknown, p. 246. Office of the Historian of the United States Postal Service, Folder: "Uniforms: Letter Carriers, Histories."
10  Photocopy, "Letter Carriers' Uniforms," *The Postal Record*, February 1894: 45. Office of the Historian of the United States Postal Service, Folder: "Uniforms: Letter Carriers, Histories."
11  Paul du Gay, Stuart Hall, Linda Janes, Anders Koed Madsen, Hugh Mackay and Keith Negus, *Doing Cultural Studies: The Story of the Sony Walkman*, 2nd edn. (Los Angeles, London, New Delhi, Singapore, and Washington, DC: Sage and The Open University, 2013). See also Susan B. Kaiser and Denise N. Green, *Fashion and Cultural Studies,* 2nd edn. (London: Bloomsbury, 2022).
12  Philip Montgomery (photos) and Vauhini Vara (text), 2020, "The Couriers of Democracy," *The New York Times Magazine*, November 2, 2020 (nytimes.com, accessed March 5, 2021).
13  Other articles included: Ted Widmer, "The Postal Service Is the Most American Thing We've Got," *The New York Times*, May 15, 2020 (nytimes.com, accessed March 5, 2021); Kelsey Ables, "We now know that the Postal Service can change history. This museum has argued that for decades," *The Washington Post*, September 10, 2020, (washingtonpost.com, accessed March 5, 2021); and Loré Yessuff, "A Love Letter to My Mailman, and the Incomparable Camaraderie Between Black Strangers," *Man Repeller*, June 22, 2020 (manrepeller.com, accessed March 5, 2021).
14  Katy Schneider and Jane Starr Drinkard, "The Look Book Goes to the Jamaica Post Office," photographs by Kyle Dorosz, *The Cut,* June 10, 2020 (thecut.com; accessed March 5, 2021). See also posts by Anka Itskovich @the_line_up, "Christopher," October 22, 2020 (instagram.com; accessed May 22, 2022); Anka Itskovich @the_line_up, "Santiago," August 10, 2020 (instagram.com; accessed May 22, 2022).

15 For a clear introduction to street style images, see Agnès Rocamora and Alistair O'Neill, "Fashioning the Street: Images of the Street in the Fashion Media," in *Fashion as Photograph: Viewing and Reviewing Images of Fashion,* ed. Eugenie Shinkle (London and New York: I. B. Tauris, 2008).

16 According to a Pew Research Center report from 2020, "Postal workers are more racially and ethnically diverse than the U.S. labor force as a whole, according to Census Bureau data from 2018, the most recent year available. About six-in-ten of the agency's employees—including mail carriers, postal clerks, and mail sorters and processors—are non-Hispanic white (57%), compared with 78% of the overall U.S. workforce. Around a quarter (23%) of Postal Service workers are black, 11% are Hispanic and 7% are Asian. In contrast, black Americans make up 13% of the national workforce, Hispanics 17% and Asian Americans 6%." Drew Desilver and Katherine Schaeffer, "The state of the U.S. Postal Service in 8 charts," *Pew Research Center* (pewresearch.org; accessed September 2, 2022).

17 The end-of-term virtual symposium is archived on YouTube as "Contemporary Dress: Spotlight on the USPS Uniform," NYU Steinhardt, May 7, 2021 (youtube.com; accessed August 20, 2022).

18 "A Young Lady of Unusual Interests," *The Seekonk Sentinel*, January 14, 1973: 14.

19 Accession 2013.2015, National Postal Museum, Smithsonian Institution.

20 We spoke again in 2019 when Salisbury offered additional objects, including five pins and badges we accessioned in 2020. Although I asked her for a second, longer interview, it eventuated that the timing was not right for either of us.

21 Lou Taylor, *The Study of Dress* (Manchester: Manchester University Press), 242.

22 For instance, see Graham Bowley, "Museums Collect Protest Signs to Preserve History in Real Time," *The New York Times*, June 10, 2020, https://www.nytimes.com/2020/06/10/arts/design/museums-protest-signs.html; Avi Decter and Ken Yellis, "Straws in the Wind: Signs of Change in American Museums," *History News*, 76, no. 2 (Spring 2021): 4–5, and Adam Popescu, "How Will We Remember the Pandemic? Museums Are Already Deciding," *The New York Times*, May 25, 2021, https://www.nytimes.com/2020/05/25/arts/design/museums-covid-19-collecting.html

23 For instance, see Michael H. Frisch, *A Shared Authority: Essays on the Craft and Meaning of Oral History and Public History* (Albany: State University of New York Press, 1990); Marianna Pegno and Christine Brindza, "Redefining Curatorial Leadership and Activating Community Expertise to Build Equitable and Inclusive Art Museums," *Curator* 64 (2021): 343–62.

24 "History of the Smithsonian National Postal Museum," National Postal Museum, https://postalmuseum.si.edu/history-of-the-smithsonian-national-postal-museum (accessed May 17, 2022).

25 Leora Auslander, "Deploying Material Culture to Write the History of Gender and Sexuality," *Clio. Women, Gender, History* 40, Making Gender with Things (2014): 157.

26 See Victoria Kelley, "The Interpretation of Surface: Boundaries, Systems and Their Transgression in Clothing and Domestic Textiles, c. 1880–1939," *Textile* 7, no. 2 (2009): 216–35; Eva Illouz, "Emotions, Imagination and Consumption: A New Research Agenda," *Journal of Consumer Culture*, vol 9, no. 3 (2009): 377–413; Lucia Ruggerone, "The Feeling of Being Dressed: Affect Studies and the Clothed Body," *Fashion Theory* 21, no. 5 (2017): 573–93.

27 For this chapter I refer to the work of Ellen Sampson and Roggerone, who argue that experiences of being clothed are confluences of ever-changing affects, experiences that can elicit emotion, but can also be separate from an emotional response. Affect is not just the history of emotion; it also refers to bodily experience in addition to mental. Roggerone, "The Feeling of Being Dressed," 579; Ellen Sampson, "Affect and Sensation," *Fashion Studies* 3, no. 1 (2020): 4.

28 Emma McClendon, "*The Body: Fashion and Physique*–A Curatorial Discussion," *Fashion Theory* 23, no. 2 (2019): 155.

29 Some examples include "Grateful–Our Readers Sling Mail," *Postal Life* 1, no. 3 (November–December 1967): 3; "Ladies Want Skirts–Our Readers Sling Mail," *Postal Life* vol 2, iss.1 (July–August 1968): 3; "Functional fashions–Our Readers Write Letters," *Postal Life* 5, no. 1 (July–August 1971): 21.

30 "The Post Office Uniform Question," *The New York Times*, July 20, 1877: 8.

31 "What Interests Chicago–Post Office Clerks Strongly Object to Wearing Uniforms," *The New York Times*, January 29, 1899: 13.

32 At the time of writing in 2022, rural carriers still do not have uniform requirements.

33 "Woman Will Cover Free Rural Route: Miss Helen Kramer's Plans," *Courier-Journal* August 17, 1902: 5.

34 Ibid, 5.

35 "Our Readers Sling Mail–Bermudas Optional," *Postal Life* 1, no. 6 (May–June 1968): 3.

36 "Our Readers Sling Mail–Wants Skirts," *Postal Life* 1, no. 6 (May-June 1968): 3.

37 See also Rachel's mention of du Gay et al.'s "circuit of culture," above.

38 By vernacular I refer to workwear modified or adjusted to fit local, environmental, or personal needs.

39 The Postal Workwear Oral History Project has benefited from conversations with oral historians and public history practitioners who have interviewed postal employees. The United States Postal Service implemented their own oral history project to commemorate the fiftieth anniversary of the USPS and published excerpts in August 2021: "Fifty Years of Service to the Nation: Highlights from the USPS 50th Anniversary Oral History Project," Historian, USPS, https://about.usps.com/who-we-are/postal-history/fifty-years-of-service-1971-2021.pdf (accessed June 6, 2022). Folklorist Emily Hilliard created the project "Rural Free Delivery: Mail Carriers in Central Appalachia," which was supported by a 2021–2 American Folklife Center Archie Green Fellowship (https://emilyehilliard.com/work#/folklore/,

accessed August 30, 2022). The approximately twenty-five interviews, photos, and other related materials will become part of the Occupational Folklife Project Collection at the American Folklife Center at the Library of Congress.

# Bibliography

Auslander, Leora. "Deploying Material Culture to Write the History of Gender and Sexuality." *Clio. Women, Gender, History* 40 (2014): 157–78.

Buckley, Cheryl and Hazel Clark. *Fashion and Everyday Life: London and New York*. London: Bloomsbury, 2017.

du Gay, Paul, Stuart Hall, Linda Janes, Anders Koed Madsen, Hugh Mackay, and Keith Negus, eds. *Doing Cultural Studies: The Story of the Sony Walkman*, 2nd edn. Los Angeles, London, New Delhi, Singapore and Washington, DC: Sage and The Open University, 2013.

Illouz, Eva. "Emotions, Imagination and Consumption: A New Research Agenda." *Journal of Consumer Culture* 9, no. 3 (2009): 377–413.

Kelley, Victoria. "The Interpretation of Surface: Boundaries, Systems and their Transgression in Clothing and Domestic Textiles, *c*. 1880–1939." *Textile* 7, no. 2 (2009): 216–35.

McClendon, Emma. "*The Body: Fashion and Physique*—A Curatorial Discussion." *Fashion Theory* 23, no. 2 (2019): 147–65.

Ruggerone, Lucia. "The Feeling of Being Dressed: Affect Studies and the Clothed Body." *Fashion Theory* 21, no. 5 (2017): 573–93.

Sampson, Ellen. "Affect and Sensation." *Fashion Studies* 3, no. 1 (2020): 1–19.

Taylor, Lou. *The Study of Dress History*. Manchester: Manchester University Press, 2002.

Tynan, Jane and Lisa Godson. *Uniform: Clothing and Discipline in the Modern World*. London and New York, Bloomsbury, 2019.

# 10

# 1970s Fashion and Women

## Finding the Everyday at the Intersection of Image, Archive, and Oral History

Alexis Romano

Perhaps more than any other era, the 1970s have provided ample fashion stereotypes, its more outlandish looks preserved and passed down in photography, films, and television. Scholars too view it through a lens of postmodern anti-fashion. According to Valerie Steele, "As the rules of taste and propriety were deliberately violated, the fashion system spawned crushed vinyl burgundy maxi-coats, avocado-green Ultrasuede pant-suits, electric blue lycra 'second-skin' body stockings and silver lurex halter tops. Polyester shirts were open to the waist, and dresses were slit up to the crotch."[1] Yes, the US fashion industry had become a sophisticated machine of manufacture and advertising, by this time capable of producing the material to cater to a range of identities, or at least it purported to do so. "The changing consumer," as laid out in a 1971 Fashion Group *Bulletin* (based on the comments of Elyse Riley of Gimbels), "wants clothes that emphasize her personal identity in a world that often seems computerized, mechanized, dehumanized."[2] The influential trade organization went on to describe a more measured albeit individualized fashion market than Steele's characterizations, who had matured into a sophisticated, professional yet still dynamic woman:

> "Gidget is gone. The Youthquake girl of the 60s. Replaced by the woman of the 70s. A member of the fast-growing 20–34 year old group. Married and a working woman who's already changing the composition of the American working force."[3]

With a focus on this general age group, this chapter addresses American fashion of the 1970s, a historical moment of national attention on women's political and social states, and a shift into postmodern modes of dress- and image-making. It questions what a history of fashion, or history through fashion, might look like when we include, even foreground, the anonymous everyday practitioner. To this end, it adopts a methodology that cross-analyzes garment, image, and oral history. Based on the early findings of this ongoing research project, this chapter foregrounds the oral history portion, and tests the potentialities and pitfalls of this integrative approach.[4] I ask how museum clothing archives[5] and the femininities depicted in advertorial and editorial images resonate with lived experiences. Museum collecting practices have tended to privilege the rarefied designer label, and expensive fine craftsmanship. This focus on the rare, extraordinary and elite is often aligned with fashion's mediation in photography and magazines.[6] As Ellen Sampson and I have written elsewhere, "The monographic imagining of fashion in museums sits in contrast to fashion as bodily and lived; the everyday experience of wearing clothes. We produce our clothed identities through acquiring, styling and collating clothes from multiple sources."[7] As such, this research maps a fuller picture of women's visual and material experience of dress in a specific historical context, which encompasses the social and subjective practices of getting dressed, wearing clothes, and looking at fashion. I also seek to gauge oral history subjects' sensory and anecdotal notions of images and museum artifacts. Thus in addition to locating gaps and overlap in collecting and representation, I explore how the wearer's perpsective amalgamates layers of meaning into established narratives as told by such sources.

## Oral history and women's everyday

In a 1972 essay, the feminist poet and writer Adrienne Rich described politics, not as "something 'out there' but something 'in here' and of the essence of my condition."[8] Rich did not include her dress process within literary meditations of her everyday gendered life. But how would this information have enhanced her narratives? How might she have described the choice and feel of the body-hugging t-shirt and mini shorts she wore, for instance, as a sitter for Alice Neel's 1973 drawing?[9] In retrospect, how might she unpack the relationship between her embodied and pictured self? In asking these questions, everyday fashion and our dress practices function as tools to uncover the "political significance of our personal experiences,"[10] as Cheryl Buckley and Hilary Fawcett have written. This thinking chimes with Rich's statement, and the advocacy of consciousness raising—based on the belief that the personal is political—by feminist groups such as the tellingly named Redstockings. Founded in 1969 and mainly active in early 1970s New York, Redstockings addressed the gamut of women's experience, and was particularly known for its work in abortion rights. Debates on consciousness have extended to fashion and appearance, as scholars including Betty Luther Hillman have noted, generally relegating these time-consuming practices as patriarchal prescriptions. She writes that "Women's liberationist and lesbian feminist writings encouraged women to discard their makeup, high heels, skirts, and dresses, opting for the mobility and comfort provided by pants and blue jeans."[11]

Thinking beyond reductive parallels between fashion and feminism, this chapter starts from the idea that fashion is a signifying element of one's gendered experience. Oral testimony is viewed as a means to refocus fashion studies through the lens of the everyday as discussed above, both to connect personal and wider historical narratives, and position everyday wearers as agents and fashion authors. Among methodologies of studying dress history, Lou Taylor wrote that "The essence of oral history is that it can catch hold of people's memories through their own voices, a quality that is especially relevant for those marginalized by or exluded from 'big' history."[12] This chapter argues that "big history" is incomplete without these voices. Further, as Linda Sandino pointed out in an oral history themed issue of the *Journal of Design History*, "memories evoked in interviews demonstrate the connections as well as the gaps between representation and experience."[13] So, how does the narrative voice of women—a means of access to the everyday—aid in or complicate our understanding of "period eyes," or the ways in which a contemporary consumer might have viewed or interpreted a fashion image, as well as a fashion object in this case. How might it challenge 1970s stereotypes held today? How does it animate the image and object archives that document this decade? What problems occur at the level of interpretation when these worlds meet?

Twenty years after Taylor wrote her text, it is still true that "within oral history little focus has yet been placed on recollection of garments and appearance."[14] In the field of fashion studies specifically, this method is also seldom utilized, both in research that conducts new interviews or that draws on existing ones.[15] There is a longstanding tradition in museum accessioning practice whereby curators solicit donors' object-based memories, but these efforts come up against the reality of lack of time and resources.[16] Examples of its use in exhibition-making around fashion and dress are rarer still.[17] And while many repositories hold oral histories recovering the stories of fashion industry professionals, the everyday consumer is rarely represented.[18] Recent scholarship within design history and fashion and cultural studies includes Alison Slater's work on 1940s dress, and Sara Chong Kwan's research into fashion and the senses.[19] They build on the ethnographic and human interest approaches of cultural anthropology and sociology and material culture studies, seen notably in Sophie Woodward's study of women dressing.[20] As a whole, these growing examples prioritize materiality and the sensory over the visual, and the affect, phenomenology, and perspective of the (female) wearer; and can be seen as a part of the material, subjective and everyday "turns" in critical thinking.[21]

To date I've interviewed ten women for this research project located around the country, from Louisiana, Texas, and New York to Berkeley, with one example in Toronto. A teacher turned homemaker, costume designer, bank professional, patternmaker, writer, marketing director turned educator, teacher turned architect, and an art historian, the interview subjects, or narrators, experienced the 1970s during their twenties and thirties (mainly). Taking into account differences of race, class and geography, their testimonies emphasized, in the words of Raphael Samuel, "both the variety of experience in any social group, and how each individual story draws on a common culture."[22] For some this was a period of "absorbing second wave feminism";[23] the shedding of fashion's gender rules; for others a period of motherhood and thus considered as antithetical to fashion. Our discussions broached difficult topics too, failed marriages, eating disorders, family deaths, and financial problems. This chapter takes fragments of my conversations with Cricket, Joyce, and Joan who were born in the 1940s, and Andrea and Mary Jo in 1952 and 1958 respectively. I've connected these narrators around themes that emerged—namely creativity, fashionability, comfort, control, and negotiations—and, where I could, integrated established narratives, fashion imagery, and clothing archival research undertaken. The task at hand, interpreting testimonies and reconciling them with other narratives, proved a constant challenge. So, too, was making meaningful connections between the experience of dress and life events, big and small, and constructions of identity. There were moments where memory faltered or romanticized, and when the 1970s became lost in a sea of a life lived and indistinguishable from other periods.

## Mary Jo and Andrea: Creativity and reinvention

I began all interviews by situating the narrators in their earliest memories of dress to map a continuum of fashion and life experience in which to connect various points. Many relayed similar accounts of home sewing and shopping with female family members: Mary Jo's mother ("a seamstress par excellence"), Andrea's Aunt Helene; Joyce's grandmother; Cricket's mother and grandmother, and Joan's female relatives in neighborhood "sewing circles." In speaking, they relived the unbridled joys of having doll clothes made, sometimes followed by their creative awakening in home economics sewing classes. This laid the groundwork in conversation to view fashion as material, expressive and social practice. Many continued to use dress creatively into their adult years, largely up to the 1970s and 1980s when other endeavors vied for their time, when children were getting older, or in the case of Joan, to focus more on "intellectual work" over the "manual" labor of sewing. Others went on to work with clothing professionally, Cricket as a pattern cutter and Mary Jo a costume designer.

Mary Jo (b. 1958) sewed from around the age of eight, and modified her clothes as a teen in Ontario, often using denim as a starting point: she crafted skirts out of jeans, or slashed the side seam, adding a gore to construct a huge flare, during which time she also experimented with tie dye, latching on to the last legs of the flower child movement into the 1970s. "My entire life I felt like an outsider," a sentiment she associated to moving several times before settling in the provincial Port Elgin, where she felt a disconnect between her urbane family - her engineer father from Slovenia and her "highly educated," fashionable mother. Fashions filtered to her town slowly, and fabrics were subpar, so she was constantly "elevating what was available to me," through garment reinvention. Overall, making was a means of elevation for Mary Jo—of materials, skills—to bridge her outsider sense of self.

A bit older, Andrea (b. 1952), who was also skilled at sewing from a young age, once combined her denim Wrangler jacket with her mother's old furs, an act of bricolage that merged her American and Russian heritage, and her utilitarian and luxury sides. Her immigrant parents, of Russian, Italian, and French descent, were constant style exemplars, and the aim to impress them informed how she styled herself, to project a sophisticated, cultured image. In one 1972 photograph she is at the stables in a tweed and leather riding jacket she designed and made, posed with her leg extended to display her go-to booted silhouette. Andrea's glamourous pose matches her privileged setting, and her role as maker underlines her self-styling and representation, while the image marks a subtle tension between her new and old worlds.

One (re)fashioned item with lived experience she fondly recalled was the fur coat that she had made for a large sum in New York, where she grew up, from which she removed some fur to trim a dress. She wore the coat to her brother's wedding, and to go out dancing—like to the Hippopotamus (the Hip) on 62nd Street. This jogged the memory of the night it got raided and her precious coat had to be thrown through the window from the coat check during her escape. I asked her what else she wore to the clubs, and she vaguely recalled trousers, high heels, and feathery tops, while dancing the "Hustle." Whilst the denim, homemade,

**Figure 10.1** Andrea at Riding Academy, Rockville Centre, New York, 1972. Image courtesy of A. Andrea Licari-LaGrassa.

and unlabeled garments discussed above would not typically elicit high museum interest, they illustrate how clothing functions as holders of memory, through the input of the wearer.

Disco also featured into Mary Jo's conception of the decade, which she divided into two sartorial periods: disco and punk. When she first traveled to Europe in 1976 it was the disco period, she explained. This trip was highly anticipated, as she had aspirations of locales (and lifestyles) beyond Canada, many of which were formed reading *Vogue*. She therefore needed to fashion her own wardrobe, to surpass what Port Elgin retailers could offer her. This included pencil skirts, which rode up and were uncomfortable, and pencil leg trousers. When, not long after, she moved to Toronto to attend the Ontario College of Art, she was still dressing to appear elegant and well off.

But this changed once there, when Mary Jo rebelled against this look and what it signified.

> Well, I came from a small town in Ontario to live in Toronto…when I first arrived I was still thinking probably disco…Trying to be…It was kind of a snooty time, people always wanted to look rich and so I was still probably trying to come off as a privileged kind of a person…And then it did not take long, it was by the sort of middle of the first year that I was starting to get influenced by punk and then of course you're sneering at all that stuff…Trying to look anti-establishment as much as possible.

It was as though this transition to punk was inevitable: she laughed and said, "What else would you do at art college." Her younger age in relation to the other

**Figure 10.2** Mary Jo in drawing class with her professor, Madame Wibaut, Banff Centre for the Arts, Alberta, Canada, 1978. Image courtesy of Mary Jo Pollak.

respondents also factors into this fashion shift. Mary Jo's style became about the "street", and she started to wear vintage—she saved her favorite piece, a 1940s grosgrain dress with a tight-fitting bodice. Otherwise, she dressed in a "uniform" of oversized men's blazers over jeans, largely influenced by musicians like Lou Reed and those she knew as friends such as Martha and the Muffins. Mary Jo was always on the hunt for black clothing during this period, which she said was hard to find. She wore a black turtleneck and bandana, in one image from 1978, the year she turned twenty, after transferring to the Banff School of Fine Arts.

She is captured at a drafting table lost in the creative process, in parallel to her thoughtful styling, the contrasting light-colored skirt, complete with jewelry and oversized glasses. Like her teacher alongside her, her image is one of sophistication, a merger of her disco and punk eras. This was the moment Mary Jo embarked on costume design studies and began to think critically about the "language" of dress as it related to character construction, which she furthered the following year, in New York at Julliard's costume department. In her personal life she likewise used clothing creatively to delineate shifting identities and worldviews—and her social difference. Yet she learned this language at an early age, thanks to her mother. As this section illustrates, making connections between various periods of a respondent's life, informed understandings of her 1970s experience. It also presents examples, which are disconnected from museum artifacts but informed by pictured fashion, of creative agency bridging aspects of one's identity across geographic locales.

## Joan and Cricket: Inside and outside fashion

Even before our conversation, Joan (b. 1947) communicated her negative views of 1970s fashion. When we spoke, she said in reference to its more exaggerated styles, "Fashion got so much more out there in the 1970s, it was so absurd." Yet, like the majority of testimonies which contained hesitant, ambiguous, or even contradictory ideas, hers encompassed alternative examples of her engagement with the decade's fashion culture. Views of what it meant to be in fashion and how that affected conceptions of self, were not straightforward for most respondents. Many shied away from the marker of being trendy but prided themselves on having fashion knowledge. In their words, they dressed according to their individual tastes, regardless of trends, and this was the case for Joan, whose comment illustrates a sense of ambivalence vis a vis group identity: "I knew what I liked, and I knew what I didn't like...I'm not sure many of us had a sense of fashion, I mean maybe it was just me, maybe I was just oblivious..."

Looking further back, she recalled not possessing many clothes as a child—she doesn't know whether this was financial, or because her single mother didn't have the time to take her shopping. Or was this a way shrugging off fashion, which wouldn't have been valued growing up in the bohemian Portland, Oregon college town? In high school, Joan wore A-line skirts, which she explained befit her thin, curvaceous frame, even though straight skirts were in style, highlighting her individuality in relation to trends. Of the 1970s Joan said, "There were various fashions that came and went and some of them I was very glad to see go." She disliked in particular tailored shirts with very pointy collars yet wore them out of necessity—as they were what was available in shops. Early in the decade she stopped wearing miniskirts and transitioned to trousers: "I remember being at a faculty party and sitting down and thinking that if the skirt were any shorter everything would be exposed [she laughs]. I had that experience and I thought, you know, why am I doing this? This is absurd, I don't really need to look like everybody else."

Joan's individualism also translated to her college plans, opting to forego the Reed College family tradition for Swarthmore, a school on the other coast of the country in Pennsylvania. In 1969, she and her husband moved to Berkeley for graduate school one year after their marriage. The same ambivalence about fashion was present: "I don't remember thinking about clothing at all during this period." She was busy with her studies and preoccupied with the war in Vietnam. It also conflicted with her academic identity ("academics aren't really into fashion"), budget, and lifestyle, needing to be comfortable while "researching in libraries."

It was abundantly clear, however, hearing her recount stories of shopping in the boutiques near campus, that Joan delighted in her clothing. She dressed in ways she felt suited her appearance. She loved color, especially blue and autumnal shades, but also found it necessary to mention those she perceived as unflattering on her. One trend she embraced were the peasant blouses, Indian, and other bright "ethnic" prints, which were (often) inexpensive and comfortable. Similar styles connected various points of her life and her art studies—from the blue wool skirt, with Guatemalan embroidery, she shared with her mother as an adolescent, to her current collection of Kashmir scarves, which counts as one of the best in the world.

In 1974, Joan relocated to Princeton, a move which came with a new elevated identity—that of professor's wife—which perhaps contradicted her own status as a graduate student, although advancing in her career and scholarly pursuits. This sort of limbo had a parallel in fashion. She laughed at the idea of donning a black blazer, the working woman's accessory of the moment. She deemed them uncomfortable and out of sync with her personality. Whereas she related to fashion much better in the following decade, when she would have been in a different place professionally and personally. In revealing stories of personal aversion, body image and identity, her testimony added meaning to archive objects that document historical trends.

At the outset of the 1970s, Cricket (b. 1941) launched her career as a patternmaker in the fast-paced New York garment industry. Before that, in the exact opposite direction to Joan, she attended Reed College in Portland, far from her east coast upbringing. She was orphaned during university, so the subsequent period was one of transition, trauma, and reinvention. She left this and the "radical West Coast politics" behind, and threw herself into travel and work, living in New Zealand, Bermuda, and Concord, Massachusetts where she even opened her own business. Perhaps fashion work suited this mental need for constant activity, but her self-fashioning was highly considered, in relation to her tastes, comfort and work-led lifestyle.

After these experiences she landed in New York to study at the Mayer School of Fashion Design to get a "hands on" education in illustration, sewing, draping, and patternmaking, as she already had a degree in philosophy. This was the only design school located in the garment center, and after a ten-month course she had acquired the skills to find work there. She changed jobs often, a reflection of the dynamic yet dying fashion industry. For her, it represented raw capitalism, and international access through immigrant colleagues: "It was so fun. It was the world, people from all over the world." She even became the president of the Craftsmen of Ladies Apparel in 1977, only three years after it opened up membership to women. Much of Cricket's wardrobe revolved around her physical job, which entailed standing, handwork and reaching across a big table.

Comfort prevented Cricket from wearing on-trend knitwear, as it made her too warm. She learned her lesson after the purchase of a knitted dress at Henri Bendel, which she first saw in a magazine. Because of its physical effect on her, she wore knitwear as outerwear in the instance of a long, olive-colored sweater with a cuff neck by Sonia Rykiel. It was a splurge and she even called her friend beforehand to ask if she should buy it, then added a lining to transform it into a coat. It also paired well with her colorful ethnic clothing, like her ikat scarf in aqua, fuchsia, and gold, which her good friend brought back from her travels to the Soviet Union. Cricket, too, loved to travel and had ikat coats from central Asia, and one from Iceland, one of her favorite places to visit. Similar to Joan, her "street clothes" were embroidered Indian tunics (kurtas) in cotton or silk, which she had in all colors, cut with a high arm hole and therefore comfortable.

After working for a sportswear company at 1407 Broadway, she moved into more formal clothing at Muney Design. The firm made clothing in jersey only, matte in the summer and wool jersey for the winter season, which Cricket normally couldn't afford herself. In 1977, however, she bought an outfit to wear to her aunt's anniversary party, at a discount: a taupe-colored blouse and skirt

**Figure 10.3** Barbara and Kevin Walz, Publicity Poster, Adri for Royal Clothes, c. 1971. Adri fashion design business records, The New School Archives and Special Collections, The New School, New York, NY. Image courtesy of Shari Robertson.

with an elastic waistband, and a band edging the neckline in a glossy satin-like fabric. She described it as her most trendy 1970s look, as "matte jersey was very big in those days." The popularity of jersey is well represented in museum archives, where I viewed, for example, high end Norma Kamali and Holly Harp dresses, trousers by Bonnie Cashin, and at a lower price point, a matte jersey wrap skirt by Bonnie August for the dancewear company Danskin.

The same prevalence marks visual culture, as 1971 campaign imagery for Royal Robes by Adri attests. In the photographs by Barbra Walz, one model engages with her anonymous loft-like interior space sparsely in a wardrobe made up almost entirely of jersey, including blousy dresses, skirts, and trousers.

**Figure 10.4** Publicity photograph for the Spring 1972 Clothes Circuit collection by Adri. Adri fashion design business records, The New School Archives and Special Collections, The New School, New York, NY. Image courtesy of Shari Robertson.

Adri, or Adrienne Steckling (1934–2006), frequently worked in jersey at this time. She graduated from Parsons School of Design in 1958 and worked at B. H. Wragge and Anne Fogarty before establishing her own lines in the late 1960s and throughout the 1970s, including Sportsthoughts and Royal Robes. Another photo campaign of models on Manhattan streets and alleyways, dressed in the Spring 1972 collection for Clothes Circuit (a division of Anne Fogarty), further connected the fabric to urban life. In a wide-legged stance with hands touching her body, framed by a wooden fence, and the rear views of brick buildings, one model shows the flexibility and sensuality of her ensemble: a cardigan and tube top over a matte jersey skirt, with a matte jersey turban, wedge sandals and a two-tone belt. These brand photographs were disseminated to the press, including regional papers across the country, for potential wide viewership. From jersey ensembles to miniskirts and blazers, according to interviews, the visually omnipresent, fashionable garments of the decade were considered but often impeded by financial constraints, ambivalence to trends, or a disconnect to body image or identity construction.

## Joyce and Andrea: Comfort and control

Touch and comfort are central threads in Joyce's (b. 1948) sartorial recollections. This was apparent from a childhood memory in Baton Rouge, Louisiana, of the difficulty of walking in hand-me-down shoes, with another person's "creases" already embedded. It also factors into her love of trousers in the 1970s (and today), as a reaction to earlier life experiences. She described the containment and fuss of the "girly" dresses with starched slips and frilly details, which her mother and grandmother would make for church or other special occasions for her and her sisters. They were worn with lacy socks and hats that didn't sit right on her head—something for which she was poked fun at. Perhaps due to the centrality of the Baptist church in the Black south, or the sensory dimension of the experience, these memories were strong for Joyce. She still doesn't like to wear dresses.

In grade and high school, she wasn't allowed to wear pants, which meant that her legs were out and she was cold. The constraints of wearing skirts further contrasted the liberating transition to trousers in college, and although she didn't pursue her dream of military training, which went against her father's wishes, she had more freedom in fashion at Southern University as a Fine Arts major, when she could wear pants and go sockless. There she was free from the hand-me-down clothes so necessary in a household with many children. In college she also started wearing an Afro, a cutting-edge and symbolic fashion choice which connected to the "Black is Beautiful" movement and, according to Tanisha C. Ford, "the language of soul."[24] Ford writes how "Collegiate spaces became important sites for soul style innovation and cultural discourse about blackness."[25] Continuing in this avant-garde mode Joyce wore a lime green minidress to her wedding in 1971. This overall sartorial freedom was tempered by the constraints of marriage within which Joyce continued to test the boundaries of her independence.

The materiality of dressing "down" resonated strongly for Joyce, and she wanted to keep her old jeans to the point that they were worn out enough to be soft against the skin. According to her mother, however, they were no longer new and needed to be thrown away. Her mother criticized her casual style, and perhaps this influenced how Joyce characterized herself, not as fashionable, but as a "tomboy," "simple" and true to self. Other items she recalled from her college years into her twenties were her burgundy corduroy jacket and a crocheted grey poncho. They felt good to the touch, and she felt like herself wearing them.

One image from the 1970s shows the seamless connection between her body, self, and environment – through comfortable dress. Seated on a sofa, she poses glamorously with one hand grazing her face and the other holding a camera. She

**Figure 10.5** Joyce surrounded by her grandmother, mother and daughter after Christmas dinner, Baton Rouge, *c.* 1975. Image courtesy of Joyce Square.

**Figure 10.6** Joyce at work at the copy center, Baton Rouge, 1975. Image courtesy of Joyce Square.

is wearing wide-leg pants, in the fashionable 1970s silhouette, a fitted striped sweater over a buttoned shirt, paired with gold hoop earrings, glasses, and a watch. Her eyes meet the lens, while three other female relatives in the scene look in a different direction caught in a candid moment. She authored other photos taken that day, the proof in her hand, but she is undoubtedly this picture's focus. Joyce recounted how she preferred taking pictures to being in them, and fondly remembers her childhood Brownie Starflash camera. The remnants of Christmas wrapping paper and the traces of decoration hint at the date of the event. The accessories she wore reappeared in another photo with a very different setting, where she is depicted confidently at the bank where she had a long career from 1974, but she traded her sweater for a jacket and soon after discarded her Afro.

To dress up she wore pantsuits and other pant ensembles. Trousers bridged Joyce's leisure and work worlds. They meant freedom, independence, maturity, and professionalism. By 1973, Andrea had a career in marketing at TWA, which led her to Wall Street later on. Working so young as a woman in a powerful position left her feeling vulnerable so she wore long coats, trousers, blazers, and menswear fabrics. She made sure to assert her confidence to me, however, adding that she did not "emulate" men's dress to give them the power, but to wear them "like a woman." Several years into her career, in 1977 John T. Molloy published *The Women's Dress for Success Book* in which he outlined the sartorial formula to aide women in moving up the corporate ladder and the ways they needed to align to and distinguish themselves from their male counterparts. A skirted suit was optimal and the jacket, as Patricia A. Cunningham wrote, would fill the need for women's appearance of authority.[26] This strategy differed widely among narrators, thinking back to Joan who was uncomfortable in black blazers: "I always thought it was odd that women who were feminists were starting to dress like their male counterparts. And I really kind of rebelled against that." The divergence perhaps also owed to their respective professional milieu: the corporate office, the university, the fashion, and theatre industries.

For Andrea, fashion was also about control. An adept seamstress with New York's resources at her disposal, as discussed above, she felt in control having the knowledge to make things. This was the case leading up to the 1970s. From her mid-teens in 1967 until her early twenties Andrea modeled, mainly for her aunt's Madison Avenue shop. Here too, she sought control of the image, to see and comment on the male photographer's work. This same impulse was perhaps behind her professional wardrobe.

Like most of the narrators, Andrea considered herself to be "ahead" of feminism, alone in her sex in both school and at work. She jumped between gender "worlds," where she could present herself differently. The established high-end sportswear firm Anne Klein provided clothes to negotiate these worlds, often selling blazers with both skirts and trousers during the 1970s, several examples of which are evident in the collection of The Costume Institute.[27] Klein's eponymous label, which was run by Donna Karan and Louis Dell'Olio after her death in 1973, targeted female professionals who sought streamlined clothing, and was widely pictured in the fashion press. This consumer market, representative of most respondents, also grew up with skirt dress codes and matured into a society that was still unclear about these terms. Joan even noted a job in the late 1980s, that only allowed skirts and sheer pantyhose. In most conversations, the subject of trousers triggered a thoughtful and animated reflection, demonstrating its contentiousness. While many archives contain Anne Klein garments to illustrate the work woman's wardrobe of the 1970s, just as they symbolized this ideal for consumers including those interviewed here, they remained financially inaccessible for many. Further, our conversations unpacked the various topics layered into the construction of professional identities, not limited to comfort, control and consciousness.

## Negotiating the gaze

"I'm trying to reach women who are committed to a contemporary lifestyle which, at times, approaches the paradoxical," Adri says. "'My' woman lives a life which is both fast and relaxed, casual and elegant. She needs clothes that can keep up with all the changes her fast-paced existence calls for."[28]

That clothing needed to mediate and facilitate the complete lives of women—from work to leisure, "single working woman" to motherhood, from morning to evening—was still a central message in the 1970s fashion press, as well as in commentary from the growing group of women designers such as Adri. As seen above, this was a moment of ambiguity for women, given more opportunities yet alert to the reality of their second-class rights, within the context of feminism's "second wave." As Joan remarked to me, "Our antennas were up as we were learning more and more about our place in the world." That the decade began with real legislative steps taken to approve the Equal Rights Amendment (ERA) to the Constitution (according to which, "Equality of rights under the law shall not be denied or abridged by the United States or by any state on account of sex.") which ended in failure after years of campaigning, helps us situate it as a period in limbo, caught between the ideals of liberalism and the New Right.

Speaking with Andrea in particular underscored the various, divergent roles women played, in relation to their clothing choices. One was the conservative and refined image she upheld when working, in contrast to dressing "provocatively," in for instance the low-cut black dress she made with a high slit, with a thick gold trim around the center seam, which she was photographed wearing in 1975 for an evening out. She also spoke, as mentioned previously, of dressing elegantly to impress her parents. She dressed with "the ambient gaze," in mind, defined by Chong Kwan as "how the wearer experiences the gaze and, moreover, how they might employ individual agency to negotiate this disciplinary gaze," based on a "social system that constructs and disciplines the body" to act (and dress) according for various situations.[29] Andrea characterized her dressing strategy as "design and management," a way of demarcating and negotiating her creative expression and professional life. Long wrap dresses, she cites Diane von Furstenberg's design, functioned as the perfect negotiation, as they were suggestive but not flashy, of a simple cut but a colorful motif, and which could be dressed up or down (with boots). Every archive I visited to date regardless of collecting aims had several models of von Furstenberg's dresses, and many more

**Figure 10.7** Andrea at the Law School Prom, St. John's University, New York, 1975. Image courtesy of A. Andrea Licari-LaGrassa.

designers had their own versions. This remarkable commonality attests to this adaptable garment's popularity.

For Andrea, they were "Clothes you can count on," as one of *Harper's Bazaar*'s regular sections was titled. It provided support during a period of anxiety and choice, in guiding readers through garment options that would work for them. Andrea had the means to afford "go-to" pieces which allowed her to travel lightly for her job: a blazer (Ralph Lauren's in particular), a trench coat, and a scarf, and the colors black or navy. For Joan and Joyce, this meant soft and comfortable clothing, simple cuts and minimalism: Joan used word "flouncy" to describe what didn't work for her. As Figure 10.2 illustrates, Mary Jo relied heavily on bandanas, which she could wrap and style in a number of ways: "It was also a way of coping with my crappy hair [which] I tried to wear long…so if I wrapped it up in a bandana it would look good." In another *Harper's Bazaar* example, in 1976 and 1977 it featured the section, "Nobody is Perfect: How to make the most of what you've got," which instructed the right garment silhouette according to body type. Respondents had precise ideas of what didn't what didn't work for them. For Joan it was pastels, straight skirts and blazers, while, according to Mary Jo, "I'm tall and I've got big hands and big feet, so I could never really pull off the totally delicate styles." These ideas were formed out of comfort, visual perceptions of self, and the potential gaze of the onlooker. In parallel, the magazine's section allowed for imperfections, yet it also encouraged readers to compare themselves to an ideal, in a social framework of looking at female bodies.

Many narrators discussed the sexual objectification they encountered in life, often in relation to clothing. Mary Jo noted the attention and rules surrounding women's bodies. In a waitressing job interview she was asked to "twirl" in her uniform. More generally, "It was hard walking down the street anywhere, it wasn't just catcalls and whistlers there were gross comments being made, graphic and everything." While, as mentioned previously, Joan remarked,

> "I hated the miniskirt…Even though I probably looked…well I got flattering comments wearing them you know that was the other thing…clothing was very sexualized I think at that point with the miniskirt and the tights and men seemed to…felt they could make more commentary about your clothing as a result of that so um I wasn't really interested in having that kind of commentary."

They discussed learning to negotiate the male gaze, to divert attention, through appearance choices. Andrea trained herself to downplay (during choice moments) her beauty and her femaleness through dress, or by hiding her long blond hair.

Indeed, the press disseminated mixed messages and a multi-directional gaze, so that sections on practical and reliable clothing or those addressing "working women," were read alongside images of sexualized bodies. Mary Jo was the most avid magazine reader of this group, and the others vaguely recalled consulting them without clear recollections of titles or particular images, with the exception of Joyce who didn't read them and Cricket who discussed one post-magazine garment purchase. Conversely, she also described magazines as reminders of the "patriarchal culture we were leaving." Mary Jo was sixteen or seventeen when she got her *Vogue* subscription, which provided access to a wider world: "I was looking at all the fabulous clubs in Paris and New York and looking at what the women were wearing there." Ideological changes stemming from feminist discourse influenced how she looked at models represented in imagery, pushing her to cancel her *Vogue* subscription in the 1980s. These were the very concerns of the Task Force on the Image of Women, created in 1966 to "change the stereotyped image and denigration of women in all the mass media." This was one of the seven task forces set up by the National Organization for Women (NOW) the year it was established. Yet by the early 1970s it deemed fashion codes as open to interpretation. According to a 1972 memo, "more and more women are making a free choice of what to wear and how to look based on what is uniquely suited to their personal style and individual lives."[30] As we saw from the 1971 FGI Bulletin quoted at the start of this essay, industry leaders were adopting a language of choice and individuality, which paralleled the centrality of "choice feminism" to the women's movement by the mid-1970s, according to Hillman.[31] Despite moments of ambivalence or hesitation, all narrators clearly communicated to me their perceived sense of authenticity and individuality vis a vis self-fashioning. It was as Andrea recounted: "I dressed for me."

## Conclusion

Downstairs at the Fashion Archives and Museum of Shippensburg University there are racks of garments, divided by period. They are not stored according to their illustrious maker as elsewhere in the archive, in fact, many have no labels. Repositories such as these are where we inch closer to finding the "every day." Very few designer names came up in the oral testimonies discussed, and probing narrators to remember them often cut off conversation. This proved similar in discussions of magazine imagery. Whereas the Fashion Archives racks resemble the ordered chaos of personal closets, a mixture of styles and quality, that seem to contain the imprint (and experiences) of the wearer more than they operate as exemplars of workmanship, trends, or designer genius. Experiential testimony supplements and animates what is held within archives, including as we've seen here, knitwear, jeans, wrap dresses and the "professional" woman's wardrobe, whilst shedding light on what is missing. This chapter contends that "big history" is incomplete without women's voices, which expose fashion narratives, such as those explored here regarding creativity, fashionability, feel, control and negotiations. The inconsistencies which occur at the intersection of image, object and voice when these worlds meet is a good place to begin our study of history.

## Acknowledgments

This research was made possible thanks to a 2020–1 postdoctoral fellowship at the Costume Institute of the Metropolitan Museum of Art. I wish to thank the staff there as well as at the following institutions where additional research was undertaken: The New School Archives and Special Collections, Manuscripts and Archives Division of the New York Public Library, de Young Museum, FIDM Museum, Los Angeles County Museum of Art, The Museum at FIT, Fashion Archives and Museum of Shippensburg University and Robert and Penny Fox Historic Costume Collection at Drexel University.

## Author interviews

Mary Jo Pollak, February 24, 2021
Cricket Giese, March 17, and March 23, 2021
A. Andrea Licari-LaGrassa, March 24, and March 31, 2021
Joan Hart, May 12, 2021,
Joyce Square, August 14, 2021

## Notes

1 Valerie Steele, "Anti-Fashion: The 1970s," *Fashion Theory* 1, no. 3 (1997): 279–96.
2 "The Changing Consumer," *Bulletin, The Fashion Group, Inc.*, October 29 (1971).
3 Ibid.
4 The wider research project examines women designers as well as consumers in its aim to expose various modes of female creative participation that have remained largely absent from history annals.
5 I've conducted research at the following archives: Costume Institute, Metropolitan Museum of Art, New York; de Young Museum, San Francisco; Fashion Institute of Design and Merchandising Museum, Los Angeles; Fashion Archives and Museum of Shippensburg University, Shippensburg; Los Angeles County Museum of Art, Los Angeles; The Museum at FIT, New York; Robert and Penny Fox Historic Costume Collection, Drexel University, Philadelphia.
6 This research project has studied the magazines *Harper's Bazaar*, *Essence*, and *Vogue*, as well as campaign imagery from a number of brands they disseminated to the national presses and used in advertising.
7 Alexis Romano and Ellen Sampson, "The Auteur is Alive and Well Dressed," *Vestoj*, 2018.
8 Adrienne Rich, "When We Dead Awaken: Writing as Re-Vision," *College English* (1972): 44.
9 Ink on paper, collection of Doug Woodham and Dalya Inhaber, www.metmuseum.org/art/collection/search/835039

10 Cheryl Buckley and Hilary Fawcett, *Fashioning the Feminine: Representation and Women's Fashion from the Fin de Siècle to the Present* (London: I. B. Tauris, 2002), 2.

11 Betty Luther Hillman, *Dressing for the Culture Wars: Style and the Politics of Self-Presentation in the 1960s and 1970s* (Lincoln, NE, and London: University of Nebraska Press, 2015), 71.

12 Lou Taylor, *The Study of Dress History* (Manchester and New York: Manchester University Press, 2002), 242.

13 Linda Sandino, "Oral Histories and Design," *Journal of Design History* 19, no. 4 (2006): 278.

14 Taylor, *The Study of Dress History*, 242.

15 For the latter see Evan Casey and Deirdre Clemente, "Clothing the Contadini: Migration and Material Culture, 1890–1925," *Journal of American Ethnic History* 36, no. 4 (2017).

16 See, for example, Claire Wilcox, "Covering Up," in *Oral History in the Visual Arts*, eds., Linda Sandino and Matthew Partington (London and New York: Bloomsbury, 2013), 153–9.

17 A notable exception is "Memory of Clothes," by Helen Barff and Suzanne Joinson at Worthing Museum (2019). See also Svetlana Kitto, *Sara Penn's Knobkerry: An Oral History Sourcebook* (Sculpture Center and New York Consolidated, 2021).

18 See, for instance, "Ebony Fashion Fair Oral History Project," Minnesota Historical Society; "Oral History Project," Gladys Marcus Library, Fashion Institute of Technology; "Fashion Group International St. Louis Oral Histories," Washington University in St. Louis; "An Oral History of British Fashion," British Library; and "Garment Industry Oral History Collection," Kansas City Public Library.

19 See Alison Slater, "Wearing in memory-materiality," 2014; Alison Slater, "Listening to Dress," 2020; Sara Chong Kwan, "Making sense of everyday dress," 2016; Sara Chong Kwan, "The Ambient Gaze," 2020. See also Liz Linthicum, "Oral History, Dress and Disability Studies," 2006.

20 Sophie Woodward, *Why Women Wear What They Wear* (Oxford and New York: Berg, 2007).

21 This growing body of work includes Lucia Ruggerone, "The Feeling of Being Dressed," *Fashion Theory* 21, no. 1 (2017); and Ellen Sampson, *Worn* (London: Bloomsbury, 2020).

22 Raphael Samuel and Paul Thompson (eds.), *The Myths We Live By* (London: Routledge,1990), 2.

23 Author interview, Cricket Giese, March 2021.

24 Tanisha C. Ford, *Liberated Threads: Black Women, Style, and the Global Politics of Soul* (Chapel Hill: The University of North Caroline Press, 2015), 102.

25 Ibid., 95.

26  Patricia A. Cunningham, "Dressing for Success: The Re-Suiting of Corporate America in the 1970s," in *Twentieth-Century American Fashion*, eds. Linda Welters and Patricia A. Cunningham (Oxford and New York: Berg, 2005), 204.
27  1977.362.26a–c; 1977.362.28a–h
https://www.metmuseum.org/art/collection/search/96824
https://www.metmuseum.org/art/collection/search/96825
28  Press release, Adri for Clothes Circuit, Spring 1972, Adri Fashion Design Business Records.
29  Chong Kwan, "The Ambient Gaze: Sensory Atmosphere and the Dressed Body," in *Revisiting the Gaze: The Fashioned Body and the Politics of Looking*, eds. Morna Laing and Jacki Willson (London: Bloomsbury Visual Arts, 2020), n.p.
30  Image of Task Force News, July 1973 memo, box 30, folder 65, series VIII, NOW records. Cited in Hillman, N99209.
31  Hillman, *Dressing for the Culture Wars*, 82.

# Bibliography

Buckley, Cheryl and Hilary Fawcett. *Fashioning the Feminine: Representation and Women's Fashion from the Fin de Siècle to the Present*. London: I. B. Tauris, 2002.

Chong Kwan, Sara. "Making sense of everyday dress: integrating multi-sensory experience within our understanding of contemporary dress in the UK" (PhD Diss., 2016).

Chong Kwan, Sara. "The Ambient Gaze: Sensory Atmosphere and the Dressed Body." In *Revisiting the Gaze: The Fashioned Body and the Politics of Looking*, edited by Morna Laing and Jacki Willson. Bloomsbury Visual Arts, London, 2020.

Cunningham, Patricia A. "Dressing for Success: The Re-Suiting of Corporate America in the 1970s." In *Twentieth-Century American Fashion*, edited by Linda Welters and Patricia A. Cunningham (Oxford and New York: Berg, 2005), 191–208.

Ford, Tanisha C. *Liberated Threads: Black Women, Style, and the Global Politics of Soul*. Chapel Hill, NC: The University of North Caroline Press, 2015.

Guy, Ali, Eileen Green and Maura Banim, eds. *Through the Wardrobe: Women's Relationships with their Clothes*. Oxford: Berg, 2001.

Hillman, Betty Luther. *Dressing for the Culture Wars: Style and the Politics of Self-Presentation in the 1960s and 1970s*. Lincoln, NE, and London: University of Nebraska Press, 2015.

Linthicum, Liz. "Integrative Practice: Oral History, Dress and Disability Studies." *Journal of Design History* 19, no. 4 (2006): 309–18.

Romano, Alexis and Ellen Sampson. "The Auteur is Alive and Well Dressed: What Designer Retrospectives Miss About Fashion." *Vestoj*, 2018, http://vestoj.com/the-auteur-is-alive-and-well-dressed/

Samuel, Raphael and Paul Thompson, eds. *The Myths We Live By*. London: Routledge, 1990.

Sandino, Linda. "Introduction. Oral Histories and Design: Objects and Subjects." *Journal of Design History* 19, no. 4 (2006): 275–82.

Slater, Alison. "Wearing in memory-materiality and oral histories of dress." *Critical Studies in Fashion and Beauty* 5, no. 1 (2014): 125–39.

Slater, Alison. "Listening to Dress: Unfolding Oral History Methods." In *Mundane Methods: Innovative Ways to Research the Everyday*, edited by Helen Holmes and Sarah Marie Hall. Manchester University Press, 2020.

Steele, Valerie. "Anti-Fashion: The 1970s." *Fashion Theory* 1/3 (1997): 279–96.

Taylor, Lou. "Approaches Using Oral History." In *The Study of Dress History*. Manchester and New York: Manchester University Press, 2002, 242–71.

Wilcox, Claire. "Covering Up." In *Oral History in the Visual Arts*, edited by Linda Sandino and Matthew Partington. London and New York: Bloomsbury, 2013, 153–9.

Woodward, Sophie. *Why Women Wear What They Wear*. Oxford and New York: Berg, 2007.

# 11

# Preserving the Latinx Sartorial Experience Through Digital Archives

Michelle McVicker

In September 2020, *The New York Times* fashion director and chief fashion critic Vanessa Freidman published an article titled, "The Incredible Whiteness of the Museum Fashion Collection," which explicitly pointed out an issue many of us participating in the field of fashion studies have been aware of for decades. The article details how in the small group of world-renowned high-culture institutions historically charged with preserving and protecting the art of fashion seldom collect or exhibit pieces designed by Black or female designers.[1] Notably, there was no mention of the percentage of pieces in collections attributed to designers representing any other marginalized community, including Latinx. Due to the homogenization of the terms Latino and Hispanic, we are currently experiencing an awakening of intersectional, gender-neutral identifiers. One is the increased usage of the term Latinx—being both American and Latino/a—with which I personally identify and will unpack and contextualize later. The inclusion of garments that represent marginalized communities and discarded histories in museums can provide a more diverse understanding of fashion, yet Latinx sartorial representation within fashion museology has been long lacking. For this chapter, I am focusing on the visual portrayal of the Latinx experience of everyday dress through the recent emergence of multiple Instagram accounts.

I owe the inspiration for this chapter to the August 2019 *New York Times* piece "Preserving Latinx History Through Vintage Photos."[2] Author Isabelia Herrera stated, "A new wave of digital archivists is capturing the forgotten stories of Latinxs across the diaspora…using the platform [of Instagram] to recover local Latinx cultures and contextualize them as part of a broader United States historical narrative."[3] These Instagram pages include Veteranas and Rucas (@veteranas_and_rucas), founded by artist Guadalupe Rosales in 2015, which portrays Chicana youth culture in the 1980s and 1990s. The New York City based

Nuevayorkinos (@nuevayorkinos), founded in 2019 by filmmaker and archivist Djali Brown-Cepeda, highlights how important clothing and 'dressing the part' is to the immigrant and generational experience. In a special *NYT* piece published in September 2020, Elizabeth Méndez Berry and Mónica Ramírez proclaim that these virtual repositories are providing alternatives to institutional limitations, including the physical space of a gallery. Demonstrating Latinx's "thirst to see ourselves," these Instagram pages are fostering community and disrupting the country's amnesia about Latinos.[4]

Other Instagram accounts providing alternate displays of history include Quinceañera Archives (@quinceaneraarchives) by visual artist Samantha Cabrera Friend, Documenting the Nameplate (@documentingthenameplate) cofounded by Isabel Flowers and Marcel Rosa-Salas, and the Latinx Diaspora Archives (@Latinx_Diaspora_Archives) curated by photographer William Camargo. The participatory nature of the pages cover subjects across the country by encouraging followers to submit their own photographs and accompanying captions and reframe Latinx visual representation in the American cultural canon.

Chief curator and deputy director curatorial and collections at the Lucas Museum of Narrative Art in Los Angeles, Pilar Tompkins Rivas, suggests a reframing of family photographs to be thought of as part of "a larger history of vernacular Latinx photography—a national project yet to be undertaken within our annals of historicizing the American experience."[5] Until museum institutions create collecting initiatives that strategize the accession of Latinx related material culture, I argue these crowdsourced photographs serve as a valid and necessary form of fashion archive. These images and their accompanying auto-biographical text provide insight into the Latinx lived experience beyond historic garments housed within institutional settings that are often exceptional rather than ordinary. Although the fashion objects represented in these images are not preserved in museums, the photographs themselves document the importance of dress within the everyday as it pertains situationally to the Latinx community. What these and many other digital archives offer those who identify as Latinx is ownership and agency over visual representation in a sartorial history where they have traditionally been excluded.

## Latinx definition (origins and usage)

Despite the controversies surrounding its legitimacy, the term "Latinx" is the first self-identifier to be coined by the community itself and is preferred by both individuals and institutions. An important distinction between this new term and its predecessors is the gender-neutral connotation marked by the letter "X" that allows for more inclusivity. Although the term has gained traction in the art world thanks to the founding director of The Latinx Project at New York University, Arlene Dávila, its application in the realm of fashion studies is limited, and its definition inconsistent and vague. For the sake of my chapter, I will apply a combination of the following definitions toward my implementation of the term.

In 2018, The New School hosted a seminar titled, "Latinx Art is American Art." I would like to employ this statement to fashion studies as well, therefore, Latinx fashion is American fashion. The following year, the creative studio White Lines Project curated the exhibition, *Mundo Latinx*, in the Fashion Space Gallery in London. The accompanying exhibition material explained why they consider "Latino" and "Latina" highly problematic terms. Both signifiers reference an antiquated colonial origin and enforce a perceived singular stereotype and narrative on culturally vastly different countries and communities, misrepresenting people from all these places as sharing a common identity and ethnicity.[6] El Museo del Barrio, which proclaims itself as "New York's leading Latino cultural institution,"[7] added "Latinx" as one of its permanent collection categories in 2020. The section's artwork is considered reflective of a "construction of identity that references Latin American heritage and ethnicity in the US, while also intersecting with African, Indigenous, queer, and trans identities."[8] In this example, the term Latinx is employed as a verb, as the act and process of self-representation, which I argue also encompasses practices of everyday dress.

## Willful Neglect: The Smithsonian Institution and US Latinos

Although Friedman's timely article brought attention to the significant gap in fashion museological representation, there was no offering of a potential plan of action by cultural institutions to combat this lack, yet remedies have been attempted. One such example of an American museum internally investigating and systemically implementing a protocol for enacting change was the 1994 seminal report aptly titled, "Willful Neglect: The Smithsonian Institution and U.S. Latinos."

After decades of complaints from museum goers and United States Congress political representatives, the Smithsonian Institution created an internal task force to address the public's concerns regarding Latino/a representation within the permanent collection and exhibitions. Produced after a year-long investigation, the sixty-page report found a pattern of discrimination dating back 148 years.[9] The task force concluded that, "The Smithsonian Institution, the largest museum complex in the world, displayed a pattern of willful neglect towards the estimated 25 million Latinos in the United States."[10] Furthermore, the task force found consistent Latino exclusion from the work of the Smithsonian. They determined a vicious cycle of low Latino initiatives, discouraging visits from museum goers as well as a lack of support for mentoring current and past Latino staff.[11] These choices were found to be intentional and done repeatedly over time. As an effect, the report concluded these omissions and faults in accountability have projected the impression that Latino history and culture are somehow not a legitimate part of the American experience.[12]

In the report, Raul Yzaguirre, the chair of the Task Force on Latino Issues, stressed the influence of the Smithsonian in defining what America is; "It is not only that we as Latinos cannot come to the Smithsonian and be reflected and see ourselves as contributors to this nation," he said, "but it is even more disheartening [that other Americans] never understand that we are part of society."[13] Among its recommendations advised nearly twenty years ago, the task force suggested a commitment to employing, promoting, and retaining Latino staff, developing sustainable funding, and even mentioned the establishment of one or more standalone museums portraying the achievements of US Hispanics. As a result, the Center for Latino Initiatives (later renamed the Smithsonian Latino Center) was created three years later, in 1997.

Additionally, as part of the Latino Initiatives Pool—a federal fund that provides financial support to programs, exhibitions, research, collections and archives, and publications—Smithsonian museums hired experts, acquired artworks and objects, and planned exhibitions and programs to accomplish their goals of telling a more inclusive history of the US.[14] In 2010, they launched the Latino Curatorial Initiative to help Smithsonian museums produce more content that adequately represents the many contributions of Latinos to the country and has funded twenty positions for Latino curators, archivists, and curatorial assistants across the Institution.[15] In terms of costume, they specifically sourced and collected a quinceañera dress, clothing sold on Olvera Street, an escaramuza ensemble, and an outfit worn by Tex-Mex singer Selena Quintanilla Pérez.[16] On their website, the National Museum of American History states that their Costume Collection, "illustrates many of the social, cultural, technological and economic influences affecting dress made or worn in America."[17] The inclusion of Latino worn and designed clothing within such an institution cements the legacy of Latinx experience in American history.

In June 2022, the National Museum of the American Latino opened its first exhibition titled, "¡Presente! A Latino History of the United States." This inaugural exhibition offered an introduction to the important ideas, moments, and people that shine a light on the many ways Latinas and Latinos shaped the nation.[18] In regard to the inclusion of fashion objects, most items of clothing on display would arguably be considered "extraordinary." A handmade Indita dance outfit from New Mexico was featured in the "Colonial Legacies" section of the exhibition while two performance costumes worn by Cuban-American signer Celia Cruz were featured as "Shaping the Nation." What can be considered the most "everyday" fashion pieces on display was an ensemble worn by a Cuban child immigrant who came to the United States through Operation Pedro Pan (*Peter Pan*) in the section titled, "Immigration Stories." Despite its location in the Molina Family Latino Gallery at the National Museum of American History and not in a standalone building, "¡Presente!" remains the first Smithsonian Museum space dedicated to the Latino experience on the National Mall.

Although the Smithsonian is in the unique position of receiving government funding and visibility on a national scale, their immense efforts made in the two decades since the self-discovery of "willful neglect" toward Latino/as highlight how effectively addressing these issues takes time, requires systemic intervention, and ongoing support of staff, which can serve as a blueprint for other institutions. Yet museum bureaucracy and the conservatism of the national institution have somewhat hampered their response. Until specific and longstanding collecting initiatives encourage the accession of Latinx related material culture, crowd-sourced photographs curated and shared on social media are a crucial intervention and serve as a valid form of a Latinx fashion archive.

## Digital Instagram archives

Jesse Alemán is a professor of English at the University of New Mexico where he teaches American and US Latinx literary histories. In the piece, "How Can Historical Photographs Preserve Latinx Culture?" he describes how the omission of Latinx people and photographers in the history of photography in the United States and beyond led him to begin his own archive:

> I thought…[there] must be people who had the resources to document themselves, and they must have valued these pictures. As we all know and are familiar with in our own families, there is always a picture of the grandparents or some other old photograph of someone somewhere in the house.[19]

In addressing the pragmatic difficulty in collecting imagery that encapsulates the nuances of Latinx identity Alemán states, "One must track down family possessions, search through library collections and inaccessible or defunct archives to capture the complexities of Latinx lives without recirculating the same distorted and harmful images."[20] This emphasis on the cultural and collective construction of embodied identity can be applied to representation in all American museological institutions, including their costume collections. A similar sentiment was echoed in Friedman's 2020 text; "Just because museums are custodians of the past does not absolve them of responsibility for the present. And in that sense, their collections and the sins of omission enshrined therein speak to the very essence of the current problem."[21]

I believe the same statement can be said about the lack of Latinx fashion collected and displayed in relevant public exhibitions in the United States. When describing collective history, cultural anthropologist Aleida Assman states, "Autobiographical memories cannot be embodied by another person, but they can be shared with others."[22] Groups, social networks, and communities are important because they keep memory active, reclaiming the narrative, which is demonstrated in the image based social media platform, Instagram. Crowd-sourced Instagram pages visually mediate how the individual Latinx sartorial memory relates to the collective history of fashion within the context of the United States. The community that emerges on such pages serve as a form of communal validation. The power of fashion/dress, and especially everyday dress, in preserving the Latinx experience reclaims the narrative through "belonging-in-difference" and shared experience.[23]

## Veteranas and Rucas

Digital archives that use Instagram as their singular platform have been on the rise since the mid-2010s. One of the earliest, Veteranas y Rucas, was founded in 2015 by Los Angeles based multidisciplinary artist and educator Guadalupe Rosales and has inspired other independent collectors.[24] Rosales views the historical misrepresentations of how Latinx communities have been portrayed and represented over her lifetime as acts of erasure and violence. Veteranas documents Chicana youth culture in Los Angeles in the 1980s and 1990s. With over 274,000 followers, the current bio of the page describes itself as a, "Platform for self-representation & Collective memory. Reframing our past by sharing our stories for better futures."[25]

In her project statement, Rosales describes how the archive "celebrates, humanizes, and reflects the positive and honest attributes of our shared culture."[26] When she began her Instagram page, the terms "marginalized" and "under/mis represented" were new to her because she felt seen where she grew up in Los Angeles, and her culture was heavily represented. Once she moved to New York, she felt homesick and tried to look for ways to understand her past and reconnect with family and friends but struggled to find material that accurately depicted her community. In a post from October 2020, Rosales stated that before this Instagram platform, she had nowhere to turn for representation. She has since noticed the emergence of pages focusing on other locations and subcultures and is encouraged by the creation of space for collective healing and storytelling where we "celebrate together, grieve together and empower one another."[27]

Rosales's archives explore how history and culture are framed and who does the framing, emphasizing how time is not only constructed but enacted through constant memory.[28] Using philosopher and sociologist Maurice Halbwachs's definition of collective memory, we learn from memory for affirmation, yet memory is active and performative.[29] In an interview with the *LA Times*, Rosales explicitly describes how her Instagram archive serves as collective memory by representing physical places, objects, and style (that may or may not still exsist) digitally.[30] Fashion and dress perform in this process by documenting the embodied experience of its wearers. Archiving such performances through publicly submitted and shared Instagram photos is a method of self-framing, actively combating exclusionary fashion history, and creating community.

## Nuevayorkinos

Nuevayorkinos, founded by filmmaker and archivist Djali Brown-Cepeda, is a digital archive documenting and preserving New York City Latin and Caribbean culture and history through family photographs and stories.[31] With over 70,000 followers, many submissions share family members' participation in the fashion system, whether through factory work or as seamstresses. Posts also often highlight the importance of clothing and "dressing the part" as part of the immigrant and generational experience.

In its mission statement, "Nuevayorkinos takes a stand against widespread hate by storytelling—sharing the endless experiences and stories of New York City Latinxs from various countries in itself combats the stereotypes affecting Latinx and immigrant communities and destroys the one-note narrative. In colonial spaces, storytelling by the historically disenfranchised is a means toward decolonization." The archive is highly localized, catalogued by New York City's five boroughs: the Bronx, Brooklyn, Manhattan, Queens, and Staten Island, with the intention of dispelling gentrification through the historical documentation of residents.

## Personal tensions of ethnography

Throughout my research for this chapter, I have been aware of the contradiction between the deeply personal nature of the family histories being shared on immensely public Instagram platforms. Although I have seen aspects of my life reflected in their images and find comfort in the community that develops in the comment section, I also came across ethical concerns when reaching out to submitters and requesting image permissions for their photographs to be a part of this chapter.

For every submission I was interested in publishing in print, I first contacted the owner of the Instagram page hosting the image. I received a variety of responses, including many "no"s, due to the layered and complicated nature of requesting such permission. In other instances, the owner of the Instagram page requested I reach out to the submitter directly and include them in my correspondence. In others still, the owner of the page provided me with the image and signed permission, choosing to reach out to the submitter on my behalf. In specific cases, the family member of the person photographed wanted to discuss the potential publication of their likeness with the subject before granting permission. In most, the submitter was initially taken aback by my interest, and enthusiastic to cement their family history in print. This begs the question, when an image is uploaded to Instagram, then shared though a third party, who does that image belong to, and what relationship does it then have to the subject?

I also encountered technical resolution issues since most of the images were not scans of the physical photograph but cell phone snap shots of family albums. In some instances, the images posted varied slightly from their original Instagram submission, having been altered with Instagram's own enhancing filters and cropped. In these cases, family members physically scanned a higher quality version of the original image for this publication. As a result, I was unable to secure the image permissions for some of the most powerful examples illustrating the role that everyday dress plays in these accounts. I will share the accompanying captions for three of my personal favorites, all sourced from Nuevayorkinos.

These images and their corresponding testimonies are important examples of Latinx individuals as not only participants within the fashion system, but as vital

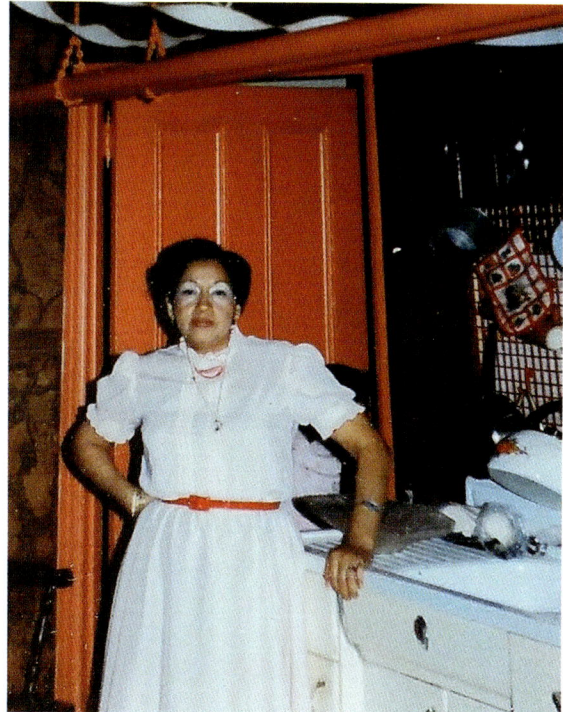

**Figure 11.1** Mercedes Marina Arambulo, The Bronx, 1980s. "This is my mother, Mercedes Marina Muñoz. She migrated from Ecuador along with her siblings and my grandmother. They all ended up in The Bronx sometime in the early 1960s. She would have four children, including me. As a teen, my parents separated, and she became the breadwinner for us all. She was a seamstress and worked in some of the sweatshops that were still in operation around The Bronx. It was piece work, so she would at times bring work home and sew gowns into the night. She worked hard to make sure we had a roof over our heads and food on the table. I am eternally grateful for what she did for us. This is an image of her in our basement before a family party, love you and miss you mom."

contributors. They played an active rather than passive role in their own and others' everyday sartorial representation as laborers, seamstresses, and designers in fashion production. Additionally, these examples highlight the impact such exposure to the different facets of the fashion system ultimately had on younger Latinx generations. Unlike the relationship between text and a static, printed image featured in a physical publication, Instagram's digital platform allows for a continued, ever-changing participatory converstation from the public in the comments section. The images and captions often trigger others' own memories, with expressions of mutal understanding, awe, and comradery in the comments, further solidifying this archive as collective memory.

**Figure 11.2** A typical day at the office, *c.* 1991/1992. "From about the mid 1980s to the mid 1990s, my mom was a professional fashion designer in children's wear. She's been sewing clothes since childhood pretty much. Growing up, I got to reap the benefits of a designer mom with all the free swag! More than anything though, it was a massive source of pride for the family to have the matriarch working in a grand place such as an office in the Empire State Building. I've always said my fashion education started with her, pounding pavement up and down the garment district. Seventh Avenue, a whole untapped world for little me. By 1997, she made the decision to leave fashion design and work in special education (and has been enjoying the retiree life since 2019. She still sews for fun too!). And I've similarly followed in her design footsteps with perusing costume design in film and TV. Every time I feel down on myself for not having connections or being in the place I want to be in at work, I remind myself that nobody has anything on me because nobody else has their education and hustle come from a sassy Dominican woman who made a place for herself high up in the Empire State Building."

*Preserving the Latinx Sartorial Experience Through Digital Archives* 237

**Figure 11.3** Jaime Restrepo, Kristina Lopez's *padrino*, at the ribbon factory. Long Island City, Queens, late 1980s. "When my godfather was on his death bed, he repeated hand motions that no one could understand at first. During small moments of consciousness his hands would get busy—putting things together, pulling them apart, getting frustrated, starting the process over. It took us a while to realize he was busy working. He had worked in a ribbon factory in L.I.C. for more years than I know. At first, I was saddened by this realization when it happened. All of a life, reduced to work in the end. But that work is also what made so many opportunities possible for me too. Since then, my studies in Tibetan Buddhism have accelerated. Something compelled me to dig deeper and deeper behind the meanings of my experiences…Thankful to all the tears cried over sickness, death, and loss that brought me here. Without them I might never have wanted to find a way out of the cycle. Love you Padrino."

## Latinx diaspora archives

Artist, arts educator, and advocate William Camargo is the curator of Latinx Diaspora Archives. The page aims to "center family photos of the Latinx Diaspora through the Instagram account in order to combat erasure throughout the US and the Americas."³² The captions in these submissions tend to be the least sartorially related of the previous pages I have mentioned, but there is still plenty of fashion to be seen and disseminated. Considering himself a non-traditional archivist, to give a voice to the narratives of the community, the ownership of each family photograph that he receives remains with the family and is returned to the owner unless directly gifted to him. An example from Latinx Diaspora Archives:

**Figure 11.4** Submitted by @jen.mar10, an ode to her tia. "♥ Rest In Peace Tia Olgis, may you enjoy your time with Tia Carmina and the other 'Chicas Doradas' in heaven. This photo of my grandmother (left), Tia Carmina (center) and Tia Olga (right) was taken in Guatemala in the mid 1950s before all immigrating to the United States. My grandmother told me when she and her friends were teenagers in Guatemala they all used to work together in the customs department at the airport. They charmed the men checking in international shipments into sneaking them fancy bottles of perfume and cutting off yards of imported beautiful fabrics. They'd split the perfume bottles, make clothes from European silks and be the best dressed girls in the neighborhood."

This older example offers a rare insight into how older generations of Latinx already knew the value of sartorial representation prior to living in the US. With their self-taught construction skills, they resourcefully created garments using highly coveted imported materials. Despite not having immediate access to expensive fabrics or fashion media, their ingenious method of self-fashioning promotes the vital role everyday dress plays in these accounts.

## Quinceañera Archives

In September 2019, Chicago native visual artist Samantha Cabrera Friend founded the Quinceañera Archives, which she describes as a visual repository, fostering public dialogues and community-driven research around the historical importance of one's lived experience. A quinceañera is a celebration marking the right of passage for young women of Latin-American descent that marks a girl's transition into womanhood. Since the height of their popularity in the 1980s and 1990s, many first and second generation Latinx are intentionally choosing unconventional celebrations that uniquely represent the intersectionality of their cultural identities. Friend has posted images of quinceañeras from different regions of the United States as well as Cuba, Mexico, and Argentina and often features the work of other artists. Her work centers on communities accessed by her lived experience and strengthened by historic pinnacles drawn through extensive, independent research."[33] Regarding concerns around ownership on social media, Friend explains how their page employs a post-custodial model to gather their archival materials. With this model, Friend takes a non-extractive approach and leaves the physical or digital copy with their original owners while they organize and catalog a copy of those materials offline.[34] With a clear focus on young women within these communities, the passage of time and coming of age through clothing and style markers is an integral thread of the work shared on the Quinceañera Archives.

## Documenting the Nameplate

Documenting the Nameplate is a project celebrating nameplate jewelry culture, aiming to foreground plurality and nonlinear history-making.[35] The nameplate is such a powerful, and ordinary, dress object. For many people in the Latinx community, purchasing or receiving personalized gold jewelry is a rite of passage, while wearing it every day is a means of sartorially ascertaining personal identity from a young age.[36] Cofounders Isabel Flowers and Marcel Rosa-Salas have encouraged as wide-ranging a submission base as possible, having hosted open-call events in New York City, Houston, and Los Angeles, where attendees had their nameplates photographed and shared stories for a forthcoming book. In addition, they have an email address and online portal through which anyone, worldwide, can submit images and/or anecdotes. As a result of such posts, I was inspired to submit an image of my own to their archive which was then reposted on their page:

**Figure 11.5** Submitted by @michelle.korinna. "She's back! A little story about my nameplate: I used to wear it all the time in middle school. One day my family's apartment got robbed (not that we had much to steal) and the only piece of real jewelry that survived was this necklace because I happened to be wearing it that day. I can't exactly remember why I stopped wearing it. Perhaps out of fear of having it taken away, or because I didn't think it was 'cool' anymore or mainstream enough; too much of a marker of a bi-cultural identity I've always had difficulty with. In 2011, times got tough, and I had to sell the chain. I've had just the nameplate in this tiny Ziplock bag in Chicago until now. I got a chain again and am so proud to wear it. Thanks to @documentingthenameplate, and everyone who wears their nameplates for encouraging me to do the same. Also go support El Dorado Jewelry on 3425 W Lawrence Ave in Chicago!"

## Personal archiving as activism

William Camargo of Latinx Diaspora Archives is an advocate of the archive as activism movement. Camargo describes the movement as, "An attempt to question the institution of the archive: Who holds the majority of archives [of] Latinx communities and other marginalized groups? Who has access to them? How are they displayed?"[37] His desire to center communities of color as part of the "American experience" came from encountering difficulty in accessing archives, only to realize the resources didn't exist. During the California wildfires in September 2019, Guadalupe Rosales of Veteranas and Rucas encouraged followers in an Instagram post to take care of their archives. She provided specific, approachable instructions to followers that included starting by "scanning your photos, getting your documents together in a safe place and please share your resources or advice on how to take care of our precious material. Spend time indoors if you can and go through your valuable things." It is clear Rosales feels a strong responsibility to preserve Latinx history and motivate others to do the same. This call to action is a common sentiment in many of these Instagram pages.

In the article, "Archiving Through Social Media," museum educator Onyx Montes details the reach of such online archives. Through the accessibility of not only content, but navigation as well, the pages are democratizing the process of historical preservation:

> There are museums, libraries and other institutions that constantly stipulate a legitimate need for academic research, special permission or qualifications to access their archives, rendering access restricted. With social media, archive-like materials propose that we all can access photographs, objects, and ephemera that no academic will find in a library or museum archive.[38]

In the piece "How Latinos can win the Culture War," Berry and Ramírez insist on the need to support more self-representation further stating, "The United States must reckon with the fact that Latinos are essential to its survival and to its splendor and have been for generations. We Latinos need to know it, too." This sentiment is echoed by Jorge N. Leal, curator of another Instagram page Rock Archivo de LÁ, the Archive of Southern California's Latinx Youth and Musical Cultures.[39] The page's "about me" states, "By making sense of our collective history, we understand ourselves as historical agents."[40] For him, this form of digital stewardship is a reminder that Latinx history is a fundamental thread in the cultural fabric of this country, and urges Latinx people to recognize that. This call to action is echoed by Elizabeth Méndez Berry and Mónica Ramírez when they ask, "What if we weren't perceived as casualties of culture but as its owners?"[41]

## Conclusion

In direct response to Vanessa Friedman's *New York Times* piece, the New York-based Fashion Studies Alliance hosted an online discussion in October 2021, followed by a collective group action to implement diversity in the field of fashion studies.[42] The participants included fashion scholars, archivists, curators, and designers, and were encouraged to select an item of fashion or dress they felt would strengthen diversity in a museum collection. While most submissions were of actual garments, some submissions included editorial fashion spreads and historical illustrations. I presented my own photograph of a "re-tailored" Pachuca zoot suit that was featured in the Museum of Fine Arts, Boston 2019 exhibition "Gender Bending Fashion." The accompanying label text described how the museum purchased this vintage gabardine suit and retailored it in the way a Pachuca many have done decades ago. Curator Dr. Michelle Finamore acknowledged the larger pervasive lack of representation in museum objects by stating,

> Early collections tended to prioritize the designer dress of wealthy white women. Marginalized groups were rarely represented in mainstream institutions. As a result, fashion trends that originated in these communities have been obscured or erased, the garments themselves lost to history. Our intention in altering this zoot suit is to acknowledge one such history.[43]

I was inspired by this attempt to solve the issue of missing material objects and look forward to other museum's approaches. This suit remains the most significant clothing object on display I have had the privilege to witness and the closest example I have come to seeing someone like myself represented sartorially within fashion museology. I found this virtual exercise to be an example of communal storytelling—of reframing how history is being told. But there are unfortunate limitations to this method, including the issue of access to such material resources, further proving the strengths of community-built platforms for archiving, democratizing, and sharing dress histories formerly resigned to the margins.

As guest editor of *Aperture*'s Winter 2021 issue, Pilar Tompkins Rivas addressed the images that collectively chart the history and future of Latinx culture. "What continuums emerge when we see images of young people styling their own personas…How may we understand the power of image making when we see young Latinxs rendering themselves visible through dress, style, self-possession, and acts of personal agency?"[44] For Rivas, as well as for many of the founders of these digital archives, the Latinx journey is not only a process of visibility but also a process of belonging.[45] For there to be increased and accurate Latinx sartorial representation within museological institutions, there is a need for infrastructure, qualified staff, and consistent financial support. Additionally, unconventional forms of collecting, including intangible heritage, must be encouraged and protected. To repeat what William Camargo of Latin Family Photo Archives states, "The increase of Instagram accounts lets us into these ephemeral moments in these communities, through the eyes of those that experienced them. This project is an attempt to elevate our communities and show our realities, through our own experiences and through the radical archives we are a part of."[46] Oral narratives, texts, and photographs are important props of autobiographical memory.

According to Jorge Zamanillo, the founding director of the Smithsonian's National Museum of the American Latino, the inaugural "¡Presente!" exhibition is meant to show visitors that "Latino history is part of American history."[47] Museums were created to instill tradition and nation building, and to secure a sense of your own identity. The Latinx community is constantly on the edge of erasure, not only within material archives, but in virtual spaces as well. An Instagram post, or entire page, with all its comments, likes, saves, and shares, can be deleted at any moment without warning or retrieval potential.

In my attempt to combat the lack of visibility of Latinx fashion history, I was also confronted with unanticipated hesitation from submitters. The sensibilities around sharing an image, and its accompanying family history, on an ephemeral digital archive are very different to allowing the same story manifest permanently in print. Publishing something physically risks it being misrepresented, making it perhaps less approachable; opening up one's own history to be interpreted to a wider audience can cause hesitation. This dichotomy led me to question what is saved and in what form or medium. What qualifies something as a legitimate "archive"? What determines who can claim ownership, and who the archive is ultimately for? My own experience in producing this research has emphasized how the accessible nature of social media makes this an apt medium to share such histories. Due to the plurality of the Latinx experience, it is difficult to encompass the entire group of people in a few material or digital manifestations. But I believe these Instagram pages are a start.

## Notes

1. Vanessa Friedman, "The Incredible Whiteness of Museum Fashion Collections," *The New York Times*, September 29, 2020, https://www.nytimes.com/2020/09/29/style/museums-fashion-racism.html
2. Important to note it was included in the Style section, as well as in El Espace, a NYT column dedicated to news and culture relevant to Latinx communities and is also offered to read in Spanish.
3. Isabelia Herrera, "Preserving Latinx History Through Vintage Photos," *The New York Times,* August 23, 2019, https://www.nytimes.com/2019/08/23/style/latinx-history-vintage-photos.html
4. Elizabeth Méndez Berry and Mónica Ramírez, "Elizabeth Méndez Berry and Mónica Ramírez: How Latinos can win the culture war," *The Salt Lake Tribune*, September 4, 2020, https://www.sltrib.com/opinion/commentary/2020/09/04/elizabeth-mndez-berry/
5. Pilar Tompkins Rivas, "What Can Photographs Tell Us about Latinx Identity in the US?" *Aperture*, December 7, 2021, http://aperature.org/editorial/what-can-photographs-tell-us-about-latinx-identity-in-the-us/
6. White Lines Project, "Mundo Latinx," Fashion Space Gallery.
7. El Museo del Barrio, "About," https://www.elmuseo.org/about/
8. El Museo del Barrio, "Permanent Collection," https://www.elmuseo.org/permanent-collection/
9. Jacqueline Trescott, "Smithsonian Faulted for Neglect of Latinos," *Washington Post*, May 11, 1994, https://www.washingtonpost.com/archive/1994/05/11/smithsonian-faulted-for-neglect-of-latinos/34b5076a-0b7c-4d1f-aab8-cab07dd383d9/
10. Smithsonian Task Force on Latino Issues, "WILLFUL NEGLECT: The Smithsonian Institution and U.S. Latinos," May 1994, https://siarchives.si.edu/sites/default/files/forum-pdfs/Willful_Neglect_The_Smithsonian_Institution%20and_US_Latinos.pdf
11. Ibid.
12. Ibid.
13. Trescott, "Smithsonian Faulted for Neglect of Latinos."
14. National Museum of the American Latino, "Latino Initiatives Pool," https://latino.si.edu/learn/staff-resources/latino-initiatives-pool
15. National Museum of the American Latino, "Sharing Latino History and Culture," https://latino.si.edu/

16 Aside from the Selena Museum located in Quintanilla Pérez's hometown of Corpus Christi, Texas, the National Museum of American History in Washington, DC is the only other museum to which her family has voluntarily donated performance memorabilia.
17 Smithsonian National Museum of American History, "Costume Collection," https://amhistory.si.edu/costume/#:~:text=The%20Costume%20Collection%20at%20the,17th%20century%20to%20the%20present
18 National Museum of the American Latino, "Making History Together," https://latino.si.edu/
19 Jesse Alemán, "How Can Historical Photographs Preserve Latinx Culture?" *Aperture*, January 28, 2022, https://aperature.org/editorial
20 Ibid.
21 Friedman, "The Incredible Whiteness of Museum Fashion Collections."
22 Aleida Assman, "Transformations between History and Memory," *Social Research* 75, no. 1, 49–72.
23 Susan B. Kaiser and Denise N. Greene, *Fashion and Cultural Studies*, 2nd edn. (New York: Bloomsbury Publishing, 2022), 76–7, 86–90.
24 In Herrera's piece, she states, "One of the earliest examples of these digital archives is Veteranas y Rucas, which was founded by Guadalupe Rosales in 2015. . ."
25 Guadalupe Rosales, Veteranas and Rucas, https://www.instagram.com/veteranas_and_rucas/?hl=en
26 Guadalupe Rosales, "Instagram Projects," https://www.veteranasandrucas.com/projects-1
27 Guadalupe Rosales, "Socorro Mary Ornellas and her younger sister Angelica Montenegro from East LA, in the 1940s," https://www.instagram.com/p/CGIVhT6J__k/?hl=en
28 Rosales, "Instagram Projects."
29 Maurice Halbwachs. "Space and the Collective Memory," *The Collective Memory*: 1–15.
30 Guadalupe Rosales, "'Corpo RanfLA: Terra Cruiser' is about collective memory. Guadalupe Rosales can explain," *Los Angeles Times*, November 29, 2022, https://www.yahoo.com/now/corpo-ranfla-terra-cruiser-collective-130009832.html
31 Djali Brown-Cepeda, "About," https://www.nuevayorkinos.com/about-nuevayorkinos
32 William Camargo, "Latinx Diaspora Archives," http://www.williamcamargo.com/latinx-diaspora-archives
33 Catchlight, "Samantha Cabrera Friend," https://www.catchlight.io/samantha-cabrera-friend
34 Quinceanera Archives, June 14, 2021, https://www.instagram.com/p/CQHvLYFFeBA/

35 Documenting the Nameplate, "About," http://documentingthenameplate.com/about.html
36 Michelle McVicker, "Pop Cultural References in 21st Century Latinx Fashion," *Latin American and Latinx Fashion, ¡Moda Hoy!*, London: Bloomsbury, 2024.
37 http://www.williamcamargo.com/latinx-diaspora-archives
38 Onyx Montes, "Archiving Through Social Media: An Interview With Alkebuluan Merriweather," *Sixty Inches from Center*, February 21, 2022, https://sixtyinchesfromcenter.org/archiving-through-social-media-an-interview-with-alkebuluan-merriweather/
39 While it primarily focuses on 1990s Rock Angelino, the collective archive incorporates many other music cultures and scenes such as punk, ska, dark-gothic, metal, rock urbano, and more.
40 Jorge Leal, "About Rock Archivo LÁ," https://rockarchivo.com/about/
41 Berry and Ramírez, "How Latinos can win the culture war."
42 The Fashion Studies Alliance is a New York-based network and support system for professionals and students working in the fields of fashion studies including archiving, curating, conservation, design, and research that fosters collaboration, growth, support and the development of individuals and the community.
43 Dr. Michelle Finamore, label text, "Gender Bending Fashion," MFA 2019.
44 Rivas, "What Can Photographs Tell Us about Latinx Identity in the US?"
45 Ibid.
46 Camargo, http://www.williamcamargo.com/latinx-diaspora-archives
47 Miranda Mazariegos, "A new exhibit takes visitors closer to the National Museum of the American Latino," *NPR*, June 18, 2022, https://www.npr.org/transcripts/1105847319

# Bibliography

Assman, Aleida. "Transformations between History and Memory." *Social Research: Collective Memory and Collective Identity* 75, No. 1 (2008): 49–72.

Halbwachs, Maurice. "Space and the collective memory." *The Collective Memory* (1950): 1–15.

Kaiser, Susan B. and Denise N. Green. *Fashion and Cultural Studies*, 2nd ed. (New York: Bloomsbury Publishing, 2022).

Montez, Oynx. "Archiving Through Social Media: An Interview With Alkebuluan Merriweather." *Sixty Inches from Center*. February 21, 2022, https://sixtyinchesfromcenter.org/archiving-through-social-media-an-interview-with-alkebuluan-merriweather/

Trescott, Jaqueline. "Smithsonian Faulted for Neglect of Latinos." *Washington Post.* May 11, 1994, https://www.washingtonpost.com/archive/1994/05/11/smithsonian-faulted-for-neglect-of-latinos/34b5076a-0b7c-4d1f-aab8-cab07dd383d9/

# 12

# Self-Fashioning, Participatory Research, and the "Will to Adorn"

Diana Baird N'Diaye

Look at almost any autobiography written by persons of African descent and you will find references to dressing and grooming. From Frederick Douglass to Malcolm X, Maya Angelou to Michelle Obama, and Beyoncé to Lizzo, rituals of adornment are remembered as significant parts of growing up, essential elements of Black creative expression, and assertions of agency, liberation, and resistance. Indeed, so central are dress and grooming to the Black experience that it was inevitable that the subject of African American style would eventually be recognized in a growing number of books, articles, exhibitions, and other forms of documentation. As a cultural scholar and long-term personal enthusiast of the arts of dress who was trained in a Harlem-based design school, I have long been interested in conducting a first-person exploration into how African Americans of many walks of life have curated their everyday fashion and presented themselves to the world. Yet, I wondered, would it even be possible to identify an African American dress aesthetic? With so many different styles of dress within the African American population of the United States, the quest to find one definitive set of aesthetic principles that would apply to African American style seemed elusive if not impossible. At the same time, there seemed to be something about the way that everyday fashion has held a special place—a place of power and agency—in African American cultural life and production that goes beyond the specifics of style that merited investigation.[1]

As conceptualized within the "Will to Adorn"—a ten-year research and public programming initiative that examined the diversity and cultural aesthetics of African American identities through the arts and traditions of dress and personal adornment—traditions of everyday dressing:

... reveal continuities of ideas, values, skills, and knowledge rooted in the African continent and the American experience. They have been shaped by identities born of African heritage, legacies of bondage and resistance, and encounters and alliances between people of African, indigenous Americans, Europeans, and, more recently, African, and Caribbean diasporas. They may reflect, for example, shared experiences of the Civil Rights and Black Power Movements; group commitments to faith; and the politics of gender.[2]

Conceived at the Smithsonian Institution's Center for Folklife and Cultural Heritage (CFCH), the Will to Adorn project began in 2010 with funding from the Center for Craft and a Smithsonian Scholarly Studies Grant, and continued through 2019 following a trajectory that interspersed research and public presentations. Several Smithsonian museums contributed to and participated in the project, including the new National Museum of African American History and Culture, the Anacostia Community Museum, the Cooper Hewitt, Smithsonian Design Museum, and the National Museum of African Art. The Smithsonian Affiliations division of the Institution also coordinated the involvement of four regional Affiliate museums and a cultural education center, each of which developed its own research project and programmatic initiative under the guidance of the CFCH.

**Figure 12.1** Rosemarie Reed Miller at the 2013 Smithsonian Folklife Festival. Photo by John Larrimore. Courtesy Ralph Rinzler, Folklife Archives and Collections, Smithsonian Institution, Washington, DC.

In my role as principal investigator and director of the project, I developed the conceptual framework and curriculum, led the training and research teams, and curated the Folklife Festival Program with the assistance and collaboration of individuals with many levels of expertise from interns still in school through seasoned scholars, educators, and other museum professionals. The research involved both inviting narrative sartorial autobiographies from "style artisans," or people whose occupation it is to create the artifacts of style. (In doing so, however, my collaborators and I recognized, of course, that many individuals both create and curate their own everyday fashion.) Although there were several points in the project where researchers and interview subjects participated in public in sessions at libraries, museums, and online, the most expansive public vetting of the project was the 2013 Smithsonian Folklife Festival Program involving more than 250 participants over a two-week span of time and a two-month long bricks-and-mortar exhibition at the Institute for Texan Culture in San Antonio, Texas. These individuals and groups came together to tell a powerful and complex story about the role of everyday fashion in the lives and expressive culture of African Americans.

Drawing upon a much larger body of work, this chapter foregrounds the research with the artisans of style whose narratives formed the backbone of the Will to Adorn project, while giving an account of the participatory methods and approaches that revealed the intersections between everyday fashion, craft, and cultural identity in African American creative expression.

## Understanding the Will to Adorn

The project's title was inspired by a 1934 essay by Zora Neale Hurston in which she famously and somewhat wryly declared "the will to adorn" as one of the primary characteristics of African American creative expression. Though Hurston focused on flourishes and embellishment in African American speech, she references the seductive and confident self-presentation of a young man posing on a street corner "possessed of only his clothing, his strength, and his youth."[3]

The title, the Will to Adorn, beautifully captured the core of the project, and specifically how style across diverse communities of African descent functions powerfully as a tool of self-definition, aspiration, and resistance, and as an art form. Dress scholar Carol Tulloch applies the construct of "style-fashion-dress" to the study of the sartorial practices of people throughout the African Diaspora as a way of understanding how the presentation of self through the choice of attire itself becomes a visual autobiographical narrative. Both in an important essay, "Style-Fashion-Dress: From Black to Post-Black," and in her masterful work, *The Birth of Cool*, Tulloch has brilliantly argued for the use of the term "style" as a synonym of agency in reference to "the construction of self through the assemblage of garments and accessories, hairstyle, and beauty regimes that may, or may not, be 'in fashion' at the time of use."[4] The findings of the Will to Adorn research resonate with Tulloch's work concerning intentionality and agency as central principles of African American fashion aesthetics. As exemplified in a popular response to the greeting, "It's good to see you!", "It's good to be seen!"

Rooted in studies of folkloristic notions of ethnicity and groups, the Will to Adorn was premised on the idea that all of us belong to communities of style framed by common understandings, ideas, and values about what is pleasing, appropriate, or beautiful.[5] Ideas about dressing are shaped by similar experiences, knowledge, interests, learned skills and practices, and access to the resources to shop and get dressed. In every style community, some individuals stand out as masters of the arts of dress and body arts. These exemplars of style capture the essence of a community's ideas of what it is to be well-dressed through their artful assembly of hair, apparel, accessories, and body art. They intentionally acquire collections of dress and personal adornment that they use to "curate" their appearance on a daily basis. Other influential literature for this project traced the history and significance of African American style. This included the work of cultural historians Shane White and Graham White, particularly *Styling: African American Expressive Culture from Its Beginnings to the Zoot Suit* (1998) and Monica L. Miller's enlightening study, *Slaves to Fashion: Black Dandyism and the Styling of Diasporic Identity* (2009).

The Will to Adorn research considered individual expression and creativity, but it focused on the details of social dressing and the conventions that define what it means to be well-dressed or appropriately attired in different communities. From its beginnings in 2010 through to 2019, the initiative developed a participatory research methodology grounded in community self-study and "sartorial autobiography,"[6] and realized in multiple iterations at several partnering venues across the United States.[7] The project identified and interviewed community "exemplars of style"—individuals who, in their own choices of attire impeccably captured the essence of the shared ideals of their time and locales regarding hair, apparel, accessories, and body art. The project also documented the experiences of "artisans of style," such as milliners, hairdressers, and tailors, who use their creativity and specialized skills to meet their clients' distinct tastes and cultural aesthetics. Moreover, it solicited individual and group narratives recording the language and discourses related to dress and adornment in African American communities. Since this chapter focuses particularly on the methodology of the project regarding collecting narratives of barbers, dressmakers, tattoo artists, and other such artisans of African American style, it is perhaps useful to give some definition and historical context for the research on artisans of style before discussing methods in greater depth.

## Artisans of style

Skilled style artisans of the body arts use their creativity, special skills, and knowledge of community aesthetics and standards to support the specialized needs and desires of clients who rely on them to achieve a style that articulates a visual construction of self. Contemporary definitions of craft and crafts persons have been matters of intense global discussion and debate and the subject of several articles and books in the past few decades. In the United States, prevailing definitions of "artisan," "maker," or "craftsperson" have, until the recent past, been applied to technicians of materials such as clay, metals, fiber, glass, wood, and leather (some of which is wearable) but not artisans who work directly on the body—barbers, stylists, tattooists. Yet, it can be said that style artisans are heritage-based makers, trained within a tradition through imitation, apprenticeship, and other learning systems grounded in local and ethnic communities. These categories of craft have been united by the skilled use of materials and culturally determined aesthetics. Barbers and hairdressers, tattoo artists, and menders of clothing would all fit under this rubric but have not, until recently, been included under the rubric of craftsperson. In her ground-breaking work, *The Grace of Four Moons* (2008), Pravina Shukla illustrated how artisans collaborated with their clients to create appealing styles in Southern India. Similarly, in the Will to Adorn project, the emphasis on the connection between community aesthetics and style-making occupations as heritage crafts was fundamental. The occupational traditions of dress and the body arts are passed on from those who are more experienced to those who are learning the ropes. The knowledge and skills that are transferred include not just techniques, skills, and tools of the trade but also how to interact with clients, find source materials, get a better rate, and keep customers coming back.

Throughout their history in the United States, people of African descent have used occupations related to adornment and the body arts to achieve economic and social success as entrepreneurs. Their economic independence in turn often allowed them a measure of political independence to participate in activism. Before Emancipation, African American couturier Elizabeth Keckley built a thriving business in the mid-1800s with African and European American clientele that later enabled her to purchase her freedom. As Mary Todd Lincoln's designer and confidante, Keckley was able to support the movement for Emancipation both financially and through her influence in the White House.[8] Illinois born chemist, educator, and entrepreneur Annie Turnbo Malone, born in 1869, invented and developed hair products for African Americans in the 1920s. Her model inspired and guided a proliferation of African American created beauty products and schools—including that of her equally successful student, Madame C. J. Walker. Rosa Parks, a central figure of the Civil Rights Movement, was working as a skilled dressmaker in 1963 at the time her activism—refusing to sit in the back of a segregated bus, initiated the Montgomery Bus Boycott that led to the end of legal segregation throughout the United States. Pioneering scholarship by Rosemary E. Reed Miller for her book, *Threads of Time, The Fabric of History: Profiles of African American Dressmakers and Designers, 1850 to the Present* (2003), along with more recent work by Elaine Nichols (2013), Jonathan Michael Square (2021), and Elizabeth Way (2021), provide additional context on the work and legacy of Keckley and other nineteenth and twentieth century African American fashion designers.

African American everyday fashion as a form of activism and entrepreneurship also manifested in the businesses in African American neighborhoods that

**Figure 12.2** Rufus Isley outfitting a client at his Mister Mann store in Washington, DC. Photo courtesy the Isley-Jackson family.

allowed people to shop for clothing with dignity. For many years, when African Americans were banned from dressing rooms in upscale department stores, clothiers opened stores specifically for an African American clientele. In the 1970s, Rufus Isley's Mr. Mann stores in Washington, DC, occupied a niche in African American communities catering to upwardly mobile clients.

In recent years, immigrants from Africa, the Caribbean, and Latin America have brought custom tailoring, dressmaking, braiding, and other hairstyling techniques and traditions to the barber shops and the beauty salons that are still mainstays in African American neighborhoods.

Many African Americans in the fashion or beauty business can point to an older family member or mentor who was a seamstress, barber, hairstylist, or even a dry cleaner. Master couturiere Zelda Wynn Valdes—designer of the first Playboy bunny outfit—founded one of the first African American businesses on Broadway and 57th Street in New York City where she designed iconic gowns for Joyce Bryant, Josephine Baker, Ella Fitzgerald, Dorothy Dandridge, and other celebrities. I had the good fortune to be one of her students from 1965 through 1968. As head of the fashion design program at HarYou-Act, a Harlem youth summer arts program established by social psychologists Kenneth and Mamie Clark,[9] she introduced a new generation of young people, including me, to the skills of couture design—teaching us draping and flat patternmaking, and helping us to create our first collections that we presented at the 1967 World's Fair in Montreal. This remains one of my fondest accomplishments. Later, Ms. Wynn took up the invitation to lead the design team of Arthur Mitchell's Dance Theatre of Harlem where she was employed until her death at the age of ninety-five.

Ms. Wynn Valdes was born in 1901, to a thriving African American family in Chambersburg, Pennsylvania. She was the oldest of seven children. Her grandmother recognized her fashion precocity and ignited her love of fashion at an early age. When I interviewed Ms. Wynn at the age of ninety-three she recalled:

> My grandmother always had her clothes made and so one day, when she went to the dressmakers. I was at that time eleven years old, and I didn't like the way the dressmaker was pinning the gown on my grandmother. So, I suggested it be done in another way. The dressmaker didn't like it because she says I was interfering and so when I got home, I said to my grandmother, "Grandma can I make that dress for you." And my grandmother says, "Yea, if you think you can do it."

That early experience began a career that lasted over seventy years. Zelda Wynn Valdes' garments are in the fashion collection of the National Museum of African

American History and Culture and the Fashion Institute of Technology, but images of her fashions grace album covers and film footage of the vocalist Joyce Bryant, Eartha Kitt, and others that she dressed.

The artisans of style interviewed for the Will to Adorn project spoke similarly about how they perceived their work and their relationship to their clients. In the context of a presentation on fashion of African American faith communities, Washington, DC researcher and trainer/coordinator Camila Bryce La Porte interviewed milliner Anthony Gaskin on the stage of the Will to Adorn Program at the Smithsonian Folklife Festival. Gaskin observed,

> Everybody has their own personality and so does every hat. When people find that hat that suits them, it brings their inner self out—and that's what I do with my work—that's the goal of my work—to bring something out in a person that they didn't know was there.

Through our research, it became clear that the artisan-client relationship was paramount—as, for instance can be evidenced in Gaskin's comments above, as well as in remarks made by Atlanta tattoo artist Charity "Cake" Hamidullah. In a 2012 interview conducted at her shop by students from Frank McClarin High School in Atlanta, Georgia, Hamidullah remarked on the connection between her and her clients, observing, "The [tattoo art] pieces definitely have to do with the relationship that I have with my client. That really helps how much better that tattoo is, and I just like the artistry, doing something that nobody has ever seen in the tattoo community."

Artisans also spoke about how they learned the craft and the business of fashion and about their artistic signatures. Brenda Winstead, designer, for her brand Damali Afrikan Couture, learned about the textiles she uses in her work from trips abroad to Senegal, Mali, and Mauritania. In a 2012 video interview with designer Brenda Winstead published on the Smithsonian Folklife website,[10] Winstead spoke about how she was inspired by the everyday fashion she saw in the streets of Senegal. "I swore, these Senegalese women were changing clothes three times a day and I was like, what is this all about? They just had on all this gorgeous fabric!" She discovered a love for traditional African artisanal textiles and returned to develop close relationships with the textile artisans from whom she acquired the materials for her work. She noticed a growing appreciation in the United States for the handcrafted. Her clients typically came to her looking for something different in an age of cookie cutter fashions. They also sought to express their recognition of their African heritage in cosmopolitan and sophisticated ways that drew on Winstead's combination of African American and African design sensibilities.

## Methods

The Will to Adorn project was initially conceived as an experiment in collaborative community-centered research and presentation. Some interviews with artisans of style were conducted by research groups of high school and college-aged interns guided by an experienced research coordinator and recorded with equipment supplied by the Smithsonian. Others were done in public as part of community presentations or at the Folklife Festival where visitors had the opportunity to ask their own questions at the end of the interview. In St. Croix, US Virgin Islands, research with style artisans took the form of recorded conversations, reciprocal interviews (with artists paired to interview each other) and studio visits on the island. In this way the research was both participatory and shared publicly throughout the project.

It was also envisioned as a project that would draw upon decades of curatorial practice and take advantage of twenty-first-century technologies such as social media, virtual conferencing, and the growing recording quality and capacity of mobile tools to create and link community-centered research communities that could work with each other and share their fieldwork across distance. The initiative paired seasoned, academically-trained scholars with high school-aged students and others interested in exploring everyday dress cultures in their communities. This kind of community engagement, especially with high schoolers, was a priority for the project because it taught students to critically evaluate what they read about themselves and their communities. It also taught them that they could do their own research and, in the process, develop their own bodies of knowledge and present it to their peers and the world. Furthermore, it taught research, listening, and analytic skills that would be valuable to them as they progressed in their lives. More than anything, we wanted to further the notion that their voices and their culture matter. With the help of our community partners, the project grew into a ten-year endeavor that not only revealed much about the diversity of African American style and aesthetics but also proved to be an extraordinarily enriching and generative experience for the individuals and groups who participated in ways that went far beyond initial expectations.

Carrying out the research required developing a framework that adequately encompassed what we wanted to discover, including guiding definitions and a methodology appropriate for community-centered work. The goals of the project were clear: this was a self-study. The primary researchers and the initial beneficiaries and audience for the research and presentation were members of the style communities they studied. This substantial value of research, by and in the service of the study's subjects, drove the project.

There were several phases of research. From 2010 to 2011, a small cadre of researchers in New York City, Atlanta, Baltimore, Washington, DC, Detroit, Chicago, Oakland, and New Orleans mapping out possible contacts and sites. From 2012 through 2013, seasoned researchers with community partners conducted seminal work identifying potential African American style communities, interviewing and documenting artisans at research sites. Between January 2012 and December 2012, thirty-one interviews were completed with artists and exemplars, along with photographs. Recordings augmented the interviews at narrative sessions conducted publicly at the 2013 Folklife Festival.

The 2013 Smithsonian Folklife Festival was the largest-scale activity of the Will to Adorn research project. Organized by the Smithsonian's Center for Folklife and Cultural Heritage, the Folklife Festival is an annual summer event highlighting the traditions and cultural expressions that help to define communities all over the globe, the event typically features artists including craftspeople and cooks, musicians, storytellers, and other cultural specialists who are experts in the cultural expressions of their communities. It is their work that often gives definition to the cultural identities of the communities that they represent. On the National Mall the importance of their work and their voices are literally and figuratively amplified. The Smithsonian Festival usually has between two and four different programs per year. Each program is based on research in the countries, regions, and localities to be featured and undertaken to identify how to respectfully portray the communities and their cultures. Visitors to the Festival number in the hundreds of thousands each year and regular visitors compare the experience of the festival to that of a tourist in an unfamiliar locale.

The 2013 Will to Adorn Festival Program was presented at the Smithsonian Folklife Festival in the green space between the Capitol building and the Washington Monument. The program was co-sponsored by the National Museum of African American History and Culture (then still in the throes of construction), the Center for Folklife and Cultural Heritage, and the Office of the Assistant Secretary of Education. It unfolded over ten hot and sweaty days in the two weekends culminating in the Fourth of July weekend in the same space that had seen the March on Washington and the inauguration of the first Black President of the United States, and which would later on see the Black Lives Matter protests. Each day, participants in the program from across the United States demonstrated the diversity and multiplicity of African American identities expressed through the arts of everyday dress through fashion shows, craft demonstrations, narrative sessions, and panel discussions. The program and the project of which it was a part were conceptually grounded in the notion that the arts of adorning the body are among the most potent and universal expressive forms—and that the cultural and occupational traditions that exist relating to dress and style are particularly vital, complex, and of historical importance within populations of African descent within the United States.

The ten-day program included forty runway presentations and thirty discussion sessions and interviews. However, research set the stage for the program and the many activities that were generated in the aftermath. On the National Mall, participants explored the spectrum of African American engagement and agency relating to the contemporary arts of the body and solicited sartorial autobiographies from a wide swath of individuals from across the United States.

I conceived the 2013 Will to Adorn Folklife Festival program as part of a broader initiative that aimed to use the lessons learned from previous research and education projects at the Center for Folklife and Cultural Heritage to develop better ways to train community-based groups and students to research their own expressive culture and organize their own public folklore projects. One such project was the African Immigrant Folklife Study project, which documented the emergence of new community culture in recently arrived immigrant groups from Africa. The African Immigrant Folklife project, which I co-curated with Dr. Betty Belanus, also sought to explore community curated and organized public folklore presentations online and at venues such as neighborhood schools, libraries, and museums. Unlike the climate in the museum and professional research world a decade earlier—when the idea of laypersons doing fieldwork made academically-trained scholars cringe—the concepts of participatory museology, citizen science, and community engagement in the research and curatorial process in 2010 were welcomed in principle if not entirely in practice. However, we encountered training, management, guidance, and interpersonal gymnastics issues in actualizing the practice.

As principal investigator for the Will to Adorn project (and for the African Immigrant Folklife Project), I developed a conceptual framework for the project and the methodology, and the training strategies for community researchers. This work was based on long term interests in both in the aesthetics of dress and in community-based participatory research.

In directing the research, I developed guidelines for the research based on a combination of standard research directives used at the Center for Folklife and

Cultural Heritage, including a publicly accessible Oral History Interview Guide developed by Smithsonian colleague and folklorist Marjorie Hunt.[11] The Will to Adorn Research guidelines included several sample questionnaires oriented to different style communities. For example, one questionnaire made suggestions directed towards interviews with style artisans, another, provided guidelines for writing a sartorial autobiography, and yet another for interviewing members of faith-based communities. Will to Adorn research teams were instructed to:

> ...look for and identify key individuals within a community—artisans of style, exemplars of style, et cetera. In some cases, you may be working with individuals you already know. In others, you will make new contacts within the community in question. The interview should include an oral biography, anecdotal narratives, responses to open-ended questions, and a detailed description of the relevant tradition.[12]

Questions for style artisans were also modifications on suggestions developed over the course of years by the curatorial staff of the Center. Sample questions for style artisans included:

> What is the artisan's repertoire of skills? What is the artisans' repertoire range within a tradition? For example, a hair braider may also be trained in other types of hair styling. What are the styles associated with a tradition? How have they changed over time? Are there criteria for excellence? For example, what makes a good milliner? A skilled seamstress or haberdashery? A talented hairdresser? How is their knowledge learned? How is it passed on? Are particular meanings associated with the tradition? (For example, historical, religious, ethnic, or other forms of identity.) Are there any associations to other cultural events or chronological cycles? What skills and knowledge are needed to belong and to perform in a particular occupationally defined community? What skills must a beautician or barber possess? What does an Afrocentric clothing designer need to be aware of?[13]

The motivation to work with smartphones, tablets, and other tools on the general market came from my experience in a previous project that I had developed with African immigrant researchers who used conventional research tools. We purchased professional cameras, audio recorders, and video equipment for the earlier project and held several training workshops. After receiving several rolls of exposed film with no images, recordings obliterated by static noise, and even unreadable field notes, we learned that the technology was one of the steepest learning curves for lay researchers. With the Will to Adorn, we relied mainly on the access technology that our partners were already familiar with but added microphones and other peripherals to enhance the sound quality. This strategy proved to work in most cases with young researchers. For older researchers, the new technology, including uploading research to the site, remained challenging.[14]

From 2010 onward, the Will to Adorn project relied on institutional partners both within and outside of the Smithsonian.[15] At the time that the project began, the Smithsonian encouraged their nineteen museums and research centers to find ways to work on collaborative ventures. Taking advantage of this, the Will to Adorn project created programming in collaboration with the National Museum of African American Culture (who co-sponsored the Folklife Festival Program), the National Museum of African Art for a program of Hair and Heritage, and the Cooper Hewitt, Smithsonian Design Museum (which hosted workshops for research teams on using design thinking methods in research). Outside the Smithsonian, all of our research teams in various cities were partners. A sampling of many partners included: the Takoma Baptist Church Mustard Seed Youth Ministry, McClaren High School, Spellman College, the Institute for Texan Cultures the Museum of the African Diaspora, and Mindbuilders, Inc.—a cultural center and heritage school in Bronx, New York. Scholars and advisors from the partnering academic and community institutions participated in both virtual and in person meetings in which we had intensive discussions about how to circumscribe the project scope. These gatherings had the cumulative effect of solidifying partnerships and in determining the project's content and scope of activities, research, and documentation.

A significant portion of this research involved using mobile handheld devices, including smartphones and tablets, as research equipment for ethnographic fieldwork and oral history interviews alongside standard professional still cameras, audio, and video equipment. Opportunities to share fieldwork and reflections with fellow researchers were accomplished through a dedicated social media platform that worked similarly to Facebook for multi-sited collaborative research, explicitly developed for the Will to Adorn project, and periodic online conference calls that students and teachers joined by smartphone, tablet, and computer. This took place before the availability of Zoom, Microsoft Teams, and other meeting platforms, but anticipated their use in facilitating collaborative research.

From 2012 through 2017, the project received a series of grants from the Office of the Smithsonian Secretary for Education and Community Outreach as part of an initiative to engage young people K through 12th grade in projects with various Smithsonian museums and research units. The 2012 to 2013 training that the project developed focused on documenting style communities and culminated

**Figure 12.3** Marilyn Davies on the 'Will to Adorn' program runway. Photo by John Larrimore. Courtesy of the Will to Adorn Collection, Smithsonian Institution, Washington, DC.

with the 2013 Folklife Festival. Research professionals along with youth and community-based researchers and educators came to the festival where they introduced the style artisans that they had interviewed, participated in discussions about researching African American style on narrative stages, and documented the daily runway shows that took place during the ten days of the festival.

The office was a major supporter of the Smithsonian Folklife Festival Will to Adorn Program. After the 2013 festival, Claudine Brown, the Assistant Secretary for Education at the Smithsonian, invited us to apply for Youth Access funds that allowed us to expand and deepen the work. We developed a logic model to map out goals, audience, and strategies, and developed two more training workshops over the course of three years for community-based educators museum educators and curators.

In addition, we funded internship programs at museums and cultural centers around the country, the focus of which being to collect community stories about style and on using design thinking to create community and school-based projects from the documentation. In 2017, a third grant received by the project made it possible to work with museum educators and their middle and high

*Self-Fashioning, Participatory Research, and the "Will to Adorn"* 263

**Figure 12.4** Interns enrolled in the Will to Adorn summer teen program. Photo by Melanie Schwebke. Courtesy of the 'Will to Adorn' Collection, Smithsonian Institution, Washington, DC.

school-aged interns to focus on documenting and presenting the artifacts of style in a community context. The 2017 project emphasized learning and practicing the skills of observing, describing, interpreting, and curating exhibitions of style artifacts.

After a training program that the project organized for museum educators, the educators in turn conveyed the skills of critical interpretation, digital collection, exhibition, and social media dialogue skills to their student interns who collected stories that communicated the meanings and impact of "artifacts of style" in everyday life through public programs in their respective cities. All of this work sought to document the expression of concerns through dress, social justice, and cultural affirmation as articulated in the work of artisans of style. Specifically, students working with museum curators and educators became what dress scholars Ingrid Mida and Alexandra Kim call "dress detectives" and digital storytellers.[16]

Educators and curators from each museum guided and supported the intern curators in conducting original research and developing local exhibitions, public programs, online collections, and digital exhibitions that they shared through the Will to Adorn social media platforms. Each of the five teams interviewed collectors and artisans of style—barbers, milliners, sewers, and T-shirt designers, and people with style in their local communities. The intern curators also collected artifacts and photographs in digital form that reflect local style and identities. These objects—including headwraps, beauty tools, apparel, and accessories—were used as the basis to curate online exhibitions and bricks-and-mortar exhibitions at the Institute of Texan Cultures and the University of Texas, San Antonio, as well.

## Conclusion

Dress is a visual narrative. The Will to Adorn project engaged participants in making the visual explicit through written and verbalized narratives as sartorial autobiographies. It further extended this conversation to include artisans of style who provide the lexicon and vocabulary for everyday fashion. The aesthetics of everyday African American fashion are shaped by values and viewpoints that grew from the history, heritage, and experiences of Black life in the United States and other parts of the African Diaspora. These influences have flowed back and forth across the Atlantic Ocean through dispersed and tight-knit style communities. The two projects sought to facilitate and highlight community, small-scale artisan/entrepreneurs, and individual sartorial agency over "big fashion" and the celebrity/fashion designer complex.

African American everyday dress is internally diverse but also culturally distinctive in the US. This is because of the circumstances of African Americans in this country, beginning with slavery and continuing through segregation. Separation—no longer enforced legally, economically, or socially—is often still present in the beauty shop, barber's chair, heritage festivals, music, bespoke neighborhood fashion businesses and, increasingly, online. African American style is also cultivated in distinct social and cultural spaces, including historically Black colleges and universities and Greek fraternities and sororities such as Alpha Phi Alpha and Delta; high schools with predominantly black enrollment; Black churches; gatherings and organizations of African, Caribbean, and Afro Latino immigrants; music subcultures; and of course, convenings of social justice movements such as Black Lives Matter. Yet, how do people obtain the elements of clothing that satisfy a particular aesthetic? In addition to identifying the spaces where African American style is cultivated, the Will to Adorn also revealed where the raw materials of dress and self-fashioning were obtained. As we learned over the course of our research, for many decades, individuals interested in asserting their identities as persons of African heritage have had to acquire their style artifacts at annual African cultural festivals such as the East Festival (in Brooklyn) and similar festivals in cities with high African American cosmopolitan populations. At these events, vendors from Africa and the Caribbean sell clothing items and provide services not available elsewhere.

Another finding of the Will to Adorn Project was that apparel and clothing choices also follow differing aesthetic community rules. Appropriate dress and grooming in any population can vary according to occasion or circumstance. An example of this is the difference between what an individual might wear to work during the week, versus what the same individual might wear to hang out with friends, on the weekend, or to worship services. Just as people code-switch in language, code-switching inevitably occurs in the visual dialects of everyday fashion, too. This code-switching can take on differing meanings if individuals dress in one way in reaction to the imposition of rules in Euro-American controlled educational and workspaces, or within African American cultural and family spaces where a wider spectrum of dress choices are acceptable. For example, an individual working in a corporate setting might avoid styles that embrace natural textures or signal affirmation of African/diaspora heritage—like wearing cornrows (however neat) or African textiles (even with European tailoring) that might be read as threatening within a Euro-American space.

None of these findings would have been made, however, without the contributions of our vast network of museum specialists, academics, community educators, artists, high school students, and others interested in exploring the sartorial traditions of their own neighborhoods and style communities. The involvement of these partners representing different regions, cultural communities, skills, and age groups was critical to the project's commitment to identifying, documenting, and representing a range of perspectives and approaches related to dress and adornment. Projects such as the Will to Adorn bring new perspectives to the study of everyday fashion; however, they can do more than add to the canon. For members of communities engaged in auto-ethnographic research and public programs, such projects can create opportunities for building inclusive communities of practice based on intergenerational, cross-regional, and intra-community appreciation of difference.

# Notes

1 Diana N'Diaye, "The Will to Adorn: African American Diversity, Style, and Identity," The Will to Adorn: African American Diversity, Style, and Identity," Smithsonian Folklife Festival Program Book, 27–31 (Washington, DC: Smithsonian Institution, 2013).
2 Ibid.

3   Zora Neale Hurston, "Characteristics of Negro Expression" in *Within the Circle*, ed. Angelyn Mitchell (Durham, NC, and London: Duke University Press, 2012), 79–94.
4   See Carol Tulloch, *The Birth of Cool: Style Narratives of the African Diaspora* (London: Bloomsbury, 2016) and Carol Tulloch, "Style-Fashion-Dress: From Black to Post-Black," *Fashion Theory: The Journal of Dress, Body amd Culture* 14, no. 3 (2010): 273–303.
5   Dorothy Noyes, "Group" in *Eight Words for the Study of Expressive Culture*, ed. Burt Feintuch (Urbana and Chicago, IL: University of Illinois Press, 2003), 7–41.
6   Pravina Shukla, *The Grace of the Four Moons: Dress, Adornment, and the Art of the Body in Modern India* (Bloomington, IN: Indiana University Press, 2015).
7   Diana N'Diaye, "Community Curation as Collaborative Pedagogy" in *Folklife and Museums: Twenty-First Century Perspectives*, eds. Patricia Hall, Charlie Seeman, and C. Kurt Dewhurst (New York: Rowman & Littlefield, 2016), 139–55.
8   Elizabeth Keckley, "Behind the Scenes, or, Thirty years a Slave, and Four Years in the White House," Documenting the American South, [1868] 1999, https://docsouth.unc.edu/neh/keckley/keckley.html (accessed February 14, 2023).
9   The Clarks' research in the late 1930s and early 1940s on the traumatic effects of systemic racism on the self-worth of African American children was used as evidence in Brown vs. the Board of Education of Topeka. Kenneth and Mamie Clark offered a choice of a white or black doll to 253 Black children in schools in the Northern and Southern United States. Three quarters of the children chose the white dolls over the black dolls. This 1954 landmark case was one of the first blows in ending legal segregation. By unanimous decision the Supreme Court established school segregation as unconstitutional. See Tim Spofford, *What the Children Told Us: The Untold Story of the Famous "Doll Test" and the Black Psychologists Who Changed the World* (New York: Sourcebooks, 2022).
10  Excerpts from the interview with Brenda Winstead are available at https://festival.si.edu/blog/2013/brenda-winsteads-joyful-quest-for-west-african-textiles/
11  Marjorie Hunt, "The Smithsonian Folklife and Oral History Interviewing Guide," Smthsonian Center for Folklife and Cultural Heritage Education Resources (2016), https://folklife.si.edu/the-smithsonian-folklife-and-oral-history-interviewing-guide/smithsonian (accessed February 15, 2023).
12  Diana N'Diaye, *Will to Adorn Research Guidelines* (Washington, DC: Center for Folklife and Cultural Heritage, 2011).
13  Ibid.
14  N'Diaye 2016.
15  A selected list of projects and research teams is available on the Will to Adorn website at https://folklife.si.edu/will-to-adorn/projects-networks
16  Ingrid E. Mida and Alexandra Kim, *The Dress Detective A Practical Guide to Object-Based Research in Fashion* (London: Bloomsbury Press, 2015).

## Bibliography

Hunt, Marjorie. "The Smithsonian Folklife and Oral History Interviewing Guide." Smthsonian Center for Folklife and Cultural Heritage Education Resources, 2016, https://folklife.si.edu/the-smithsonian-folklife-and-oral-history-interviewing-guide/smithsonian (accessed February 15, 2023).

Hurston, Zora Neale. "Characteristics of Negro Expression." In *Within the Circle*, edited by Angelyn Mitchell, 79–94. Durham and London: Duke University Press, 2012.

Keckley, Elizabeth. "Behind the Scenes, or, Thirty years a Slave, and Four Years in the White House." Documenting the American South [1868] 1999, https://docsouth.unc.edu/neh/keckley/keckley.html (accessed February 14, 2023).

Mida, Ingrid E. and Alexandra Kim. *The Dress Detective A Practical Guide to Object-Based Research in Fashion*. London: Bloomsbury Press, 2015.

Miller, Monica L. *Slaves to Fashion: Black Dandyism and the Styling of Diasporic Identity*. Durham, NC and London: Duke University Press, 2009.

Miller, Rosemary E. Reed. *Threads of Time, the Fabric of History: Profiles of African American Dressmakers and Designers, 1850–2003*, 2nd edn. Washington, DC: Toast and Strawberries Press, 2003.

N'Diaye, Diana. *Will to Adorn Research Guidelines*. Washington, DC: Center for Folklife and Cultural Heritage, 2011.

N'Diaye, Diana. "The Will to Adorn: African American Diversity, Style, and Identity." Smithsonian Folklife Festival Program Book, 27–31 Washington, DC: Smithsonian Institution, 2013.

N'Diaye, Diana. "Agency, Reciprocal Engagement and Applied Folklore Practice: Beyond the Folklife Festival." In *Curatorial Conversations: Cultural Representation and the Smithsonian Folklife Festival*, edited by Sojin Kim, and Diana Baird N'Diaye Olivia Cadaval, 275–302. Jackson, MS: University of Mississippi Press, 2016.

N'Diaye, Diana. "Community Curation as Collaborative Pedagogy." *In Folklife and Museums: Twenty-First Century Perspectives*, edited by Patricia Hall, Charlie Seeman, and C. Kurt Dewhurst, 139–55. New York: Rowman & Littlefield, 2016.

Nichols, Elaine. "Decked Out Accordingly: the Adornment of African American Women from Enslavement tothe Mid-Twentieth Centrury." Smithsonian Folklife Festival Program Book, 37. Washington, DC: Smithsonian Institution, 2013.

Noyes, Dorothy. "Group." In *Eight Words for the Study of Expressive Culture*, edited Burt Feintuch, 7–41. Urbana and Chicago, IL: University of Illinois Press, 2003.

Oring, Eliot. *Folk Groups and Folklore Genres: An Introduction*. Logan, UT: Utah University Press, 1986.

Shukla, Pravina. *The Grace of the Four Moons: Dress, Adornment, and the Art of the Body in Modern India*. Bloomington, IN: Indiana University Press, 2015.

Spofford, Tim. *What the Children Told Us: The Untold Story of the Famous "Doll Test" and the Black Psychologists Who Changed the World*. New York: Sourcebooks, 2022.

Square, Jonathan Michael. "Slavery's Warp, Liberty's Weft: A Look at the Work of Eighteenth and Nineteenth-Century Enslaved Fashion Makers and their Leagacies." In *Black Designers in American Fashion*, edited by Elizabeth Way, 29–46. London: Bloomsbury, 2021.

Stern, Stephen and John Allan Cicala. *Creative Ethnicity: Smbols and Strategies of Contemporary Ethnic Life*. Logan, UT: Utah State University Press, 1991.

Tulloch, Carol. "Style-Fashion-Dress: From Black to Post-Black." *Fashion Theory: The Journal of Dress, Body amd Culture* 14, no. 3 (2010): 273–303.

Tulloch, Carol. *The Birth of Cool: Style Narratives of the African Diaspora*. London: Bloomsbury, 2016.

Way, Elizabeth, ed. *Black Designers in American Fashion*. London: Bloomsbury, 2021.

White, Shane and Graham White. *Stylin': African American Expressive Culture from its Beginnings to the Zoot Suit*. Ithaca and London: Cornell University Press, 1998.

# Index

Numbers in italics indicate figures. (897 lines)

accessories
   *Heirlooms and Accessories* (Marshall) 82, *83*, 86–88
   slave jewelry 159–175
ACLU *see* American Civil Liberties Union
activism, personal archiving 241–242
adornments, political 88–89
Adri *213–214*, 214–215, 219
Africa, jazz and the plantation 168–169
African American
   and African design 256
   agency 249, 253, 259
   everyday fashion 254
   style 249, 262
African descent
   adornment occupations 253–254
   self-definition 251
African Immigrant Folklife project 259
Afro hair 216, *216*
agency 1, 21, 39
   African American 249, 253, 259
   of communicator 86
   economic 134
   individual 219
   Latinx 183, 228
   legislative 134
   personal 2, 243
   political 121–122, 133–135
   and style 252
   white women 170
Aguilera, Christina, music video 173, *173*, 174
aloha attire 54
Aloha Week 44
America 3–4
*America*, Simon and Garfunkel 3
American Civil Liberties Union (ACLU) 90
American fashion 3–4, 7–8
   Northwest Coast 17
   versus *haute couture* 95–96
American flag jackets 108
American Legion 126–130
   Seminole costumes 126–127, *127*, 128–129
   swamp reclamation 129–130
American Museum of Natural History (AMNH) 25–27
   archives 133
   Tsimshian robe 25, *26*, 27–28
American symbols, indigenization 25–28
Anna Wintour Costume Institute 79
appliquéd crest jacket 25
Arambulo, Mercedes Marina *235–236*
Archer-Straw, Petrine, Black culture and Parisian avant-garde 164–165
archives
   American Museum of Natural History 133
   Broward County Historical Archives 126
   East Texas Digital Archives 61
   Fashion Archives Shippensburg University 222
   Latinx Diaspora Archives 228, 238–239, 241
   Nuevayorkinos 228, 233
   Quinceañera Archives 228, 239
   Veteranas and Rucas 232–233
archiving, as activism 241–242
Areeayl Yoseefaw earrings, Indya Moore 88
art and fashion, Northwest Coast 21–25
artful self-fashioning 13
artisans of style 252–256
assimilation design, potlatch cape 27

Baden-Powell, Lord Robert 130
Baker, Himikalas Pamela 23
bandanas 220

Bayonet Constitution, Hawaiian League 41
BC *see* British Columbia
beats 101
Beitler, Lawrence Henry (photographer) 83
*Big Blouses 30*
big shirts
    Patchwork *128*
    Seminole men 125, *125*
BIPOC *see* Black, indigenous, and people of color
black blazers 211–212
Black culture
    and Parisian avant-garde 164–165
    whites consuming 168–169
Black deco 165
Black design
    opportunities for 149–150
    politics of 153–155
    promoting 146–150, *149*
Black designers, NAFAD 143–145, 147–148
Black empowerment, style of 150–152
Black fashion, and National Association of Fashion and Accessories Designers (NAFAD) 141–155
Black, indigenous, and people of color (BIPOC) 3
*Black is Beautiful* movement 216
Black life
    experience of death 82, 85–86
    photography 85
Black Lives Matter 2
    Covid-19 pandemic 194
    identity 264
    postal workers 189
    protests 258
Black Panthers 103
Black women, slave jewelry 171–173, *173*
Blackness 82, 87–88, 90, 163, 165, 167, 172–173, 216
    antiblackness 82, 91
blazers, black 211–212
blouses
    *Big Blouses* 29, *30*
    gingham 64
    Heiltsuk Nation 29
    peasant 211
    and skirts 62, 63–65, 67
    sleeveless 65
    Texas 63
bohemians 101, 104, 211
bookstore, Stephen F. Austin State College 65, 66
boutiques 102
Boy Scouts of America 130–133
    Native reenactment 130
    Order of the Arrow (OA) 131–133
    racism 131
    Seminole jackets 131–133
boy scouts (UK) 130
bricolage 207
British Columbia (BC) 23, 25–26, 28, *31*
Broward County Historical Archives 126
Brown, Jeanetta Welch 141, 144, 150
Brown, Michael 81
Brown-Cepeda, Djali, Nuevayorkinos 227–228
button blanket 25, 31

Campo, Talaysay 17
    Raven Transformation dress *18*
*Can't Hold Us Down*, Lil' Kim *173*
cape, sheer 31–32
Carmina, Tia *238*
catalogs, everyday clothing 70
Center for Folklife and Cultural Heritage (CFCH) 183, 250, 258–259
ceremonial dress *see* regalia
CFCH *see* Center for Folklife and Cultural Heritage
Chicana youth culture 227
Chicas Doradas *238*
Chief dress, feasts 25
city letter carrier's uniform 188, *188*
civil rights 83, 102, 142, 144–146, 148
Civil Rights Movement 3, 153, 250, 254
Clavin, Cliff, *Cheers* postal uniform 185
Cleopatra bracelets 163
clothes
    country 63
    hand-me-downs 215–216
    work 66–69
*clothes you can count on* 220
clothing, flouncy 220
Cohn & Rosenberger, Inc. advertisement, *Slave Bracelets 164*
colors, Hawaiian shirts 46–47

comfort and control, Joyce and Andrea 215–218
community uplift 32–33
consumer culture, 'raceless' 84
consumerism, and youth boom 102
consumption 69–72
continuity 69–72
coppers 29
corduroy jacket 216
cotton
    dresses 64, *65*
    frocks 68
    shirts 123
counterculture 99, 101–109, 112–113, 115
    dress 103–104
    Indians 134
    publications 103–104
country clothes 15, 63
couriers of democracy, US postal workers 189
Covid-19 pandemic
    *Black Lives Matter* 194
    effect on fashion 1
    US postal workers 189
Crawford, Joan, *Our Dancing Daughters* 159, *162*
creativity and reinvention, Mary Jo and Andrea 206–210
crests 22, 24
    Grandpa's Frog Crest *24*
Crist, Charlie, shirt 119, *119*
Cruz, Celia 231
cultural aesthetics 23
cultures, of display 25
Cypress, Mitchell, Seminole shirt 119, *119*, 120, 135

daguerreotypes 85
Davies, Marilyn, Will to Adorn program *262*
Davis, Daphne, *Vanity Fair* 113
de Certeau, Michel 4, 9
death, Black experience of 82
*Death Becomes Her* exhibition 79–81
denim 68
    jacket 207
*Denise Poiret at 'The Thousand and Second Night' party*, Georges Lepape *166*
department stores, everyday clothing 70

design motifs, Northwest Coast 23
designers
    Andrea Licari-LaGrassa *208*
    Barbara Walz *213*
    Kevin Walz *213*
    Mary Jo Pollak *209*
Diggers 112–113
digital Instagram archives 231–232
disco, dressing for 209
display, cultures of 25
dress
    in American life 1
    appropriate 13, 219–220
    counterculture 103–104
    feminists 103, 218
dress codes 196
dresses
    flour sack 72–73
    girly 215
    housedresses 68, 71
    quinceañera 230
    wash 66–69
dressing
    for comfort 215
    for disco 209
    down 216
    for elegance 208
    individualism 211
    the part 233
    provocatively 219
    for punk 209
    for success 218
    for taste 210–211
    to avoid male gaze 221
    for work 212
dressing sovereign 28–32
Drive, Dahlia, *Big Blouses 30*

earrings, Areeayl Yoseefaw 88
East Texas Digital Archives 61
East Texas Research Center (ETRC) 61, 64–66
economic agency 134
Egyptomania 164
Eisenhower jacket 131
emancipation 84
Emmerich, Korina (Puyallup) 32
enfranchisement, and white femininity 161

Equal Rights Amendment (ERA) 219
escaramuza ensemble 230
ethnic diversity, Hawai'i 39
ethnography, personal tensions 234–238
ETRC *see* East Texas Research Center
Euro-American men, power dressing 119–120
everyday
   life 4–5
   recovering 181–183
   refashioning 13–15
   revisiting 95–97
   women and oral history 204–206
everyday clothing
   catalogs 70
   department stores 70
   home sewing 71–73
   postal uniform 187
   Texas 60
everyday fashion 5, 59
   African American 254
   Cuban child immigrant 231
   East Texas oral history 61–62
everyday life, Adrienne Rich 204
everyday, the 1
everyday togs, finding 61–62
exemplars of style 252
exoticism 165, 167, 172
   and primitivism 163–166
*Eye* magazine 102

fabrics
   corduroy 216
   cotton 123
   denim 207
   jersey 213–215
   menswear 217–218
   poplin 68
   practical work 68
   sailcloth 68
   washable 66–67
fabulousness 13
fashion 1–3, 6
   in American life 1–9
   high 60
   invisible 62
   non-Native 20
   objects 5
   self-fashioning 249–265

   and underground press 100–105
Fashion Archives Shippensburg University 222
fashion cities 5
fashion designers, NAFAD 142–143
Fashion Institute of Technology (FIT) 7, 9, 223, 256
fashion media, revolution in 107
fashionable dress 20
fashioning 2
feasts, Chief dress 25
female imagery, and feminists 221
female networks, crafting 143–146
feminism
   ahead of 218
   second wave 219
feminists
   Adrienne Rich 204
   dress 103, 218
   and female imagery 221
   groups 204
   lesbian writings 205
   photography 85
   T-shirt 90
FIT *see* Fashion Institute of Technology
flappers, 'slave bracelets' *161*
Florida swamps, Seminole refuge in 123–124
flour sack dresses 73
formline 22
found theory 60
frocks, cotton 68

garment reinvention 207
Garner, Eric 81
gaze, negotiating the 219–222
Giese, Cricket 206–207, 210, 212–213, 221
*go-to pieces* 220
Granata, Francesca, in-between-ness 181
*Grandpa's Frog Crest* 22, 24, *24*
Grant, Dorothy, cultural aesthetics 23
Greenblatt, Stephen, self-fashioning 2, 13
groups, feminists 204

Haida art 21
Haida Gwaii 17, 22
Haiìzaqv's regalia 32
haole hegemony 41
haoles

Hawaiian shirts 50–51, 53–54
and locals 40–42
Harlem
Blackness 167
jazz clubs 168
Renaissance photography (Van Der Zee) 81
*Harper's Bazaar* 100
clothes you can count on 220
Hart, Joan 206–207, 210–212, 218–221
*haute couture*, versus American fashion 95–96
Hawai'i, ethnic diversity 39
Hawaiian Islands, immigrants 41
Hawaiian League, Bayonet Constitution 41
Hawaiian mo'oelo *46*
Hawaiian shirts
in 1930s *43*
colors 46–47
David Shepard *46*
haoles 50–51, 53–54
identity 42–53
local haoles 51–53
locals 44–47, 50–52
reverse 45
Reyn Spooner *48*
tourists *47–49*, *48–49*
on TV 51
Waikiki 44, 47, *49*, 51
Hawaiian social values 42
hegemony 103
Heiltsuk Nation
Big House 30, *31*
blouses 29, *30*
dress 29
symbolism 29–30, *30*
*Heirlooms and Accessories*, Kerry James Marshall 82, *83*, 86–88
Hells Angels 103
high fashion 60
*Vogue* 100
Highmore, Ben 4, 9
Hillman, Betty Luther, women's liberation 205
hip-hop 2
repackaging 173
style 173–174
hippies 99, 101–102, 112
*History of the Indian Tribes of North America*, Charles Bird King *124*
Hollywood, slave bracelets 159, *161–162*, 162
home sewing, everyday clothing 71–73
housedresses 68, 71

*I Can't Breathe* T-shirt 90
identity 1
African 229
*Black Lives Matter* 264
Hawaiian shirts 42–53
Indigenous 32, 229
queer 229
Thalia Massie case 41–42
trans 229
whiteness 40, 42
immigrants, Hawaiian Islands 41
Indians
counterculture 134
stereotyping culture 120
indigenization, American symbols 25–28
Indigenous fashion
identity 32
Northwest Coast 17–33
system 19
Indita dance outfit 231
individual agency 219
individualism, dressing 211
*Inside Fashion* 99, 104, 108
Instagram archives, digital 231–232
Institute for Texan Culture 251
interns, Will to Adorn program *263*
invisible fashion 62
Iron Arrow students, Seminole jackets 120
ironing 64

jackets
American flag 108
appliquéd crests 25
corduroy 216
denim 207
fuel oil drips 29
letter carrier 188, 191–193, *192*
painted leather 103
patchwork 131, *131*, 132
riding 207
Seminole 120, 131–132
for success 218

jazz
    culture 161, 170–171
    dancing 167–168, 174
    plantation and Africa 168–169
    primitivism and exoticism 163–166
*Jazz*, Toni Morrison 85
jazz clubs, Harlem 168
Jazz Moderne 165
Jean-Raymond, Kerby, T-shirt 82, 89–90
jersey 213–215
Jim Crow laws 80
Joel Gutman & Co. advertisement, *Slave Jewelry 160*
Johnson, Betsey 108
    *Rags 106*
jumper 62, 63–64

Keckley, Elizabeth 254
killer whales, T-shirts 23
King, Charles Bird, *History of the Indian Tribes of North America 124*
kitsch 52
Korinna, Michelle, nameplate *240*

Lahaina Sailor shirt, Reyn Spooner 47–48, *48*
Latino Curatorial Initiative 230
Latino Initiatives Pool 230
Latinos, at Smithsonian Institution 229–231
Latinx
    agency 183, 228
    definition 228–229
    experience 227–244
    self-identifier 228–229
Latinx Diaspora Archives 228, 238–239, 241
Lauren, Ralph 220
Leaphart, Becky 65, *67*
Leaphart, Frances Maxine 65, *67*
Lefebvre, Henri 4, 9, 60
legislative agency 134
Lepape, Georges, *Denise Poiret at 'The Thousand and Second Night' party 166*
lesbian writings, feminists 205
letter carrier 186–188, *188*, 190, *190*, *192*, 193, 196
    jacket 188, 191–193, *192*

    shorts 197
    uniform 188, *188*, 190, *192*, 193, 196
Licari-LaGrassa, Andrea *208*, 215–218, *220*
Lil' Kim, *Can't Hold Us Down* 173
Lili'uokalani, Queen 41
liminal place 181
locals
    and haoles 40–42, 51–52
    Hawaiian shirts 44–47, 50–52
Long, Lois, slave bracelets 159–160
Look Book, US postal worker 189–190, *190*, 191
Lopez, Kristina, padrino *237*
lynching, Thomas Shipp and Abram Smith 82–83

McDowell, Deborah, post-mortem photography 81
Maher Brothers, letter carrier's uniform 188, *188*
Malone, Annie Turnbo 254
Marshall, Kerry James
    *Heirlooms and Accessories* 82–83, *83*, 86–88
    Signifyin(g) 82–88
Martin, Trayvon, and George Zimmeran 81, 89
Mary Jo and Andrea, creativity and reinvention 206–210
Massie, Thalia, Hawaiian identity 41–42
material culture
    and oral history 195–198
    postal workwear 191–195
men, Seminole fashion 119–136
Miccosukee 120, 122, 132–133, 135
Miller, Rosemarie Reed, Smithsonian Folklife Festival *250*, 254
minis versus midis 111–112
Miyamoto, Koichiro (Musa-Shiya) 42–43
mo'oelo 54
    Hawaiian shirt *46*
Moore, Colleen, slave bracelets 159, *161*
Moore, Indya, Oscar de la Renta gown 88
Morrison, Toni, *Jazz* 85
Moss, Pyer, *They Have Names* T-shirt 88–91
motifs, identity 46–47
mourning adornment, and antiblack violence 88

## Index

mourning dress 79, 84
   signifyin(g) 86
mourning jewelry 84–85
   *Heirlooms and Accessories* (Marshall) 82, *83*, 86–88
Musa-Shiya 42–43
music video, Christina Aguilera *173*

Nadolleck, Indian Agency 186
NAFAD *see* National Association of Fashion and Accessories Designers
nameplate
   documenting 240–241
   Michelle Korinna *240*
National Association of Fashion and Accessories Designers (NAFAD/NFAD) 96–97
   Black empowerment 150–152
   and Black fashion 141–155
   collection *149*
   emblem *146*
   networking 148–149
   politics 153–155
   San Francisco Chapter 153–154, *154*
   teaching 148
National Council of Negro Women (NCNW) 142, 144–145, 147–148
National Museum of the American Latino 231
National Organization for Women (NOW) 222
National Postal Museum (NPM) 185, 188–189, 191–192, 194–195, 197–198
Native Northwest Coast style 17
Native peoples, settlers clothing 122
Navajo Nation, and Urban Outfitters 2
NCNW *see* National Council of Negro Women
New York University (NYU) 185–187, 189, 229
NFAD *see* National Association of Fashion and Accessories Designers
non-Native fashion 20
Northwest Coast
   art and fashion 21–25
   design motifs 23
   Indigenous fashion 17–33
   style 17

NOW *see* National Organization for Women
NPM *see* National Postal Museum
Nuevayorkinos
   archive 228, 233–234
   Djali Brown-Cepeda 227–228
NYU *see* New York University

OA *see* Order of the Arrow
Olgis, Tia *238*
*on the street* 96, 106–110, 113–114
OOTD *see* outfit of the day
oral history
   everyday fashion East Texas 61–62
   garments 205
   and material culture 195–198
   and women's everyday 204–206
orientalism 160, 162, 165–167, 169
Oscar de la Renta gown, Indya Moore 88
*Our Dancing Daughters*, Joan Crawford *162*
outfit of the day (OOTD) 96
outfitters, Rufus Isley *254*
*Outside Fashion* 104–107, 112

padrino (godfather), Kristina Lopez *237*
painted leather jackets 103
pantsuits 217
Parks, Rosa 254
patchwork clothing 126–127, 130–131
   big shirt 96, *128*
   jacket 130–131, *131*, 132
   Seminoles 127, 130
Peacock, Mary, *Rags* 106
peasant blouses 211
period eyes 205
personal agency 2, 243
personal archiving, as activism 241–242
personal tensions, ethnography 234–238
photography
   feminists 85
   lynching 82–83
   Patrick Shannon 17, 19, *19*, 32–33
   post-mortem 81
   street style 108
plantation, jazz and Africa 168–169
poi dog 47
political agency 121–122, 133–135
politics, of Black design 153–155

Pollak, Mary Jo 206–210, *209*, 220–221
Polynesian prints 47, 52
poplin 68
Post Office Department uniform contract 187–188
postal uniform
    Ann Salisbury 191–194, *192*
    fabric 196–197
    shorts 197
    skirts 197
    workers complaints 196
postal workers 187–191
    *Black Lives Matter* 189
    oral history 186
    as stakeholders 194
postal workwear 185
    material culture 191–195
    personalization 188
    women 191–194, *192*
Postal Workwear Oral History Project 182, 186, 194–195, 198
potlatch cape, red wool 25–27, *26*, 28
potlatch gifts, T-shirts 24
primitivism 160, 162, 165, 167, 169
    and exoticism 163–166
    and sexuality 167–168
protests, *Black Lives Matter* 258
publications, counterculture 103–104
punk, dressing for 209
Puyallup (Korina Emmerich) 32

queer
    aesthetics 13
    identity 229
Quinceañera Archives 228, 239
quinceañera dress 230
Quintanilla Pérez, Selena 230

'raceless' consumer culture 84
racial groups, mortality rates 80–81
racism
    Boy Scouts of America 131
    daguerreotypes 85
    *The Scourged Back* 85
    'white superiority' 85–86
*Rags*
    birth of 105–107
    covers *100*, *114*
    first issue *106*

niche clothing 99–101
*On the street* 108, *109*, 113–114
    *Stud & Patch & Paint & Bleach* 111
Raiford, Leigh
    commodity culture 84
    consumer culture and desegregation 84
    lynching 83–84, 86–87
Ramirez, Manuel, and family 68, *69*
Raven Transformation dress, Yolanda Skelton *18*
Redstockings 204
refashioning 207–208, *208*
regalia 21
resourcefulness 72–73
Restrepo, Jaime, ribbon factory *237*
revolution, in fashion media 107
ribbon factory, Jaime Restrepo *237*
Rich, Adrienne
    everyday life 204
    feminists 204
Rickard, Jolene 20
riding jackets 207
Rohrer, Judy, haoles 40, 42
*Rolling Stone* magazine 105–107
Roosevelt Jr., Theodore 121
Rosales, Guadalupe, Veteranas and Rucas archive 227, 232–233, 241
Royal Robes by Adri 213, *214*
Rufus Isley, outfitters *254*
runway, Will to Adorn program *262*
Rusk, Dana *62*, 63–64
Rusk, Louise Jenkins *62*, 63–64

Sabol, Blair 104–106
    *Rags* 106
sailcloth 68
salesladies 70
Salisbury, Ann, postal uniform 191–194, *192*
San Francisco Chapter, NAFAD 154
Seaweed, Henry 23, *24*
self-fashioning 1–2, 249–265
    artful 13
    Steven Greenblatt 2, 13
Seminole
    refuge in Florida swamps 123–124
    and settler history 122–126, *125*
    swamp reclamation 126, 129
    Tribal Charter and Constitution 132

Seminole chief, Tuko-See-Mathla (Tukose Emathla) 123, *124*
Seminole Compact, celebration 119, *119*
Seminole dress, Veterans of Foreign Wars *127*
Seminole jackets
　Boy Scouts of America 131–132
　Iron Arrow students 120
Seminole men
　Euro-American accessories 125, *125*, 126
　political fashion 119–136
Seminole War reenactors 133–134
separates, sportswear 63–66
Seton, Ernest Thompson, Woodcraft Tribe 130
settler Boy Scouts of America 130–133
　wearing Native dress 130
settler states 22
settlers
　going Native 120–121, 129–130
　Miccosukee 132
　national borders 14
　and Seminole culture 120, 122–126
sewing 71–73
sewing circles 206–207
sexuality, and embodied primitivism 167–168
Shannon, Patrick, photography 17, 19, *19*, 32–33
Shepard, David, Hawaiian shirt *46*
Shipp, Thomas, lynching 82–83, 86–87
shirtdresses 63
shirts
　of the movement 89
　patchwork 96, *128*
　polyester 203
　Seminole 119–120, *119*, 135
　and ties 119, *119*
*Shop Hound*, Vogue 63
shorts, letter carrier 197
signifyin(g)
　Kerry James Marshall 82–88
　mourning dress 86
silhouettes, in woman's attire 79
Simmeran, George, and Trayvon Martin 81, 89
Simon and Garfunkel, *America* 3
Skelton, Yolanda 17, *19*

Raven Transformation dress *18*
　studio 23–24, *24*
skirted suit 218
skirts
　A-line 211
　and blouses *62*, 63–65
　pencil 208
　postal uniform 197
　for school 215
　straight 64
　and sweater 65, *67*
　taffeta 64
slave bangles 163
　and jazz 163
*Slave Bracelets*, Cohn & Rosenberger, Inc. advertisement *164*
slave bracelets
　Colleen Moore 159, *161*
　Hollywood 159, *161–162*, 162
slave jewelry
　accessories 159–175
　Black women 171–173, *173*
　contingent meanings 169–171
　as gifts 163
　Joel Gutman & Co. advert *160*
　origins of 164
　precious metals 163
　white women 169–171
slavery
　afterlives of 83
　wake of 82
Slett, Chief Marilyn 28, 30–32, *30–31*
Smith, Abram, lynching 82–83, 86–87
Smithsonian Folklife Festival 251
　Rosemarie Reed Miller *250*, 254
Smithsonian Institution, and US Latinos 229–231
social values, Hawaiian 42
sovereign, dressing 28–32
sovereignty, visual 20
spectacularization 2
Spooner, Reyn, Lahaina Sailor shirt *48*
sportswear separates 60, 63–66
Square, Joyce 215–218, *216–217*, 220–221
Steckling, Adrienne *see* Adri
Stephen F. Austin State College bookstore 65, 66
stitching 71
straight skirt 64

street clothes 212
street style 96, 99, 110, 113, 115, 189, 210
   photography 108
*Stud & Patch & Paint & Bleach, Rags* 111
style
   and agency 252
   artisans of 253–256
   of Black empowerment 150–152
style-fashion-dress 39
   Carol Tulloch 251–252
Suit Ensemble, Amanda Wicker *152*
Supernaturals Modelling 17
swamp reclamation
   American Legion 129–130
   Seminoles 126, 129
swamp refuges, Seminoles 124
sweater, and skirt 65, *67*
sweater sets 64
symbolism, Heiltsuk Nation *30*

T-shirts
   *Even More Names* 90
   *I Can't Breathe* 90
   Kerby Jean-Raymond 82
   killer whales 23
   for potlatch gifts 24
   *They Have Names* 88–91
   *We Should All Be Feminists* 90
taffeta skirt 64
Taylor, Breonna 2
Texas
   rural fashions 64–65, *65, 67,* 68, *69*
   rural women 59–74
*The Scourged Back,* racism 85
*They Have Names* T-shirt, Pyer Moss 88–91
Tia Carmina *238*
Tia Olgis *238*
tourists, Hawaiian shirts 47, *49*
trans fashion
   earrings for trans victims 88
   Indya Moore 88
trans identity 229
transphobic violence 88
trousers
   for warmth 215
   women 68–69, *69,* 166
Tsimshian robe 25–28, *26,* 31
Tuko-See-Mathla (Tukose Emathla) 123, *124*

Tulloch, Carol, style-fashion-dress 251–252
turbans, Seminole men 123, *124–125*
Turtle Island 3, 8

underground press 100–105
uniform, letter carrier 188, *188,* 190, *192,* 193, 196
United States Postal Service (USPS) 185–198, *192*
United States postal workers
   Black Lives Matter 189
   couriers of democracy 189
   Covid-19 pandemic 189
   Look Book 189–190, *190,* 191
Urban Outfitters, and Navajo Nation 2

Van Der Zee, James, Harlem Renaissance photography 81
Van Riesen, Wendy
   *Big Blouses* 30
   Heiltsuk symbolism 29
*Vanity Fair* 2
   Daphne Davis 113
Veteranas and Rucas archive 232–233
Veterans of Foreign Wars, Seminole dress *127*
visual sovereignty 20
*Vogue* 2, 84
   aspirations from 208, 221
   classics 63
   country clothes 63
   high fashion 100
   *Shop Hound* 63
   street style 115
   style 102
   *Vogue's Own Boutique* 102
*Voice,* magazine 104–105

Waikiki, Hawaiian shirts 44, 47, *49,* 51
Walz, Barbara *213*
Walz, Kevin *213*
wash dresses 66–69
*We Should All Be Feminists* T-shirt 90
white Euro-American immigrants *see* settler
white femininity 159–175
   and enfranchisement 161
'white superiority', racism 85–86

white women
    agency 170
    slave jewelry 169–171
whiteness, identity 40, 42
whites, consuming Black culture 168–169
Wibaut, Madame *209*, 220
Wicker, Amanda, Suit Ensemble *152*
Will to Adorn program 249–250, 259
    interns *263*
    Marilyn Davies *262*
    methods 257–264
    runway *262*
    understanding 251–253
women
    in the 1970s 203–223
    in rural Texas in the 1950s 59–74
    stereotyping 221–222
    white femininity in 1920s 159–175
women's everyday, and oral history 204–206
women's liberation, Betty Luther Hillman 205
Woodcraft tribe 130
work clothes 15, 66–69
    for comfort 217, *217*
work fabrics 68
work-about clothes 71

Yoseefaw, Areeayl, earrings for trans victims 88
youth boom, and consumerism 102
yukata cloth 42

Zealy, Joseph T., daguerreotypes 85